Light & Easy
Holiday Cooking

BY SANDRA WOODRUFF, M.S., R.D.

Light & Easy Holiday Cooking

SIMPLE, HEALTHY MEALS THAT ARE AS GOOD-TASTING AS THEY ARE GOOD FOR YOU

Sandra Woodruff, M.S., R.D.

Avery

A MEMBER OF PENGUIN PUTNAM INC.

NEW YORK

Every effort has been made to ensure that the information contained in this book is complete and accurate. However, neither the publisher nor the author is engaged in rendering professional advise or services to the individual reader. The ideas, procedures, and suggestions contained in this book are not intended as a substitute for consulting with your physician. All matters regarding health require medical supervision. Neither the author nor the publisher shall be liable or responsible for any loss, injury, or damage allegedly arising from any information or suggestion in this book.

The recipes contained in this book are to be followed exactly as written. Neither the publisher nor the author is responsible for your specific health or allergy needs that may require medical supervision, or for any adverse reactions to the recipes contained in this book.

Most Avery books are available at special quantity discounts for bulk purchase for sales promotions, premiums, fund-raising, and educational needs. Special books or book excerpts also can be created to fit specific needs. For details, write Putnam Special Markets, 375 Hudson Street, New York, NY 10014.

AVERY

a member of
Penguin Putnam Inc.
375 Hudson Street
New York, NY 10014
www.penguinputnam.com

Copyright © 2001 by Sandra Woodruff

Library of Congress Cataloging-in-Publication Data

Woodruff, Sandra L.
Light and healthy holiday cooking : simple, healthy meals that are
as good-tasting as they are good for you / Sandra Woodruff.
p.   cm.
Includes index.
ISBN 1-58333-116-6 (pbk.)
1. Holiday cookery.   2. Low-fat diet—Recipes.   I. Title.
TX739.W6623   2001   2001022739
641.5'68—dc21

Printed in the United States of America

1   3   5   7   9   10   8   6   4   2

This book is printed on acid-free paper. ∞

BOOK DESIGN BY JILL WEBER

THIS BOOK IS DEDICATED TO MY FAVORITE TASTE TESTERS,

Wiley, C.D., and Belle.

ACKNOWLEDGMENTS

I AM GRATEFUL FOR THE GUIDANCE OFFERED by the team of professionals at Penguin Putnam, whose input at every stage of development has made this book possible. Special thanks go to John Duff for providing the opportunity to publish this book and to my editor, Dara Stewart, whose excellent suggestions and diligent attention to detail have added so much.

Thanks also go to my husband, Tom, and to my friends and family members for their long-term support and encouragement. And last, but not least, I would like to express my gratitude to the many clients, coworkers, colleagues, and readers, whose questions, ideas, and suggestions have been a constant source of inspiration.

Contents

Introduction

GREAT FOOD ADDS THAT SPECIAL TOUCH TO ANY OCCASION and makes every holiday more enjoyable and memorable. Whenever we think of Thanksgiving, Christmas, Hanukkah, Easter, and other traditional holidays, certain foods, unique to each occasion, come to mind. Turkey and stuffing at Thanksgiving, and golden potato latkes at Hanukkah, for instance, are a must for most of us.

Unfortunately, all that wonderful food that makes holidays and celebrations so special can also lead to an overdose of fat, sugar, and calories. High-fat hors d'oeuvres, indulgent entrées, rich sauces, and decadent desserts can make special occasions a real challenge for anyone who's trying to eat healthfully. Yet, when we make the switch to a more healthful diet, we face a dilemma. How can we enjoy lavish meals of holiday favorites and still prepare low-fat high-nutrient dishes? *Light & Easy Holiday Cooking* answers this question with inventive menus that combine lighter traditional dishes with exciting new fare for festive meals that are sure to delight family and friends.

Light & Easy Holiday Cooking was inspired by my previous work *Fat-Free Holiday Recipes,* which was published in 1994. This book retains some of my favorite recipes from the previous work, with an update to reflect the latest developments in nutrition and health, the availability of new products that have entered the marketplace, and cooking techniques that simplify and streamline food preparation. *Light & Easy Holiday Cooking* also features over 280 recipes including over 200 totally new, never-before-published recipes, and includes even more options that will allow you to plan menus to suit your family's tastes.

Nutrition Goals of This Book

Over the past several years, the science of nutrition has evolved, and while the fundamentals of good nutrition remain the same, some new thoughts have emerged on what constitutes a healthy diet. *Light & Easy Holiday Cooking* reflects these changes. The emphasis is on getting a healthy balance of fats by limiting ingredients that are high in saturated and trans fats, and instead, using small amounts of healthful fats like olive oil and canola oil, as well as moderate amounts of nuts and seeds. Lean meats and low-fat dairy products are featured in recipes, and vegetables, fruits, and whole grains are used in generous amounts. Most of the recipes in this book are compatible with a diet that is low in fat and rich in fiber, vitamins, minerals, and health-promoting phytochemicals and antioxidants. In addition, I have strived to keep sugar and salt at low to moderate levels.

The wide availability of lighter products today, as well as a greater knowledge of healthful cooking techniques, means that fabulous food no longer need be rich and fattening. For instance, festive dips, spreads, and other hors d'oeuvres are easily slimmed down using lower-fat versions of sour cream, mayonnaise, and cheese. Elegant entrées can be made using ultra-lean cuts of meat, and spectacular side dishes can be created from a glorious bounty of fresh produce and wholesome whole grains. Even pumpkin pie and other desserts can be made with a lighter hand, thanks to ingredients like low-fat evaporated milk and egg substitutes.

Timesaving Considerations

During holidays and special occasions, the expectation for fabulous food that is beautifully presented is at an all-time high. Unfortunately, this is also precisely when time is in short supply and stress is at an all-time high. But don't fear. Many excellent products are now available that can simplify holiday meal planning. Prewashed gourmet salad greens and other ready-to-use produce items help us add beautiful color and textures to holiday meals. A wide variety of frozen foods and carefully selected canned products can also help simplify meal preparation. With a little imagination, even convenience products like cake mixes, pudding mixes, canned pie fillings, flavored yogurts, and whipped toppings can be used to create show-stopping holiday desserts that won't blow your fat or calorie budget.

In planning the holiday menus in this book, I have strived to include dishes that are not only easy to make but can also be partially or entirely prepared ahead of time. Advance planning strategies accompany each menu to help you organize food preparation, avoid a last minute rush, and allow you to enjoy your own party!

How This Book Is Organized

Part One of *Light & Easy Holiday Cooking* introduces you to the basics of healthful eating upon which this book is based. You'll also learn about the many ingredients that will help you lighten up your holiday dishes without sacrificing flavor, and you'll discover a wealth of tips for giving your own holiday dishes a healthy makeover.

Following this important information, this book is divided into four additional parts, each of which focuses on a specific type of party or holiday food, or presents complete menus and recipes for special-occasion meals. Part Two offers a cornucopia of light finger-food recipes that are perfect for any gathering. Included in this section are recipes for both hot treats, like kabobs and meatballs, and cold treats, like finger sandwiches and dips. Also included are recipes for hot and cold beverages that round out party menus and add to the festivities.

Part Three presents menus and accompanying recipes for five traditional holidays: Thanksgiving, Christmas, Hanukkah, Passover, and Easter. Each menu is composed of a variety of taste-tempting, light and healthy main dishes, salads, side dishes, and desserts. Whenever possible, options have been provided to allow you to tailor the meal to suit your family's tastes. The Thanksgiving menu, for instance, offers a selection of seven stuffings, eight kinds of cranberry sauces and relishes, and seven side dishes—in addition to the turkey, of course. Best of all, each menu includes plan-ahead strategies that will allow you to complete many of your preparations in advance, helping you avoid a last-minute rush on the day of your get-together.

Part Four presents menus and recipes for a variety of special occasions, including New Year's Day, Valentine's Day, Saint Patrick's Day, Memorial Day, the Fourth of July, Labor Day, and Halloween. Again, each of these complete menus include a variety of healthy, easy-to-make dishes that maximize nutrition and taste while minimizing fuss.

Part Five rounds out this collection of holiday and party recipes with a bonanza of deceptively decadent dessert and baked-goods recipes. Whether you're searching for a festive quick bread to complement a simple luncheon dish or a dazzling grand finale to a special-occasion dinner, this section will meet your needs.

———

$\mathcal{A}$s you will see, adopting a light and healthy lifestyle does not mean giving up your favorite holiday and party foods. The recipes in this book preserve the traditional tastes of holidays past, with the advantage of a healthy update. It is my hope that *Light & Easy Holiday Cooking* will prove to you, as well as to your friends and family, that party food does not have to be rich and fattening, and that light and healthy food can be satisfying, exciting, and fun. So eat well and enjoy! It is possible to do both—every day of the year.

PART ONE

Mastering Healthy Holiday Cooking

IMAGINE A HOLIDAY MEAL THAT LOOKS FABULOUS, tastes terrific, and perfectly reflects the holiday spirit. Now imagine the same meal being just as healthful as it is delicious. If that's the kind of meal you've been dreaming about, stop dreaming—it *is* possible to have both.

Light & Easy Holiday Cooking presents a variety of innovative cooking techniques and shows you how to use the latest fat- and calorie-saving products, as well as many traditional ingredients. The result? Lighter, healthier holiday favorites that are never bland or boring, that are simple to prepare, and that your entire family will love.

In these pages, you will find recipes for a wide variety of deliciously light recipes that are perfect for all your special occasions. You will be delighted by slimmed down versions of old favorites, as well as tempting new creations that will let you eat the foods you love without guilt. Perhaps just as important, this book will show you that, contrary to popular belief, changing to a light and healthy lifestyle does not have to be an ordeal. As you will see, the recipes in this book will save you not just fat and calories but time and effort too.

This part begins by explaining the light and healthy philosophy that forms the basis for the recipes in this book. Next, you will learn about the best ingredients to use in your light and healthy dishes and how to use these foods to create great-tasting sure-fire family favorites that will be requested all year round.

The Basics of Light and Healthy Eating

Volumes of research have proven that we have enormous power to prevent disease, slow the rate of aging, increase our energy level, and promote a healthy body weight simply by making smart food choices. In recent years, the old saying "You are what you eat" has proven truer than anyone could ever have guessed. And despite headlines that are often contradictory and confusing, eating healthfully is a lot easier than most people think.

Following are some simple strategies for smart eating. In fact, these strategies are so simple that people often dismiss them. But don't let their simplicity fool you—they are very powerful. By implementing the following guidelines, you will automatically get more of the antioxidants, phytochemicals, vitamins, minerals, fiber, and other nutrients that your body needs, and less of the harmful fats, sugar, salt, and calories that you don't need.

Eat Generous Amounts of Vegetables and Fruits

Vegetables and fruits offer a bounty of nutrients, fiber, and phytochemicals—all of which are powerful preventive medicines against cancer, cardiovascular disease, and many other health problems. Since not all of the protective substances present in these foods have been identified, and some of them probably never will be, it is impossible to get all the benefits of vegetables and fruits from pills or supplements.

How much is enough? Five servings of vegetables and fruits a day is the minimum recommended amount, but to maximize your health, aim for eight to ten servings per day. This is not as hard as you may think. A medium-sized piece of fruit, a half-cup of cooked or raw fruits or vegetables, a cup of leafy salad greens, a quarter-cup of dried fruit, or three-fourths of a cup of fruit or vegetable juice each constitute a serving. So if you include at least one cup of vegetables or fruits at each meal, and replace snacks like chips, pretzels, crackers, and cookies with vegetables and fruits, you can easily meet this guideline.

Watching your weight? Enjoying generous portions of produce is definitely one of the secrets of successful weight loss. Why? Low in calories and high in bulk, these foods fill you up—but not out. People who skip the vegetables and fruits at a mere 25 to 50 calories per cup, and pile on extra rice or pasta at 200 calories per cup—or who have an extra slice of bread at 80 to 100 calories—will probably find weight loss slower than they expect. (Be aware that starchy vegetables like potatoes, peas, and corn are similar to bread, pasta, and rice in calorie and carbohydrate content.)

Vegetable and fruit salads and side dishes add that special touch to holiday meals, and every family has its favorite recipes for each occasion. Unfortunately, salads drenched in oil or mayonnaise and vegetables covered with cheese or rich sauces often contain more fat and calories than the entrée! But as you will discover, spectacular salads and satisfying side dishes can also be made the light and healthy way. Fruit desserts such as pies, cobblers, and crisps are also holiday favorites. And these recipes, too, can be made substantially lighter in both fat and sugar.

This book features a fresher, lighter approach to preparing vegetables and fruits. With the creative use of lower-fat spreads and dressings, lighter cheeses and dairy products, and other healthful products, you'll find that even home-style casseroles, creamy fruit salads, and bubbling fruit cobblers can star in your holiday menus.

Choose Whole Grains Over Refined Grains

Grain products like bread, cereal, rice, and pasta have long been thought of as "the staff of life." But you should know that not all grains are created equal. To get the most from this food group, it is crucial to choose *whole-grain* products—like 100 percent whole-grain breads and cereals, oats, barley, brown rice, and bulgur wheat. Why? In recent years, whole grains have emerged as one of the foremost health-protective foods. In fact, numerous studies have shown that people who eat whole grains are about 30 percent less likely to develop heart disease and diabetes than people who eat mostly refined grains like white bread, white flour, white rice, and refined breakfast cereals. This should come as no surprise. Many of the nutrients that are present in whole grains—magnesium, copper, chromium, selenium, folate, vitamin E, and fiber, for instance—are essential for the protection of the cardiovascular system and the metabolism of carbohydrates. In addition, whole grains contain lignans, phytates, flavonoids, and other health-promoting phytochemicals, the benefits of which are just being recognized.

Unfortunately, most people are not reaping the benefits of whole grains. In fact, a whopping 85 percent of all grains eaten by Americans are refined! Refining strips grains of most of their fiber, vitamins, and minerals, and causes a 200- to 300-fold loss of phytochemicals. Therefore, a diet based on refined products will actually hasten the development of heart disease, diabetes, cancer, and many other health problems. Need another reason to switch to whole grains? Fiber-rich whole grains are more filling and satisfying than their refined counterparts, so can help prevent overeating. In contrast, a diet of low-fiber refined foods will leave you feeling constantly hungry.

Like fresh vegetables and fruits, whole grains can be incorporated into many holiday favorites—from savory stuffings and pilafs to crumb-topped apple crisps and golden spice cookies. The last part of this section will introduce you to the whole grain products that can enhance your holiday recipes, and show you how to use these and other foods to create wholesome and delicious dishes in your own kitchen.

Eat Two to Three Servings of Protein-Rich Foods Every Day

Getting enough protein is critical for maintaining lean body mass, muscular strength, and keeping your immune system going strong. But many people who have been following low-fat diets do not eat enough protein. Why? In an effort to reduce fat and cholesterol, many people choose to eat less meat, or even give it up entirely. And while it is not necessary to eat meat to get enough protein, you *must* substitute a protein-rich alternative like dried beans, soy foods, or eggs. Unfortunately, many people do not do this. If you are watching your weight, you should know that it is especially important to include some protein in each meal. Why? Protein-rich foods are the most filling of all foods so they help stave off hunger and keep you feeling satisfied until your next meal.

Fat-fighters will be happy to know that a wide selection of ultra-lean red meats, pork, poultry, and even lunch meats and sausages is now available to choose from. This means you can have your protein without a counterproductive dose of saturated fat. The last part of this section will guide you in selecting these products. Where does fish and seafood fit in? These foods range from practically fat-free to moderately fatty. However, the oil in fish provides an essential kind of fat—known as omega-3 fat—which most people do not get enough of. Therefore, all kinds of fish—especially the more oily ones like salmon—are considered healthful and are excellent alternatives to meat and poultry. In fact, fish *should* substitute for meat at least twice a week.

Eat Two to Three Servings of Calcium-Rich Foods Every Day

Everyone knows that calcium is essential for building strong bones. But calcium also helps maintain normal blood pressure, may help prevent colon cancer, and performs many other vital functions in the body. Yet most people's diets fall short of the recommended 1,000 to 1,200 milligrams per day. Why do so many people lack calcium? Many people avoid calcium-rich dairy products believing them to be high in fat and calories. While this used to be true, these days a multitude of no- and low-fat, reduced-calorie dairy products are widely available. The last part of this section will introduce you to these products, which can beautifully replace full-fat cheeses, sour cream, and other popular foods in your favorite holiday dishes.

Prefer not to eat dairy products? No problem. But you must substitute other calcium-rich foods such as calcium-fortified soymilk, soy cheese, and soy yogurt. As a bonus, soy products also contain phytochemicals and nutrients that help protect against osteoporosis, cancer, and heart disease. Many leafy green vegetables—such as greens, kale, and bok choy—are also loaded with calcium. And legumes and tofu can add significant amounts of calcium to your diet as well.

Limit Your Use of Table and Cooking Fats

One of the most effective ways to trim fat and calories from your diet is to cut down on fats used in cooking and baking, like butter and margarine, and fats added at the table, like oily salad dressings, mayonnaise, and butter. In their full-fat versions, just one tablespoon of any of these products will add about 10 grams of fat and 100 calories to your meal, so it is well worth finding ways to cut back on these products. In addition, a diet that is low in fat leaves more room for healthful foods like vegetables, fruits, and whole grains. But can you cut back on fat and still have flavor? Absolutely! For each of these foods there is now a lighter alternative that can substitute beautifully in your favorite dishes.

In addition to going easy on added fats, it is just as important to choose the right *kinds* of fat, when you do need to use some fat in recipes. This will ensure that you get enough of the essential fatty acids needed for optimal health. The last part of this chapter will introduce you to a variety of lighter, fat-saving products and will help you select the vegetable oils with the most healthful nutritional profiles.

Eat Sugar Only in Moderation

Too much sugar has long been a problem in many people's diets, and the holidays bring a flood of sweet treats, dramatically increasing our exposure to sugar. What health threats are posed by sugar? First, sugar contains no nutrients, so high-sugar diets contribute to nutritional deficiencies and set the stage for a multitude of health problems. Second, by overwhelming the taste buds and increasing the taste threshold for sweet flavors, diets rich in sugary foods can cause us to lose our taste for the more subtle flavors of wholesome, natural foods. And last but not least, sugary foods are usually loaded with calories, making them a real obstacle to successful weight control.

Does this mean you must give up all of your favorite holiday goodies? No. The good news is that, in moderation, sugar can be enjoyed without harm to your health. What's a moderate amount? A person who needs 2,200 calories per day to maintain his or her weight should consume no more than 48 grams, or about 12 teaspoons, of added sugar per day. If you need only 1,600 calories per day, your upper limit should be 24 grams, or about 6 teaspoons—the amount present in about ¾ cup of ice cream or a piece of apple pie.

Whenever possible, the recipes in this book are made with less sugar. Many traditional holiday recipes for marinades, sauces, and even salads and side dishes are loaded with sugar. For instance, a sweet potato casserole might contain over a cup of brown sugar—and a full stick of butter. The recipes in this book strive to reduce the need for all that sugar by adding natural sweetness with fruits, fruit juices, and sweet spices like cinnamon and nutmeg. As for desserts, those that feature ripe sweet fruits frequently need only a moderate amount of added sugar. Cakes are topped with low-sugar frostings or simple glazes instead of thick icings. And many recipes give you the option of using sugar-free products such as pudding and gelatin, so that you can create dishes that best suit your personal nutritional needs.

Moderate Your Intake of Sodium

A limited sodium intake has many benefits, ranging from better-controlled blood pressure to stronger bones. But of all the guidelines for good eating, this one can be the most difficult to follow, since many lower-fat foods contain extra salt. Fortunately, with just a little effort, even this dietary goal can be met. One of the most effective sodium-control strategies is to cut back on salt used for cooking and at the table. Believe it or not, just one teaspoon of salt contains 2,300 milligrams of sodium—almost your entire daily allowance—so it pays to put the salt shaker away. You can also cut back on sodium by switching to a "light" salt, which is half sodium chloride and half potassium chloride. (Note that people with certain medical conditions should not use light salt, due to its high potassium content.)

Another effective strategy is to limit your intake of high-sodium processed foods. Read labels, and choose the lower-sodium frozen foods, canned goods, broths and soups, cheeses, and other products. Also, whenever you make a recipe that contains high-sodium cheeses, processed meats, or other salty ingredients, avoid adding any extra salt. The recipes in this book will show you how to balance high-sodium products with low-sodium ingredients, herbs, and spices to create dishes that are lower in sodium but high in flavor.

THESE GUIDELINES AREN'T GLAMOROUS and they don't make headlines, but as many people have discovered, they *do* produce results. The fact is, it is the simple things that you do day in and day out that have the biggest impact on your health. And small changes, practiced consistently, can make a *big* difference in the way you look and feel.

You'll find that the recipes and tips provided throughout this book make it surprisingly easy to follow these steps and build a healthful, enjoyable eating plan all year round.

About the Ingredients

Never before has it been so easy to eat healthfully. Light and healthy alternatives are available for just about any ingredient you can think of. This makes it possible to create a dazzling array of healthful and delicious foods, including dramatically slimmed down versions of many of your favorite holiday dishes. In the pages that follow, we'll take a look at the low-fat dairy products, spreads and dressings, eggs and egg substitutes, ultra-lean meats, and many other ingredients that will ensure success in all your light and healthy cooking adventures.

Low-Fat and Nonfat Cheeses

Cheese is an excellent source of calcium and high-quality protein. Unfortunately, these nutrients often come packaged with a large dose of artery-clogging saturated fat. Fortunately, a wide range of low-fat and nonfat products is now available, making it possible to have your cheese and eat it too. Let's learn about some of the cheeses that you'll be using in your light and healthy recipes.

COTTAGE CHEESE

Although often thought of as a "diet food," full-fat cottage cheese has 5 grams of fat per 4-ounce serving, making it far from diet fare. Instead, choose nonfat or low-fat cottage cheese. When puréed until smooth, these versatile products make a great base for dips, spreads, and salad dressings. Cottage cheese also adds richness and body to casseroles, quiches, cheesecakes, and many other recipes. Select brands with 1 percent or less milk fat. Most brands of cottage cheese are quite high in sodium, with about 400 milligrams per half-cup, so it is best to avoid adding salt whenever this cheese is a recipe ingredient.

CREAM CHEESE

This product adds creamy richness to dips, spreads, sauces, fillings, frostings, and many other recipes. Unfortunately, just one block of full-fat cream cheese contains 80 grams of fat, the equivalent of a stick of butter! But don't fear, many lower-fat alternatives are also available to choose from. Neufchâtel cheese, with 6 grams of fat per ounce, was once the only lower-fat alternative available. However, these days, a variety of light brands with 3 to 5 grams of fat per ounce are also widely sold in grocery stores. Lighter still is nonfat cream cheese, which can also be found in the dairy case.

Feta Cheese

With 6 grams of fat per ounce, this semisoft cheese has about one-third less fat than most other kinds of cheese, and is considered moderately high in fat. However, a little bit goes a long way, so used moderately in recipes that contain little or no other fats, you can enjoy this product without exceeding your fat limits. An even better choice, though, is a reduced-fat brand, which will have about 4 grams of fat per ounce. Nonfat feta cheese is also available in some grocery stores.

Firm and Hard Cheeses

Both low-fat and nonfat cheeses of many types—including Cheddar, Monterey Jack, mozzarella, provolone, and Swiss—are widely available. Reduced-fat cheeses generally have about 4 to 6 grams of fat per ounce while low-fat brands contain no more than 3 grams of fat per ounce, and nonfat cheeses contain no fat at all. Compare this with whole-milk varieties with 9 to 10 grams of fat per ounce, and your savings are clear.

For cooking purposes, you should know that reduced-fat cheeses work best in recipes in which you need a cheese that melts well—atop a casserole or pizza for instance. Nonfat brands work fine atop a salad or in a sandwich. The recipes in this book will indicate which type of cheese can be used in recipes that contain this ingredient.

Parmesan Cheese

Parmesan typically contains 8 grams of fat and 400 milligrams of sodium per ounce. As with most cheeses, reduced-fat versions are available. A little bit of this flavorful cheese goes a long way, so used moderately in recipes that call for few or no other high-fat ingredients, even the "real thing" will not blow your fat budget.

Process Cheese

Typically sold in one- or two-pound blocks as well as in shredded and sliced forms, this cheese is designed to melt smoothly, and so is a good choice for use in soups and sauces. Most grocery stores sell brands like Velveeta Light. Process cheeses tend to be high in sodium, but you can avoid a sodium overload when using these cheeses by leaving out the salt and avoiding the use of other high-sodium ingredients in your recipe.

RICOTTA CHEESE

Ricotta is a slightly sweet, creamy cheese that may be used in savory or sweet fillings, mousses, cheesecakes, and many other recipes. As the name implies, nonfat ricotta contains no fat at all. Part-skim ricotta, on the other hand, has 2 to 3 grams of fat per ounce, while whole-milk ricotta has about 4 grams of fat per ounce.

SOFT-CURD FARMER CHEESE

This soft, slightly crumbly white cheese makes a good low-fat substitute for soft goat cheese and, when blended until smooth, can replace cream cheese in many recipes. Brands made with skim milk have about 3 grams of fat per ounce compared with cream cheese's 10 grams. Nonfat brands are also available in some grocery stores and specialty shops. Some brands are made with whole milk, so read the label before you buy.

YOGURT CHEESE

A good substitute for cream cheese in dips, spreads, and cheesecakes, yogurt cheese can be made at home with any brand of plain or flavored yogurt that does not contain gelatin or vegetable thickeners such as carrageenan or guar gum. Simply place the yogurt in a funnel lined with cheesecloth or a coffee filter, and let it drain into a jar in the refrigerator for eight hours or overnight. When the yogurt is reduced by half, it is ready to use. The whey that collects in the jar may be used in place of the liquid in breads and other baked goods. Note that some stores now sell a firm block-type "yogurt" cheese, alongside other firm cheeses like Cheddar, Monterey Jack, and Swiss. This product is not interchangeable with the soft yogurt cheese made from drained yogurt.

NONDAIRY CHEESE ALTERNATIVES

If you choose to avoid dairy products because of a lactose intolerance or for another reason, you'll be glad to know that low-fat cheeses made from soy milk and nut milk are now available in a variety of flavors. Be aware that some nondairy cheeses do contain casein, a milk protein that you may want to avoid.

Other Low-Fat and Nonfat Dairy Products

Of course, cheese isn't the only dairy product we use in our everyday cooking. How about the sour cream in dips, casseroles, and sauces, and the buttermilk in your favorite biscuits? Fortunately, there are low-fat and nonfat versions of these and other dairy products as well.

BUTTERMILK

An essential ingredient in the low-fat kitchen, buttermilk adds a rich flavor and texture to all kinds of breads and baked goods, and lends a "cheesy" taste to sauces, dressings, frozen desserts, and many other dishes. But isn't buttermilk high in fat? Contrary to what its name implies, most buttermilk is quite low in fat. Originally a by-product of butter making, buttermilk should perhaps be called "butterless" milk. One-percent low-fat brands of buttermilk are widely available in grocery stores, and many stores offer nonfat brands as well. Choose these for your low-fat cooking needs.

The flavor and texture of real buttermilk works best in the recipes in this book, but if you do not have buttermilk on hand, you can make a substitute by mixing equal parts of nonfat yogurt and skim or low-fat milk. Alternatively, place a tablespoon of vinegar or lemon juice in a 1-cup measure, and fill to the 1-cup mark with skim or low-fat milk. Let the mixture sit for 5 minutes before using.

EVAPORATED MILK

This ingredient is available in both skim (nonfat) and low-fat versions and can be substituted for cream in sauces, gravies, quiches, puddings, and many other dishes. Not only do you save 620 calories and 88 grams of fat for each cup of evaporated skim milk you substitute for cream, but you also add extra calcium, protein, potassium, and other nutrients to your recipe. If you don't have any evaporated skim milk on hand, you can make a substitute by mixing ⅓ cup instant nonfat dry milk powder with ⅞ cup skim or low-fat milk. This will yield 1 cup.

MILK

One gallon of whole milk contains 130 grams of fat—the equivalent of one and one-half sticks of butter! And while you may not drink a gallon at a time, the fat you consume from milk can really add up over time. What are the best milk choices? Choose nonfat (skim) milk for the very least fat. Next in line is 1-percent low-fat milk with about 2.5 grams (½ teaspoon) of fat per cup. What about 2-percent milk? By legal definition, a low-fat product can have no more than 3 grams of fat per serving. With 5 grams of fat per cup, 2-percent milk is not low fat.

People who cannot tolerate milk sugar (lactose) will be glad to know that most supermarkets stock Lactaid milk in a nonfat version. Nonfat Lactaid milk may be used in place of milk in any recipe.

NONFAT DRY MILK

Like evaporated skim milk, this product adds creamy richness, as well as important nutrients, to quiches, cream soups, sauces, custards, and puddings. One-third cup of nonfat dry milk powder mixed with seven-eighths cup of skim- or low-fat milk can replace cream in most recipes. Or add this ingredient to low-fat baked goods to enhance flavor and promote browning. For best results, always use *instant* nonfat dry milk powder, as this product will not clump.

SOUR CREAM

As calorie- and fat-conscious people know, full-fat sour cream contains 48 grams of fat and almost 500 calories per cup! Use nonfat sour cream, though, and you'll eliminate at least half of the calories and all of the fat. Light sour cream, with half the fat of regular sour cream, is another good option. Made from cultured nonfat or low-fat milk thickened with vegetable gums, these products substitute beautifully for their fatty counterpart in dips, spreads, sauces, and many other dishes.

YOGURT

Yogurt adds creamy richness and flavor to sauces, baked goods, and casseroles. And, of course, it is a perfect base for many dips and dressings. Be aware though, that yogurts thickened with pectin will curdle if added to hot sauces or gravies. To prevent this, first let the yogurt warm to room temperature. Then stir 1 tablespoon of cornstarch or 2 tablespoons of unbleached flour into the yogurt for every cup of yogurt being used. You will then be able to add this ingredient to your dish without fear of separation. Yogurts that are thickened with vegetable gums and modified food starch are usually heat-stable without the addition of cornstarch or flour. In your low-fat cooking, select brands of yogurt with 1-percent or less milk fat.

Nonfat and Low-Fat Spreads and Dressings

Like dairy products, spreads and dressings have long been a major source of fat and calories in many people's diets. Happily, many lighter alternatives to our high-fat favorites are now available. Let's learn a little more about these fat-saving products.

Butter and Margarine

Which is better, butter or margarine? Neither should have a prominent place in your diet. Butter is a concentrated source of artery-clogging saturated fat, while margarine often contains harmful trans fats. In addition, both are pure fat and loaded with calories. If you are used to spreading foods with butter or margarine, you can easily reduce your dietary fat by switching to a nonfat or reduced-fat spread and using it sparingly. When selecting margarines, look for those that list liquid canola or soybean oil as the first ingredient. This will help reduce your exposure to trans fats and boost your intake of essential fats. Some "trans-free" margarines are also now available, so choose these whenever possible.

Though you cannot sauté, fry, or brown with nonfat spreads, the reduced-fat products can be used for many of your cooking needs. For instance, most brands melt well enough to toss with steamed vegetables or rice dishes when you want added moisture and flavor. In some cases, you can also bake with light butter and reduced-fat margarine. Simply replace the desired amount of full-fat butter or margarine with three-fourths as much of a light brand. For baking, select a light spread that contains 5 to 6 grams of fat per tablespoon, as brands with less fat generally do not perform well for this use. The recipes in this book will specify which kind of spread is most appropriate for each recipe.

Mayonnaise

Nonfat and reduced-fat mayonnaise are highly recommended over regular mayonnaise, which provides about 11 grams of fat and 100 calories per tablespoon. How can mayonnaise be made without all that oil? Manufacturers use more water and vegetable thickeners to create creamy spreads that can replace the full-fat versions in all of your favorite recipes.

Salad Dressings

Many flavors and brands of nonfat and reduced-fat salad dressings, from creamy ranch to balsamic and raspberry vinaigrettes, are available to choose from. Although these lighter dressings tend to be low in calories, some flavors are quite high in sugar and sodium, so it pays to read labels to evaluate how well a product meets your personal nutrition goals. As for regular dressings, these can also fit into a healthful diet, provided you choose brands that are made with acceptable oils such as olive, canola, soybean, and walnut. However, if you are watching your weight, be sure to use these products sparingly as they are quite high in calories.

Oils

Like butter and margarine, oils used in cooking, baking, and salad dressings can blow your fat budget in a hurry. Many people are confused about oils because liquid vegetable oils have long been promoted as being "heart healthy." The reason? These oils are low in artery-clogging saturated fat and contain no cholesterol. Unfortunately, many people also assume that these products are low in total fat and calories and therefore may be used liberally. Not so. The fact is that all oils are pure fat. Just one tablespoon of *any* oil has 13.6 grams of fat and 120 calories. However, sometimes you do need a little oil for cooking, and some are more useful to the healthy cook than others.

CANOLA OIL

Low in saturated fats and rich in monounsaturated fats, canola oil also contains alpha-linolenic acid, an essential omega-3 fat that is deficient in most people's diets. For these reasons, canola oil should be one of your primary cooking oils. Canola oil has a very mild, bland taste, so it is a good all-purpose oil for cooking and baking when you want no interfering flavors.

EXTRA VIRGIN OLIVE OIL

Along with canola oil, olive oil should be one of your primary cooking oils. Rich in monounsaturated fat, olive oil also contains phytochemicals that help lower blood cholesterol levels and protect against cancer. Unlike most vegetable oils, which are very bland, olive oil adds its own delicious flavor to foods. Extra virgin olive oil is the least processed and most flavorful type of olive oil. And a little bit goes a long way, making this product a good choice for use in low-fat recipes. What about "light" olive oil? In this case, light refers to flavor, which is mild and bland compared with that of extra virgin oils. This means that you have to use more oil for the same amount of flavor—not a good bargain.

SOYBEAN OIL

Most cooking oils that are labeled simply "vegetable oil" are made from soybean oil. Soybean oil is also used as an ingredient in many brands of margarine, mayonnaise, and salad dressing. This oil supplies a fair amount of omega-3 fat, though not as much as canola and walnut oils do. Like canola oil, soybean oil has a bland flavor that works well in dishes where you want no interfering flavors.

Walnut Oil

With a delicate nutty flavor, walnut oil is an excellent choice for baking, cooking, and salads. Like canola oil, walnut oil contains a substantial amount of omega-3 fat. Most brands of walnut oil have been only minimally processed and can turn rancid quickly, so once opened, they should be refrigerated.

Nonstick Vegetable Oil Cooking Spray

Available unflavored and in butter, olive oil, and garlic flavors, these products are pure fat. The advantage to using them is that the amount that comes out during a one-second spray is so small that it adds an insignificant amount of fat to a recipe. Nonstick cooking sprays are very useful to the low-fat cook to promote the browning of foods and to prevent foods from sticking to pots and pans.

Eggs and Egg Substitutes

From hearty breakfast omelets to quiches, casseroles, and puddings, eggs are star ingredients in many recipes. Most people know that eggs are also loaded with cholesterol—just one large egg uses up two-thirds of your daily cholesterol budget. One egg also contains 5 grams of fat. This may not seem like all that much until you consider that a three-egg omelet contains 15 grams of fat—and that's without counting the cheese filling or the butter used in the skillet! The good news is that it is a simple matter to make dishes with more whites (which are fat- and cholesterol-free) and fewer yolks or you can use a fat-free egg substitute and enjoy your favorite egg dishes with absolutely no fat or cholesterol at all.

Just what are egg substitutes? Contrary to what the term *substitute* implies, these products are made from 99 percent pure egg whites. The remaining 1 percent consists of vegetable thickeners and yellow coloring—usually beta-carotene or the plant-based coloring agents annatto or turmeric. You will find egg substitutes in both the refrigerated foods section and the freezer case of your grocery store.

You may wonder why some of the recipes in this book call for egg whites or a combination of whole eggs and egg whites while others call for egg substitute. In some cases, one ingredient does, in fact, work better than the other. For instance, because they have been pasteurized (heat treated), egg substitutes are safe to use uncooked in eggnogs and salad dressings. On the other hand, when recipes require whipped egg whites, egg substitutes do not work.

In most recipes, egg whites and egg substitutes can be used interchangeably. When replacing egg whites with egg substitutes, or whole eggs with egg whites or egg substitute, use the following guidelines:

1 large egg = 1½ large egg whites

1 large egg = 3 to 4 tablespoons egg substitute

1 large egg white = 2 tablespoons egg substitute

Realize that although whole eggs are high in cholesterol, most health experts agree that a healthy diet can include four to seven egg yolks per week. Ask your physician or dietitian to make a recommendation for your specific needs.

Finally, some manufacturers are now feeding hens a diet that is enriched with vitamin E and ingredients like flaxseeds, marine algae, and fish meal. This produces eggs that are nutritionally superior to regular eggs because the yolks are higher in vitamin E and omega-3 fatty acids. When you eat whole eggs, choose these omega-3-enriched products most often.

Ultra-Lean Poultry, Meat, and Vegetarian Alternatives

Because of the high fat and cholesterol contents of meats, many people have sharply reduced their consumption of meat, have limited themselves to white meat chicken or turkey, or have totally eliminated meat and poultry from their diets. Happily, whether you are a sworn meat eater, someone who only occasionally eats meat dishes, or a confirmed vegetarian, plenty of lean meats, lean poultry, and excellent meat substitutes are now available. Here are some suggestions for choosing the leanest possible poultry and meat.

TURKEY

Once relegated only to Thanksgiving dinner, turkey is now a big seller all year round. Of course, skinless turkey breast is the leanest cut available, with just 119 calories and 1 gram of fat per 3-ounce serving. Below, you will learn about the cuts that you're likely to find at your local supermarket.

◆ *Turkey Cutlets.* Turkey cutlets, which are slices of fresh turkey breast, are usually about ¼ inch thick and weigh about 2 to 3 ounces each. These cutlets may be used as a delicious ultra-lean alternative to boneless chicken breast, pork tenderloin slices, or veal.

◆ *Turkey Medallions.* Sliced from turkey tenderloins, medallions are about 1 inch thick and weigh about 2 to 3 ounces each. Turkey medallions can be substituted for pork or veal medallions in any recipe.

◆ *Turkey Tenderloins.* Large sections of fresh turkey breast, tenderloins usually weigh about 8 ounces each. Tenderloins may be sliced into cutlets or medallions, cut into stir-fry or kabob pieces, ground for burgers, or grilled or roasted as is.

◆ *Ground Turkey.* Ground turkey is an excellent ingredient for use in meatballs, chili, burgers—in any dish that uses ground meat. When shopping for ground turkey, you'll find that different products have different percentages of fat. Brands that are simply labeled "ground turkey," and bear no nutrition facts label, are often made with added skin and fat, and are usually about 15 percent fat by weight—which is more than twice the amount of fat in some kinds of lean ground beef. At the other end of the spectrum is ground turkey breast, which is only 1 percent fat by weight, and is the leanest ground meat you can buy. However, many people find this product too dry and tough for their taste. A good compromise is to find a mixture that contains somewhere between 93 and 96 percent lean or look for a product that is labeled "ground turkey meat," as this should contain no added skin.

CHICKEN

Although not as low in fat as turkey, chicken is still lower in fat than most cuts of beef and pork, and therefore is a valuable ingredient in light and healthy cooking. Beware, though: Many cuts of chicken, if eaten with the skin on, contain more fat than some cuts of beef and pork. For the least fat, choose the chicken breast, and always remove the skin—preferably, before cooking.

BEEF AND PORK

Although not as lean as turkey, beef and pork are both considerably leaner today than in decades past. Spurred by competition from the poultry industry, beef and pork producers have changed breeding and feeding practices to reduce the fat content of these products. In addition, butchers are now trimming away more of the fat from retail cuts of meat. The result? On average, grocery store cuts of beef are 27 percent leaner today than they were in the early 1980s, and retail cuts of pork are 43 percent leaner. Of course, some cuts of beef and pork are leaner than others. Which are the smartest choices? The following table will guide you in selecting those cuts that are lowest in fat. Some manufacturers are now offering cuts of meat that are even leaner than the ones listed in this table. Look for these in your local grocery store.

THE LEANEST BEEF AND PORK CUTS

Cut (per 3-ounce cooked, trimmed portion)	Calories	Fat
BEEF		
Eye of Round	143	4.2 g
Top Round	153	4.2 g
Brisket, flat half	162	5.3 g
Round Tip	157	5.9 g
Top Sirloin	165	6.1 g
Bottom Round	172	6.4 g
Top Loin	176	8.0 g
Tenderloin	179	8.5 g
PORK		
Tenderloin	139	4.1 g
Ham (95% lean)	112	4.3 g
Boneless Sirloin Chops	164	5.7 g
Boneless Loin Roast	165	6.1 g
Boneless Loin Chops	173	6.6 g

While identifying the lowest-fat cuts of meat is an important first step in healthy cooking, be aware that even lean cuts have varying amounts of fat because of differences in *grades*. In general, the higher, and more expensive, grades of meat, like USDA Prime and Choice, have more fat due to a higher degree of *marbling*—internal fat that cannot be trimmed away. USDA Select meats have the least amount of marbling, and therefore the lowest amount of fat. How important are these differences? A USDA Choice piece of meat may have 15 to 20 percent more fat than a USDA Select cut, and USDA Prime may have even more fat. Clearly, the difference is significant. So when choosing beef and pork for your table, by all means check the package for grade. Then look for the least amount of marbling in the cut you have chosen, and let appearance be your final guide.

Ground beef. If you are not fond of ground turkey as a hamburger substitute, you will be happy to learn that lean mixtures of ground beef are now widely available, giving you another choice. As with ground turkey, always check labels before you buy because ground beef varies greatly in its fat and calorie content. At its worst, ground beef is almost one-third pure fat. But grocery stores also commonly sell ground beef that is 93 to 96 percent lean. As an alternative to ready-made ground beef, you can select a piece of top round and ask the butcher to trim off the fat and grind the remaining meat. The resulting product will be about 95 percent lean.

How different is the leaner ground beef from the more commonly sold product? Beef that is 95 percent lean contains 4.9 grams of fat and 132 calories per 3-ounce cooked serving. Compare this with regular ground beef, which is 73 percent lean and has 17.9 grams of fat and 248 calories per serving, and your savings are clear.

VEGETARIAN GROUND MEAT ALTERNATIVES

Looking for ways to sneak some soy into your diet? These days, many grocery stores offer a couple of ground meat alternatives, which can be substituted for part or all of the ground beef or turkey in recipes like chili, tacos, and casseroles, and can replace up to one-third of the meat in burgers and meat loafs. Here are some products to look for:

Frozen recipe crumbles. Made from soy and other vegetable proteins, this product is rich in protein and is fat-free. They are widely available in the freezer case of many grocery and health-food stores. Two cups of crumbles is the equivalent of one pound of cooked ground beef or turkey.

Tofu hamburger. Located in the produce section alongside the regular tofu, these mildly seasoned bits of tofu look like cooked ground beef. One ten-ounce package (about two cups) is the equivalent of one pound of cooked ground beef or turkey.

Texturized vegetable protein (TVP). This product has long been a staple in health foods stores and can now be found in some grocery stores as well. TVP is made from defatted soy flour and comes packaged as small nuggets that you rehydrate with water. To rehydrate TVP, simply place 1 cup of the nuggets in a bowl, pour ⅞ cup of boiling water or broth over the nuggets, and let sit for 5 minutes. The rehydrated product is equivalent to 1 pound of cooked ground beef or turkey.

LEAN PROCESSED MEATS

Because of our new health-consciousness, low-fat bacon, ham, and sausages are now available, with just a fraction of the fat of regular processed meats. Some of these low-fat products are used in the recipes in this book. Here are some examples of what you are likely to find in your local grocery store.

Bacon. Turkey bacon, made with strips of light and dark turkey meat, looks and tastes much like pork bacon. But with 20 to 30 calories and 0.8 to 2 grams of fat per strip, turkey bacon has at least 50 percent less fat than crisp-cooked pork bacon, and shrinks much less during cooking. Besides being a leaner alternative to regular breakfast bacon, turkey bacon may be substituted for pork bacon in vegetables, casseroles, salads, and other dishes.

For best results when cooking turkey bacon, prepare it in a microwave oven. This will produce a crisp texture instead of the chewy texture that results when turkey bacon is cooked in a skillet. Place the bacon slices on a microwave-safe plate lined with a paper towel, and cover with another paper towel. Then cook on high power for about 1 minute per slice, or until browned and crisp. Or follow the manufacturer's directions for making crisp bacon.

Canadian bacon, which has always been about 95 percent lean, is another useful ingredient to the low-fat cook. Use this flavorful product in breakfast casseroles and soups, and as a topping for pizzas.

Ham. Many kinds of low-fat ham, from presliced lunch meats to fully cooked whole hams, are now available. Hams made from either pork or turkey can be purchased in most grocery stores, and many of these products contain as little as 0.5 gram of fat per ounce. Of course, all cured hams, including the leaner brands, are very high in sodium, though some reduced-sodium brands are also available. However, used in moderation—to flavor bean soups or breakfast casseroles, for instance—these products can be incorporated into a healthy diet. Just avoid adding further salt or high-sodium ingredients to your recipes.

Sausage. A variety of low-fat smoked sausages and kielbasa made from turkey, or a combination of turkey, beef, and pork, is now available. These products contain a mere 30 to 40 calories and from less than ½ gram to 3 grams of fat per ounce. Compare this with an ounce of full-fat pork sausage, which contains over 100 calories and almost 9 grams of fat, and you'll see what a boon these new healthier mixtures are. Beware, though: While labeled "light," some brands of sausage contain as much as 10 grams of fat per 2.5-ounce serving. This is half the amount of fat found in the same-size serving of regular pork sausage, but is still a hefty dose of fat for such a small portion of food.

Fish and Other Seafood

Of the many kinds of fish and other seafood now available, some are almost fat-free, while some are moderately fatty. However, the oil in fish provides an essential kind of fat—known as omega-3 fatty acids—that most people do not get enough of. The omega-3 fats in fish can help reduce blood triglycerides, lower blood pressure, and prevent the formation of deadly blood clots. This means that all kinds of fish, including the more oily ones, are considered healthful.

What about the cholesterol content of shellfish? It may not be as high as you think it is. With the exception of shrimp and oysters, a 3-ounce serving of most shellfish has about 60 milligrams of cholesterol—well under the daily upper limit of 300 milligrams. The same-size serving of shrimp has about 166 milligrams of cholesterol, which is just over half the recommended daily limit. Oysters have about 90 milligrams of cholesterol. However, all seafood, including shellfish, is very low in saturated fat, which has a greater cholesterol-raising effect than does cholesterol.

Fish is highly perishable, so it is important to know how to select a high-quality product. First, make sure that the fish is firm and springy to the touch. Second, buy fish only if it has a clean seaweed odor, rather than a "fishy" smell. Third, when purchasing whole fish, choose those fish whose gills are bright red in color, and whose eyes are clear and bulging, not sunken or cloudy. Finally, refrigerate fish as soon as you get it home, and be sure to cook it within forty-eight hours of purchase.

Whole Grains and Flours

One of the best-kept secrets of healthy eating is the benefits that can be derived simply by switching from refined grains and refined flours to whole-grain products. While refined grains are practically devoid of fiber, nutrients, and phytochemicals, whole grains are loaded with these health-promoting substances. In fact, a number of studies have shown that whole grains offer protection against cardiovascular disease, cancer, and diabetes. And because they are more filling and satisfying than refined grains, making the switch may help you control your weight as well.

If you have never used whole-grain flours before, a word should be said about storing these products. Since whole-grain flours naturally contain a small amount of oil, they can become rancid more quickly than their refined counterparts. For this reason, be sure to purchase them in a store that has a high turnover rate and to keep them in the refrigerator or freezer after you take them home. Following are descriptions of some of the grain products that you may find useful in your holiday recipes.

BARLEY

This grain has a light, nutty flavor, making it a great substitute for rice in casseroles, soups, pilafs, and other dishes. Hulled or pearled barley cooks in about fifty minutes. Quick-cooking barley, which cooks in about twelve minutes, is also available in most grocery stores.

BROWN RICE

Brown rice is whole-kernel rice, meaning that all nutrients are intact. With a slightly chewy texture and a pleasant nutty flavor, brown rice can replace white rice in any of your favorite recipes. For a real treat, try basmati brown rice, which has a richer, nuttier flavor than regular brown rice. Brown rice does take forty-five to fifty minutes to cook, so when you are in a hurry, try one of the many brands of quick-cooking brown rice that are now available.

BUCKWHEAT

Buckwheat is technically not a grain but the edible fruit seed of a plant that is closely related to rhubarb. Roasted buckwheat kernels, commonly known as kasha, are delicious in pilafs and hot breakfast cereals. Buckwheat flour, made from finely ground whole buckwheat kernels, is especially delicious in pancakes.

BULGUR WHEAT

Cracked wheat that is precooked and dried, this nutty-tasting grain can be prepared in a matter of minutes. Bulgur wheat is delicious in pilafs, stuffings, salads, and casseroles.

CORNMEAL

This grain adds a sweet flavor, a lovely golden color, and a crunchy texture to baked goods. When purchasing cornmeal, look at the nutrition facts label and choose a brand that contains at least 2 grams of fiber per 3-tablespoon serving. Cornmeal may be fine, medium, or coarsely ground, and is available in white, yellow, and even blue colors. Unlike the color of bread, the color of cornmeal—white versus yellow or blue—does not indicate the product's nutritional value or the degree to which it was refined.

COUSCOUS

This is actually tiny pasta, and not a grain. Couscous, which cooks in less than five minutes, makes a great substitute for rice in pilafs and salads, and is an excellent accompaniment to stews and stir-fries. Be sure to choose whole wheat couscous for the most nutrition.

Flaxseeds

These small, nutty-tasting seeds have long been a popular ingredient with bakers in Europe and Canada, who frequently add the whole seeds or ground flaxmeal to breads and baked goods. Besides adding flavor and crunch to foods, flaxseeds are loaded with soluble fibers and healthful omega-3 fatty acids.

Both whole flaxseeds and ground flaxmeal are widely available in health foods stores. Realize that once ground into meal, flax can turn rancid quickly, so should be stored in an opaque container in the refrigerator or freezer. Even better, make your own flaxmeal as you need it by grinding the whole seeds in a blender or coffee grinder. Flaxmeal looks similar to wheat bran and can replace 15 to 25 percent of the wheat flour in many baked goods. Flaxmeal can also be sprinkled over cereals or added to smoothies for a nutrition boost.

Oats

More than just a breakfast cereal, rolled oats can replace part of the flour in baked goods such as yeast breads, muffins, quick breads, pancakes, waffles, cookies, pie crusts, and crumb toppings. And since oats have a naturally sweet flavor, you can often get by with using less sugar in recipes. Oats can also replace bread crumbs as a filler in meat loaf and meatball recipes.

Oat Bran

Made from the outer part of the oat kernel, oat bran has a naturally sweet, mild flavor and is a concentrated source of cholesterol-lowering soluble fiber. Great as a hot and hearty breakfast cereal, oat bran can also replace 25 to 50 percent of the flour in many baked goods, where its soluble fibers add tenderness and retain moisture, reducing the need for fat. In fact, oat fibers are used in a variety of commercial fat substitutes. Look for oat bran in the hot-cereal section of your grocery store, alongside the rolled oats. The softer products, like Quaker oat bran, work best in baked goods.

Oat Flour

Like oat bran, oat flour retains moisture and adds tenderness to baked goods, reducing the need for fat. To add extra fiber and nutrients, substitute oat flour for 25 to 50 percent of the refined flour in cakes, muffins, and quick breads. Look for oat flour in health foods stores, or make your own by finely grinding quick-cooking rolled oats in a food processor.

WHEAT BRAN

The outer part of the wheat kernel, wheat bran is high in fiber, minerals, and phytochemicals. Wheat bran can replace 10 to 15 percent of the flour in yeast breads, pancakes, waffles, and cookies, and up to half of the flour in muffins and quick breads.

WHEAT GERM

The inner part of the wheat kernel, toasted wheat germ has a nutty flavor and is loaded with vitamin E, trace minerals, and B vitamins. Wheat germ can replace 10 to 15 percent of the flour in muffins, quick breads, pancakes, waffles, cookies, and many other baked goods.

WHOLE WHEAT FLOUR

Ground from the whole-grain wheat kernel, whole wheat flour includes the grain's nutrient-rich bran and germ. Most of the whole wheat flour sold in supermarkets is made from a hard red wheat, which has a strong flavor that many people find overwhelming. White whole wheat flour and whole wheat pastry flour, described below, are lighter-tasting alternatives.

WHITE WHOLE WHEAT FLOUR

Made from hard white wheat instead of the hard red wheat used to make regular whole wheat flour, white whole wheat flour contains all of the nutrients of regular whole wheat flour, but is sweeter and lighter-tasting than its red-wheat counterpart. White whole wheat flour can be used for all of your baking needs, including yeast breads.

WHOLE WHEAT PASTRY FLOUR

Made from soft (low-protein) white whole wheat flour, whole wheat pastry flour has a lightly sweet flavor and soft texture that is ideal for making muffins, quick breads, pancakes, cookies, and many other baked goods. This nutritious whole-grain flour can replace 50 to 100 percent of the white flour in any recipe except for yeast bread. Whole wheat pastry flour is also a nutritious alternative to white flour for thickening gravies. Look for this ingredient in health foods stores and some grocery stores.

Nuts

Although high in fat, nuts can and should be a regular part of a healthful diet. These tasty morsels supply essential fats and a wide range of phytochemicals, vitamins, and minerals. These qualities put nuts high on the list of healthful foods. In fact, people who eat an ounce of nuts (three to four tablespoons) several times a week are 30 to 50 percent less likely to suffer from heart disease as people who avoid nuts. If you are watching your weight, be aware that a cup of nuts provides about 800 calories, so don't go overboard. However, used moderately, nuts can greatly enhance the joy of eating without exceeding your fat or calorie budgets.

Toasting Nuts

To bring out the flavor of nuts, try toasting them. Toasting intensifies the flavors of nuts so much that you can often halve the amount used. Nuts that benefit most from toasting include almonds, hazelnuts, and pecans. Walnuts are not usually toasted. Simply arrange the nuts in a single layer on a baking sheet, and bake at 350°F for 8 to 10 minutes, or until lightly browned with a toasted, nutty smell. (Watch the nuts closely during the last couple of minutes of baking, as they tend to brown quickly.) To save time, toast a large batch and store the extras in an airtight container in the refrigerator or freezer. That way, you'll always have a supply on hand.

This book is filled with creative dishes that will make entertaining elegant, simple, and satisfying. Whether you are having a few people over for coffee and dessert, a casual dinner party, or an open house, you will find something to meet your needs. So eat well and enjoy! The dishes you are about to make will not only be delicious, they will also be foods that you can feel good about serving to your friends and family.

About the Nutrition Analysis

The Food Processor version 7.6 (ESHA Research) computer nutrition analysis system, along with product information from manufacturers, was used to calculate the nutritional information for the recipes in this book. For each recipe, information on calories, carbohydrates, pro-

Holiday Meal Makeovers

*W*hen *you consider the typical holiday dinner, it's easy to see why we all feel the need to start a diet the morning after! From appetizer to dessert, a traditional holiday meal easily supplies an entire day's worth of fat, calories, and sugar. Although a once-a-year family feast is not the time or place to make drastic changes in cherished family recipes, some simple substitutions can substantially lighten your favorite holiday foods without sacrificing the flavors you love. Here are some ideas for giving a healthy makeover to each course of your meal.*

*   **Appetizers.** Dips and spreads can be dramatically slimmed down simply by substituting lower-fat brands of sour cream, mayonnaise, and cream cheese for their high-fat counterparts. For instance, one tablespoon of spinach dip made with full-fat mayonnaise and sour cream contains about 45 calories. If you were to make this dip with nonfat mayo and sour cream, it would have just 13 calories per tablespoon. Similarly, choosing leaner meats and reduced-fat cheeses can lighten up a wide variety of hors d'oeuvres, finger sandwiches, and party platters. Finally, be sure to include plenty of fresh cut vegetables, fruits, and whole-grain crackers in your appetizer selection.*

*   **Entrée.** Turkey is an ideal low-fat main course for many holiday meals. To keep it this way, baste your bird with broth, sherry, or white wine instead of fat, and cover it with foil during cooking to seal in the moisture. (Remove the foil during the last 30 minutes so that it becomes beautifully browned.) For a change of pace, try a spiral-sliced precooked ham. Brands that are up to 96 percent lean are widely available and need to be heated only before serving.*

*   **Gravy.** To make delicious fat-free gravy, defat poultry or meat drippings using a fat separator cup. This handy device, which can be purchased in most grocery stores, has a specially designed spout, which pours from the bottom of the cup. The fat, which floats to the top, stays in the cup.*

*   If you don't have a fat separator cup, allow the drippings to cool slightly, then pour them into a large, heavy-duty zip-type freezer bag. Seal the bag and allow the fat to rise to the surface of the liquid. Carefully snip a small piece off one of the bottom corners of the bag to form a spout, and allow the fat-free drippings to drain into a bowl. When all of the fat-free drippings have been removed, stop pouring, and discard the fat that remains in the bag.*

Side dishes. *Vegetable side dishes laden with butter or blanketed with sauce and cheese often contain more calories than the entrée! Fortunately, there are many ways to trim fat and calories from these dishes. Moisten mashed potatoes with evaporated low-fat or skim milk, yogurt, or nonfat or light sour cream instead of cream, whole milk, or butter. And try Yukon Gold potatoes for making mashed potatoes. This variety of potato has a naturally rich buttery flavor, which reduces the need for adding fat.*

When making casseroles, use lower-fat cheeses and low-fat cream soups. In many casseroles and pilafs you can also reduce the amount of butter or margarine called for or substitute a reduced-fat brand of butter or margarine. As for those southern-style greens and green beans, try seasoning them with ham bouillon, diced lean ham, or chunks of skinless smoked turkey instead of bacon or ham hocks.

Salads. *Contrary to popular belief, many salads are anything but "diet" food. Fortunately, substituting ingredients like lower-fat mayonnaise, salad dressings, and sour cream for full-fat versions easily lightens up salads. For instance, ¾ cup of Waldorf salad made with full-fat mayonnaise contains 329 calories and 31 grams of fat. You could trim away 70 percent of the fat and over half of the calories simply by dressing this salad with nonfat mayonnaise or a mixture of nonfat mayo and nonfat or light sour cream.*

What about the nuts in dishes like Waldorf salad? Nuts are naturally cholesterol-free and contain primarily heart-healthy unsaturated fats. They also supply a variety of vitamins, minerals, and phytochemicals that help protect against cardiovascular disease. Nuts are high in calories (about 800 per cup), but if you cut back on ingredients like full-fat mayonnaise and salad dressings, you can afford to include some nuts in recipes.

Stuffing. *Moisten your stuffing with chicken broth instead of melted butter or margarine and save about 800 calories and 80 grams of fat for each stick of butter or margarine that you replace. But don't try to substitute an equal amount of broth for butter or margarine—you might end up with an overly moist stuffing. Instead, start by replacing the butter or margarine with half as much broth. Toss the stuffing and broth together. It should be lightly moist and hold together nicely. Add a little more broth if necessary. For added nutrition, try using whole wheat or multigrain bread instead of white. You can also boost nutrition and reduce the need for salt by adding lots of celery, onions, mushrooms, and other vegetables, as well as plenty of savory herbs and spices, to your stuffing mixture.*

Dessert. *Custards, puddings, trifles, and fruit-based desserts like fruit cobblers and crisps are the most easily slimmed down dessert recipes. It is a simple matter to substitute evaporated low-fat or skim milk and fat-free egg products in pumpkin pies, custards, and puddings. As for sugar, you can often reduce this ingredient by up to 25 percent if you enhance sweetness with a little extra vanilla or a dash of nutmeg, cinnamon, or orange rind.*

You may be able to replace some of the fat in your holiday breads and cakes with applesauce, but experiment with these recipes well in advance to see how they will turn out. Try replacing just a quarter of the fat the first time, then cut back a little more if the results are satisfactory. In some recipes such as quick breads, cakes, brownies, and pie crusts, you can also replace butter, margarine, or shortening with half as much vegetable oil. Again, experiment with these recipes in advance to evaluate the results. When purchasing ready-made pie crusts, read the nutrition labels and compare brands, as the fat content of these products varies widely, ranging from 4 to 12 grams of fat per serving.

As you can see, a few simple substitutions can go a long way toward lightening up your favorite holiday recipes. By giving your favorite holiday dishes a healthy makeover, you can prepare a memorable feast that is both low in fat and calories and high in nutrition and flavor.

tein, fat, cholesterol, dietary fiber, sodium, and calcium is provided. Nutrients are always listed per one serving.

Sometimes recipes give you options regarding ingredients. For instance, you might be able to choose between nonfat and reduced-fat cheese, nonfat and light mayonnaise, or sugar-free or regular pudding mix. This will help you create dishes that suit your tastes and your personal nutrition goals. *Just keep in mind that the nutritional analysis is based on the first ingredient listed and does not include optional ingredients.*

LIGHTENING UP YOUR FAVORITE HOLIDAY RECIPES

Recipe	Healthy Makeover Tips
APPETIZERS AND HORS D'OEUVRES	Use lower-fat versions of sour cream and mayonnaise in dips and spreads. Use lower-fat cheeses and lean meats in party platters and hors d'oeuvres. Offer plenty of fresh cut vegetables and fruits along with your appetizer selection.
BURGERS, MEATBALLS	Use extra-lean ground beef or turkey. Replace up to one-third of the ground meat with vegetarian hamburger crumbles, tofu hamburger, or TVP. Add lots of finely chopped mushrooms, onions, bell peppers, and other vegetables to the ground meat mixture.
SALADS	Use lower-fat mayonnaise and dressings. Use lower-fat cheeses and leaner meats.
SOUPS	Use a gravy separator to remove the fat from stocks and broths or chill the stock or broth and remove the fat that floats to the top. Use leaner meats. Substitute skim or low-fat milk for whole milk. Add 1–2 tablespoons of nonfat dry milk powder to each cup of skim or low-fat milk for a richer flavor. Thicken soups with puréed vegetables instead of cream.

STUFFING	Moisten stuffings with broth instead of butter or margarine. (Start with half as much broth as the amount of butter called for, then add more if needed.)
	Add lots of celery, onion, and other vegetables to the stuffing mixture.
	Use fat-free egg substitute instead of whole eggs.
	Substitute whole-grain breads for white bread.
SAUCES	Substitute evaporated skim or low-fat milk for cream.
	Use less butter or margarine.
SIDE DISHES	Use lower-fat cheeses, sour cream, and cream soups in casseroles.
	Use less butter, margarine, and oil in recipes.
	Moisten mashed potatoes with evaporated skim or low-fat milk, light sour cream, or plain yogurt.
DESSERTS	Substitute skim or low-fat milk for whole milk in custards and puddings. (Add 1–2 tablespoons of nonfat dry milk powder to each cup of skim or low-fat milk for a richer flavor.)
	Use fat-free egg substitutes instead of whole eggs.
	Substitute nonfat or light whipped topping for whipped cream. (For a creamier texture, fold 1 part vanilla yogurt into 3 or 4 parts whipped topping.)

DESSERTS (*cont.*)	Use evaporated skim or low-fat milk in pumpkin pie, custards, and puddings.
	Substitute applesauce for part of the oil in baked goods.
	Toast nuts to bring out their flavor (see page 30), and you can often halve the amount used.

PART TWO

Hors D'Oeuvres for All Seasons

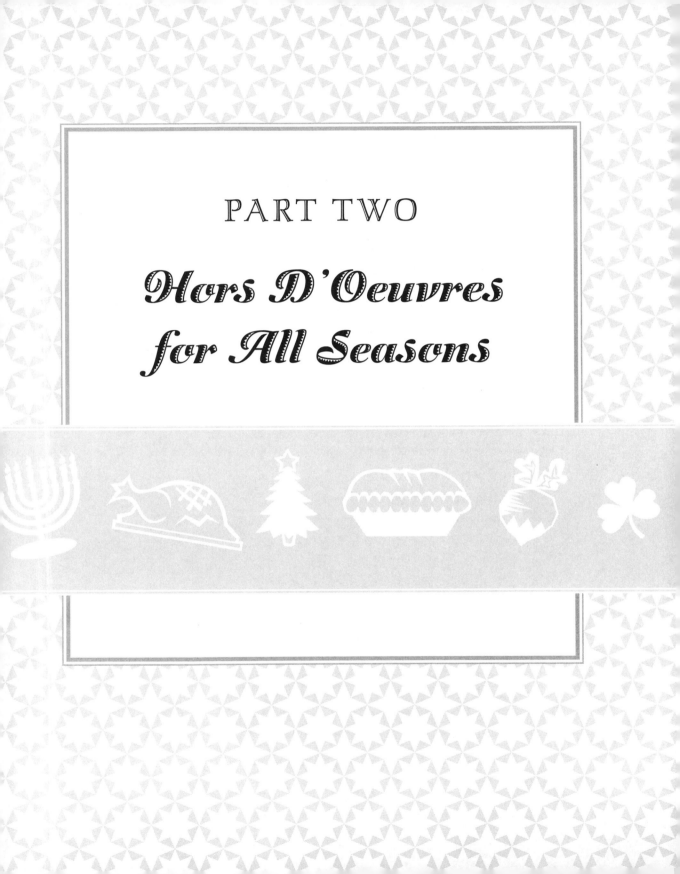

Whether you are planning to have a few people over for light hors d'oeuvres or an open house for fifty, this collection of recipes is sure to meet your needs with a wealth of ideas for lighter finger foods that are so delicious, no one will even guess that they're good for you.

As you will see, a few simple ingredient substitutions can make a big fat and calorie difference in traditional party favorites. Ultra-lean ground meats, reduced-fat and nonfat cheeses, sour cream, and mayonnaise star in meatballs, dips, spreads, and finger sandwiches that are every bit as tempting as their traditional counterparts.

The following pages first present recipes for hot treats—skewers, meatballs, hot dips, and other savory snacks that can be passed around on platters or kept warm in a chafing dish for fuss-free serving. This is followed by a tempting variety of finger sandwiches and other cold pick-up snacks, as well as a wide range of recipes for perhaps the most popular and versatile party foods of all—cold dips and spreads. Chilled beverages and hot brews, from a frosty fruit punch to steaming apple cider, round out the selection, guaranteeing that your next party will be a memorable one.

Hot Stuff

Apricot-Glazed Chicken Skewers

YIELD: 20 APPETIZERS

1¼ pounds boneless skinless chicken breast
20 six-inch skewers

MARINADE
½ cup apricot jam or fruit spread
3 tablespoons seasoned rice vinegar
3 tablespoons reduced-sodium soy sauce
1 tablespoon roasted (dark) sesame oil
1½ teaspoons crushed garlic
¾ teaspoon ground ginger

1. Rinse the chicken with cool water, and pat it dry with paper towels. Cut the chicken into thin strips (about ¼-inch), and place the strips in a shallow nonmetal container.
2. Place all of the marinade ingredients in a blender, and process until smooth.
3. Pour ¼ cup of the marinade over the chicken strips, and toss to mix well. Set aside for 20 to 30 minutes.
4. Loosely weave an 8-inch strip of the chicken onto each skewer. (If you are using wooden skewers, soak them in water for 20 minutes before using, to prevent burning.)
5. Coat a large broiler pan with nonstick cooking spray, and arrange the skewers on the pan. Broil for about 8 minutes, turning occasionally or until the chicken is nicely browned and no longer pink inside. Baste with the reserved marinade several times during the last 3 minutes

of cooking. (Alternatively, grill the skewers, covered, over medium coals for about 8 minutes, turning occasionally.) Place the skewers on a serving plate, and serve hot.

Nutritional Facts (per appetizer)
CALORIES: 44 CARBOHYDRATES: 3 G CHOLESTEROL: 16 MG FAT: 0.7 G FIBER: 0 G
PROTEIN: 7 G SODIUM: 109 MG CALCIUM: 4 MG

Teriyaki Steak Skewers

YIELD: 20 APPETIZERS

1 pound well-trimmed beef top sirloin steak
20 ½-inch wedges yellow onion
20 pieces red or green bell pepper (½ inch-by-1 inch)
10 medium-large fresh mushrooms, halved
20 six-inch skewers

MARINADE
¼ cup pineapple or orange juice
3 tablespoons reduced-sodium soy sauce
¼ cup hoisin sauce
2 tablespoons honey
1 tablespoon roasted (dark) sesame oil
¾ teaspoon ground ginger

1. Rinse the steak with cool water, and pat it dry with paper towels. Cut the steak into thin strips (about ¼ inch), and place the strips in a shallow nonmetal container.
2. Place all of the marinade ingredients in a small bowl and stir to mix well.
3. Pour ¼ cup of the marinade over the steak strips, and toss to mix well. Set aside for 20 to 30 minutes.
4. Loosely weave 1 onion wedge, 1 bell pepper piece, ½ mushroom, and a 6-inch strip of the steak onto each skewer. (If you are using wooden skewers, soak them in water for 20 minutes before using, to prevent burning.)

5. Coat a large broiler pan with nonstick cooking spray, and arrange the skewers on the pan. Broil for about 8 minutes, turning occasionally or until the skewers are nicely browned and the steak is done. Baste with the reserved marinade several times during the last 3 minutes of cooking. (Alternatively, grill the skewers, covered, over medium coals for about 8 minutes, turning occasionally.) Place the skewers on a serving plate, and serve hot.

Nutritional Facts (per appetizer)
CALORIES: 54 CARBOHYDRATES: 3 G CHOLESTEROL: 15 MG FAT: 2.1 G FIBER: 0.5 G
PROTEIN: 6 G SODIUM: 105 MG CALCIUM: 6 MG

Caribbean Shrimp Skewers

YIELD: 12 APPETIZERS

1 pound shelled and deveined large shrimp
12 six-inch skewers

MARINADE
3 tablespoons orange juice
1 tablespoon lime juice
1½ tablespoons extra virgin olive oil
⅓ cup mango chutney
1 teaspoon crushed garlic
¼ teaspoon salt
¼ teaspoon ground black pepper
¾ teaspoon dried thyme

1. Place all of the marinade ingredients in a blender and process until smooth. Remove ⅓ cup of the marinade, transfer to a covered container, and refrigerate until ready to cook the skewers.
2. Pour the remaining marinade over the shrimp, and toss to mix well. Cover and refrigerate for 30 to 60 minutes.
3. Thread about 4 shrimp onto each skewer as follows: Bend each shrimp almost in half, so that the large end nearly touches the smaller tail end. Insert the skewer just above the tail so that

it passes through the shrimp twice. (If you are using wooden skewers, soak them in water for 20 minutes before using, to prevent burning.)

4. Coat a large broiler pan with nonstick cooking spray, and arrange the skewers on the pan. Broil for about 6 minutes, turning occasionally, or until the shrimp turn pink and are cooked through. Baste with the reserved marinade during the last 3 minutes of cooking. (Alternatively, grill the skewers, covered, over medium coals for about 6 minutes, turning occasionally.) Place the skewers on a serving plate, and serve hot.

Nutritional Facts (per appetizer)
CALORIES: 52   CARBOHYDRATES: 1 G   CHOLESTEROL: 57 MG   FAT: 1.3 G   FIBER: 0 G
PROTEIN: 8 G   SODIUM: 89 MG   CALCIUM: 20 MG

Simple Shrimp Skewers

✲ *For variety, substitute Cajun or Greek seasoning or lemon pepper for the Old Bay seasoning.*

YIELD: 12 SERVINGS

1 pound shelled and deveined large raw shrimp
12 six-inch skewers
2 teaspoons Old Bay seasoning
1 tablespoon extra virgin olive oil

1. Place the shrimp in a large bowl, sprinkle with the seasoning and drizzle with the oil. Toss to mix well and set aside for 15 to 30 minutes.
2. Thread about 4 shrimp onto each skewer as follows: Bend each shrimp almost in half, so that the large end nearly touches the smaller tail end. Insert the skewer just above the tail so that it passes through the shrimp twice. (If you are using wooden skewers, soak them in water for 20 minutes before using, to prevent burning.)
3. Coat a large broiler pan with nonstick cooking spray, and arrange the skewers on the pan. Broil for about 6 minutes, turning occasionally, or until the shrimp turn pink and are cooked

through. (Alternatively, grill the skewers, covered, over medium coals for about 6 minutes, turning occasionally.) Place the skewers on a serving plate, and serve hot.

Nutritional Facts (per appetizer)
CALORIES: 48   CARBOHYDRATES: 0 G   CHOLESTEROL: 56 MG   FAT: 1.5 G   FIBER: 0 G
PROTEIN: 8 G   SODIUM: 135 MG   CALCIUM: 48 MG

Mini Crab Cakes

YIELD: 20 APPETIZERS

⅓ cup finely chopped celery
⅓ cup finely chopped onion
½ cup finely chopped red bell pepper
2 cans (6 ounces each) crabmeat, drained or 1½ cups flaked cooked crabmeat
1 teaspoon dried parsley or 1 tablespoon finely chopped fresh parsley
½ teaspoon ground paprika
⅛ teaspoon ground cayenne pepper
¾ cup sourdough bread crumbs*
¼ cup plus 2 tablespoons fat-free egg substitute
⅓ cup cornflake or Special-K cereal crumbs
Butter-flavored or olive oil nonstick cooking spray

SAUCE
½ cup plus 2 tablespoons nonfat or light mayonnaise
2 tablespoons chili sauce

1. Coat a large nonstick skillet with the cooking spray and add the celery, onion, bell pepper, and 1 tablespoon of water. Place the skillet over medium heat, cover, and cook, stirring occasionally, for about 5 minutes, or until the vegetables are soft. Add a little more water during cooking if needed, but only enough to prevent scorching. If there is excess water at the end of cooking, remove the lid and cook uncovered for a minute or two, or until the liquid evaporates.

2. Remove the skillet from the heat, and stir the crabmeat, parsley, paprika, and cayenne pepper into the vegetable mixture. Next, stir in the bread crumbs, followed by the egg substitute.

3. Place the cereal crumbs in a shallow dish. Shape the crab mixture into 1¼-inch balls and roll in the crumbs to coat evenly. Coat a large baking sheet with the cooking spray, place the balls on the sheet, and flatten slightly to form 1¾-inch cakes. Spray the tops of the crab cakes lightly with the cooking spray, and bake at 400°F for 8 minutes. Turn the crab cakes with a spatula, spray again, and bake for an additional 5 minutes, or until the cakes are nicely browned.

4. To make the sauce, combine the mayonnaise and chili sauce in a small bowl and stir to mix well. Serve the crab cakes hot, accompanied by the sauce.

Nutritional Facts (per appetizer with sauce)
CALORIES: 32 CARBOHYDRATES: 4 G CHOLESTEROL: 11 MG FAT: 0.2 G FIBER: 0.3 G
PROTEIN: 3.4 G SODIUM: 137 MG CALCIUM: 17 MG

*To make the bread crumbs, tear about 1¼ slices of sourdough bread into chunks. Put in a food processor or blender and process into crumbs.

Mediterranean Meatballs

YIELD: 60 APPETIZERS

MEATBALLS
1¼ pounds 95 percent lean ground beef
1½ teaspoons crushed garlic
1 teaspoon dried oregano
1¼ teaspoons beef bouillon granules
¼ teaspoon ground black pepper
10-ounce package frozen chopped spinach, thawed and squeezed dry
1 cup cooked brown rice or bulgur wheat
¾ cup finely chopped onion

SAUCE
2 cups bottled marinara sauce

1. Place all of the meatball ingredients and 2 tablespoons of the marinara sauce in a large bowl, and mix thoroughly.

2. Coat a large baking sheet with nonstick cooking spray. Shape the meatball mixture into 60 (1-inch) balls, and arrange them in a single layer on the baking sheet. Bake at 350°F for about 25 minutes, or until nicely browned and no longer pink inside. Transfer the meatballs to a chafing dish or Crock-Pot heated casserole to keep warm.

3. Place the remaining marinara sauce in a small pot, and cook over medium heat just until heated through. Pour the sauce over the meatballs, toss gently to mix, and serve.

Nutritional Facts (per appetizer)
CALORIES: 20   CARBOHYDRATES: 2 G   CHOLESTEROL: 5 MG   FAT: 0.5 G   FIBER: 0.3 G
PROTEIN: 2.3 G   SODIUM: 50 MG   CALCIUM: 6 MG

Ginger-Glazed Meatballs

YIELD: 50 APPETIZERS

MEATBALLS
1½ pounds 95 percent lean ground beef or ground turkey
8-ounce can water chestnuts, drained and chopped
1 cup finely chopped onion
2 egg whites
2 tablespoons reduced-sodium soy sauce
1 teaspoon crushed garlic
½ teaspoon ground ginger
¼ teaspoon ground black pepper

SAUCE
½ cup plus 2 tablespoons apricot jam or fruit spread
2½ tablespoons reduced-sodium soy sauce
2½ tablespoons seasoned rice vinegar
2½ tablespoons chicken broth
½ teaspoon ground ginger

1. Place all of the meatball ingredients in a large bowl, and mix thoroughly.
2. Coat a large baking sheet with nonstick cooking spray. Shape the meatball mixture into 50 (1-inch) balls, and arrange them in a single layer on the baking sheet. Bake at 350°F for about 25 minutes, or until nicely browned and no longer pink inside. Transfer the meatballs to a chafing dish or Crock-Pot heated casserole to keep warm.
3. Place the sauce ingredients in a blender, and blend until smooth. Transfer to a small pot, and cook over medium heat just until heated through. Pour the sauce over the meatballs, toss gently to mix, and serve.

Nutritional Facts (per appetizer)
CALORIES: 30 CARBOHYDRATES: 3 G CHOLESTEROL: 7 MG FAT: 0.6 G FIBER: 0.3 G
PROTEIN: 3 G SODIUM: 109 MG CALCIUM: 2 MG

Meatballs in Creamy Mushroom Sauce

YIELD: 48 APPETIZERS

MEATBALLS
1¼ pounds 95 percent lean ground beef
½ cup quick-cooking (1-minute) oats
1 cup finely chopped fresh mushrooms
1 cup finely chopped onions
1 egg white
1½ tablespoons finely chopped fresh parsley or 1½ teaspoons dried parsley
1¼ teaspoons beef bouillon granules
1 teaspoon crushed garlic
¼ teaspoon ground black pepper

SAUCE
10¾-ounce can condensed reduced-fat and -sodium cream of mushroom soup
½ cup nonfat or light sour cream

1. Place all of the meatball ingredients in a large bowl, and mix thoroughly.
2. Coat a large baking sheet with nonstick cooking spray. Shape the meatball mixture into 48 (1-inch) balls, and arrange them in a single layer on the baking sheet. Bake at 350°F for about 25 minutes, or until nicely browned and no longer pink inside. Transfer the meatballs to a chafing dish or Crock-Pot heated casserole to keep warm.
3. Place the sauce ingredients in a 1-quart pot, and cook, stirring frequently, over medium heat just until heated through. Pour the sauce over the meatballs, toss gently to mix, and serve.

Nutritional Facts (per appetizer)
CALORIES: 26 CARBOHYDRATES: 2 G CHOLESTEROL: 6 MG FAT: 0.8 G FIBER: 0.2 G
PROTEIN: 3 G SODIUM: 67 MG CALCIUM: 6 MG

Hot Artichoke Appetizers

YIELD: 24 APPETIZERS

2 jars (6 ounces each) marinated quartered artichoke hearts
4 ounces thinly sliced roasted turkey breast or lean ham

1. Drain the artichokes, reserving the marinade. Cut the turkey or ham into ¾-inch-wide strips. Wrap a strip of turkey or ham around each artichoke quarter, and secure with a wooden toothpick.
2. Place the artichoke pieces in a shallow baking dish, and add 2 tablespoons of the reserved marinade to the dish. Bake at 350°F for about 15 minutes, or until heated through. Transfer to a serving tray, and serve hot.

Nutritional Facts (per appetizer)
CALORIES: 13 CARBOHYDRATES: 1 G CHOLESTEROL: 2 MG FAT: 0.8 G FIBER: 0.5 G
PROTEIN: 0.7 G SODIUM: 80 MG CALCIUM: 1 MG

Chili-Cheese Quesadillas

YIELD: 32 APPETIZERS

⅔ cup nonfat or light sour cream
½ cup diced seeded plum tomatoes
⅓ cup thinly sliced scallions
8 flour tortillas (8-inch rounds)
2 cups shredded nonfat or reduced-fat Monterey Jack or Cheddar cheese
4-ounce can chopped green chilies, drained
Butter-flavored nonstick cooking spray

1. Place the sour cream, tomatoes, and scallions in separate serving dishes, and set aside.
2. Lay a tortilla on a flat surface and sprinkle with ¼ cup of cheese and a tablespoon of the chilies. Fold the top half of the tortilla over to enclose the filling. Repeat with the remaining ingredients to make 8 filled tortillas.
3. Coat 2 large baking sheets with the cooking spray, and lay the folded tortillas in a single layer on the sheets. Spray the tops lightly with the cooking spray. Bake at 425°F for 5 minutes. Turn the quesadillas over, and bake for 4 additional minutes, or until the tortillas are lightly browned and the cheese is melted.
4. To serve, place each quesadilla on a cutting board and cut into 4 wedges. Arrange the wedges on a serving platter accompanied by dishes of sour cream, tomatoes, and scallions.

Nutritional Facts (per appetizer)
CALORIES: 51   CARBOHYDRATES: 8 G   CHOLESTEROL: 0 MG   FAT: 0.5 G   FIBER: 0.5 G
PROTEIN: 3.3 G   SODIUM: 112 MG   CALCIUM: 70 MG

For variety, add any of the following to the filling:

◆ 1 cup shredded roasted chicken

◆ 1 cup flaked cooked crabmeat

◆ 3 slices turkey bacon, cooked, drained, and crumbled

◆ 8-ounce can Mexican-style whole-kernel corn, well drained

Spinach and Bacon Quesadillas

YIELD: 32 APPETIZERS

1 cup chopped fresh mushrooms

1 teaspoon crushed garlic

¼ teaspoon dried thyme

5 cups (moderately packed) fresh coarsely chopped spinach leaves

4 slices extra-lean turkey bacon, cooked, drained, and crumbled

8 flour tortillas (8-inch rounds)

2 cups shredded nonfat or reduced-fat mozzarella or Swiss cheese

Olive oil nonstick cooking spray

1. Coat a large nonstick skillet with the cooking spray. Add the mushrooms, garlic, and thyme, and place over medium-high heat. Cook, stirring frequently, until the mushrooms release their juices and are nicely browned. Periodically place a lid on the skillet if the mixture begins to dry out. (The steam released during cooking will moisten the skillet.) Add the spinach to the skillet and cook, stirring frequently, for a minute or two or until the spinach is wilted. Remove the skillet from the heat, stir in the bacon, and set aside.

2. Lay a tortilla out on a flat surface and spread one-eighth of the spinach mixture over the bottom half of the tortilla, then sprinkle with ¼ cup of the cheese. Fold the top half of the tortilla over to enclose the filling. Repeat with the remaining ingredients to make 8 filled tortillas.

3. Coat 2 large baking sheets with the cooking spray, and lay the folded tortillas in a single layer on the sheets. Spray the tops lightly with the cooking spray. Bake at 425°F for 5 minutes. Turn the quesadillas over, and bake for 4 additional minutes, or until the tortillas are lightly browned and the cheese is melted.

4. Place each quesadilla on a cutting board and cut into 4 wedges. Serve hot.

Nutritional Facts (per appetizer)
CALORIES: 50 CARBOHYDRATES: 6 G CHOLESTEROL: 3 MG FAT: 0.9 G FIBER: 0.6 G
PROTEIN: 4 G SODIUM: 121 MG CALCIUM: 70 MG

Roasted Red Pepper Quesadillas

YIELD: 32 APPETIZERS

8 flour tortillas (8-inch rounds)
2 cups shredded nonfat or reduced-fat mozzarella or provolone cheese
¾ cup chopped bottled roasted red bell peppers, drained
½ cup chopped black olives
¼ teaspoon dried Italian seasoning
Olive oil nonstick cooking spray

1. Lay a tortilla on a flat surface, and sprinkle with ¼ cup of cheese, 1½ tablespoons roasted peppers, and a tablespoon of the olives. Sprinkle some of the Italian seasoning over the filling. Fold the top half of the tortilla over to enclose the filling. Repeat with the remaining ingredients to make 8 filled tortillas.
2. Coat 2 large baking sheets with the cooking spray, and lay the folded tortillas in a single layer on the sheets. Spray the tops lightly with the cooking spray. Bake at 425°F for 5 minutes. Turn the quesadillas over, and bake for 4 additional minutes, or until the tortillas are lightly browned and the cheese is melted.
3. Place each quesadilla on a cutting board and cut into 4 wedges. Serve hot.

Nutritional Facts (per appetizer)
CALORIES: 46 CARBOHYDRATES: 7 G CHOLESTEROL: 0 MG FAT: 0.7 G FIBER: 0.5 G
PROTEIN: 2.7 G SODIUM: 134 MG CALCIUM: 61 MG

Feta and Tomato Tarts

YIELD: 24 APPETIZERS

4 pieces whole wheat or oat-bran pita bread or flatbread or
   4 small pieces focaccia bread (6-inch rounds)

TOPPINGS

1 cup finely chopped plum tomatoes (about 3 medium)

¼ cup chopped black olives

2 tablespoons thinly sliced scallions

¾ cup shredded reduced-fat mozzarella cheese

¼ cup crumbled nonfat or reduced-fat feta cheese

¼ teaspoon dried oregano

Olive oil nonstick cooking spray

1. Spread a quarter of the tomatoes, olives, and scallions over each bread round to within ¼ inch of the edges. Sprinkle first the mozzarella and then the feta cheese over the tomatoes. Sprinkle with a quarter of the oregano and spray the top of each tart lightly with the cooking spray.

2. Arrange the tarts on a large baking sheet and bake at 400°F for about 10 minutes, or until the cheese is melted and the tarts are lightly browned. Transfer the tarts to a cutting board, and cut each one into 6 wedges. Serve hot.

Nutritional Facts (per appetizer)

CALORIES: 35   CARBOHYDRATES: 6 G   CHOLESTEROL: 2 MG   FAT: 0.8 G   FIBER: 0.8 G
PROTEIN: 2.4 G   SODIUM: 103 MG   CALCIUM: 27 MG

Crab and Artichoke Tarts

YIELD: 24 APPETIZERS

4 pieces whole wheat or oat-bran pita bread or flatbread or
*   4 small pieces focaccia bread (6-inch rounds)*

TOPPINGS

6-ounce jar marinated artichoke hearts, drained and finely chopped

6-ounce can crabmeat, drained or ¾ cup flaked cooked crabmeat

¼ cup grated Parmesan cheese

¼ teaspoon dried oregano

Olive oil nonstick cooking spray

1. Spread a quarter of the artichoke hearts and crabmeat over each bread round to within ¼ inch of the edges. Sprinkle a quarter of the Parmesan cheese and oregano over the artichokes and crabmeat on each tart, then spray the tops lightly with the cooking spray.
2. Arrange the tarts on a large baking sheet and bake at 400°F for about 10 minutes, or until lightly browned. Transfer the tarts to a cutting board, and cut each one into 6 wedges. Serve hot.

Nutritional Facts (per appetizer)
CALORIES: 36   CARBOHYDRATES: 6 G   CHOLESTEROL: 5 MG   FAT: 0.8 G   FIBER: 0.9 G
PROTEIN: 2.6 G   SODIUM: 108 MG   CALCIUM: 27 MG

Mushroom and Mozzarella Party Pizzas

YIELD: 24 APPETIZERS

4 pieces whole wheat or oat-bran pita bread or flatbread or
   4 small pieces focaccia bread (6-inch rounds)

TOPPINGS
2 cups sliced fresh mushrooms
1 small yellow onion, thinly sliced
¼ teaspoon dried Italian seasoning
¾ cup bottled marinara sauce
2 tablespoons grated Parmesan cheese
¾ cup shredded reduced-fat mozzarella cheese
Olive oil nonstick cooking spray

1. Coat a large nonstick skillet with the cooking spray. Add the mushrooms, onions, and Italian seasoning, and place the skillet over medium-high heat. Cover and cook for about 4 minutes, stirring several times, until the mushrooms and onions are tender and lightly browned.
2. Place the bread rounds on a flat surface and spread each with a quarter of the marinara sauce to within ¼ inch of the edges. Top the sauce on each bread round with a quarter of the mushroom mixture, then sprinkle with a quarter of the Parmesan and mozzarella cheese. Spray the top of each pizza lightly with the cooking spray.

3. Arrange the pizzas on a large baking sheet and bake at 400°F for about 10 minutes, or until the cheese is melted and the pizzas are lightly browned. Transfer the pizzas to a cutting board, and cut each one into 6 wedges. Serve hot.

Nutritional Facts (per appetizer)
CALORIES: 37 CARBOHYDRATES: 6 G CHOLESTEROL: 2 MG FAT: 0.7 G FIBER: 0.9 G
PROTEIN: 2.6 G SODIUM: 104 MG CALCIUM: 28 MG

Pepperoni Party Pizzas

YIELD: 24 APPETIZERS

4 pieces whole wheat or oat-bran pita bread or flatbread or
  4 small pieces focaccia bread (6-inch rounds)

TOPPINGS
¾ cup bottled marinara sauce
1 cup shredded reduced-fat mozzarella cheese
28 slices turkey pepperoni
Olive oil nonstick cooking spray

1. Place the bread rounds on a flat surface and spread each with a quarter of the marinara sauce to within ¼ inch of the edges. Top the sauce on each bread round with 2 tablespoons of the mozzarella and a quarter of the pepperoni slices. Finish off each pizza with a quarter of the remaining mozzarella, then spray the top of each pizza lightly with the cooking spray.
2. Arrange the pizzas on a large baking sheet and bake at 400°F for about 10 minutes, or until the cheese is melted and the pizzas are lightly browned. Transfer the pizzas to a cutting board, and cut each one into 6 wedges. Serve hot.

Nutritional Facts (per appetizer)
CALORIES: 37 CARBOHYDRATES: 6 G CHOLESTEROL: 5 MG FAT: 0.8 G FIBER: 0.7 G
PROTEIN: 2.8 G SODIUM: 132 MG CALCIUM: 20 MG

Mini Mexican Pizzas

YIELD: 24 APPETIZERS

4 flour tortillas (8-inch rounds)
1 cup shredded reduced-fat Monterey Jack cheese
¼ cup chopped black olives
¼ cup thinly sliced scallions
Olive oil nonstick cooking spray
¼ cup plus 2 tablespoons bottled salsa
¼ cup plus 2 tablespoons nonfat or light sour cream

1. Place the tortillas on a flat surface and sprinkle each with a quarter of the cheese, olives, and scallions. Spray the top of each tortilla lightly with the cooking spray.
2. Spray 2 large baking sheets with the cooking spray and arrange 2 of the tortillas on each sheet. Bake at 500°F for about 5 minutes, or until the tortillas are puffed and lightly browned around the edges. Transfer the tortillas to a cutting board, and cut each one into 6 wedges. Serve hot accompanied by the salsa and sour cream.

Nutritional Facts (per appetizer)
CALORIES: 42 CARBOHYDRATES: 4 G CHOLESTEROL: 2 MG FAT: 1.2 G FIBER: 0.4 G
PROTEIN: 2.3 G SODIUM: 89 MG CALCIUM: 47 MG

Baked Broccoli-Cheese Spread

YIELD: 2½ CUPS

½ cup light garlic-and-herb-flavored cream cheese
¾ cup nonfat or light mayonnaise
10-ounce package frozen chopped broccoli, thawed and squeezed dry
⅓ cup chopped black olives
½ cup grated Parmesan cheese
Butter-flavored nonstick cooking spray

1. Place the cream cheese and mayonnaise in a medium-sized bowl, and stir to mix well. Add the broccoli, olives, and ¼ cup plus 2 tablespoons of the Parmesan cheese, and stir to mix well.

2. Coat a 1-quart casserole dish with the cooking spray, and spread the broccoli mixture evenly in the dish. Sprinkle the remaining 2 tablespoons of Parmesan cheese over the top, and spray the top lightly with the cooking spray.

3. Cover the dish with aluminum foil, and bake at 350°F for 25 minutes, or until the mixture is heated through. Remove the foil, and bake for 5 additional minutes, or until the top is lightly browned. Serve hot with whole-grain crackers, Parmesan Pita Crisps (page 80), or a loaf of sourdough French bread.

Nutritional Facts (per tablespoon)
CALORIES: 17 CARBOHYDRATES: 1 G CHOLESTEROL: 3 MG FAT: 0.9 G FIBER: 0.3 G
PROTEIN: 1 G SODIUM: 77 MG CALCIUM: 24 MG

Baked Artichoke Dip

YIELD: 2½ CUPS

2 cans (14 ounces each) artichoke hearts, drained and chopped
¾ cup nonfat or light mayonnaise
1 tablespoon Dijon or spicy mustard
½ cup grated Parmesan cheese
Butter-flavored nonstick cooking spray

1. Place all of the ingredients except for 2 tablespoons of the Parmesan cheese in a food processor and process for about 20 seconds, or until the mixture is well blended but still slightly chunky.

2. Coat a 1-quart casserole dish with the cooking spray, and spread the artichoke mixture evenly in the dish. Sprinkle the remaining 2 tablespoons of Parmesan cheese over the top, and spray the top lightly with the cooking spray.

3. Cover the dish with aluminum foil, and bake at 350°F for 25 minutes, or until the mixture is heated through. Remove the foil, and bake for 5 additional minutes, or until the top is lightly

browned. Serve hot with whole-grain crackers, Parmesan Pita Crisps (page 80), or a loaf of sourdough French bread.

Nutritional Facts (per tablespoon)
CALORIES: 14 CARBOHYDRATES: 2 G CHOLESTEROL: 1 MG FAT: 0.5 G FIBER: 0.8 G
PROTEIN: 0.8 G SODIUM: 68 MG CALCIUM: 23 MG

Hot Spinach and Artichoke Spread

YIELD: 2½ CUPS

10 ounces frozen chopped spinach, thawed and squeezed dry
14-ounce can artichoke hearts, well drained and finely chopped
¼ cup plus 2 tablespoons light garlic-and-herb-flavored cream cheese
¼ cup plus 2 tablespoons nonfat or light mayonnaise
½ cup grated Parmesan cheese
Butter-flavored nonstick cooking spray

1. Place all of the ingredient except for 2 tablespoons of the Parmesan cheese in a medium-sized bowl, and stir to mix well.
2. Coat a 1-quart casserole dish with the cooking spray and spread the mixture evenly in the dish. Sprinkle the remaining 2 tablespoons of Parmesan cheese over the top, and spray the top lightly with the cooking spray.
3. Cover the dish with aluminum foil and bake at 350°F for 25 minutes, or until the mixture is heated through. Remove the foil and bake for 5 additional minutes, or until the top is lightly browned. Serve hot with whole-grain crackers, Parmesan Pita Crisps (page 80), or a loaf of sourdough French bread.

Nutritional Facts (per tablespoon)
CALORIES: 15 CARBOHYDRATES: 1 G CHOLESTEROL: 2 MG FAT: 0.7 G FIBER: 0.6 G
PROTEIN: 1 G SODIUM: 57 MG CALCIUM: 29 MG

Hot and Creamy Crab Dip

YIELD: 3¼ CUPS

8-ounce block nonfat cream cheese
8-ounce block reduced-fat (Neufchâtel) cream cheese
2 tablespoons finely chopped onion
1 teaspoon white wine Worcestershire sauce
1 teaspoon prepared horseradish
1½ cups flaked cooked crabmeat or 2 cans (6 ounces each) crabmeat, drained
¼ cup sliced toasted almonds (page 30), crushed or ¼ cup finely chopped walnuts
Butter-flavored nonstick cooking spray
Ground paprika

1. Place the cream cheese, onion, Worcestershire sauce, and horseradish in a large bowl, and beat with an electric mixer until smooth. Stir in the crabmeat. Coat a 9-inch deep-dish pie pan with the cooking spray and spread the mixture evenly in the pan. Sprinkle the nuts over the top, then spray the top lightly with the cooking spray, and sprinkle lightly with the paprika.
2. Bake uncovered at 350°F for about 25 minutes, or until the edges are bubbly and the top is lightly browned. Serve hot with whole-grain crackers or Parmesan Pita Crisps (page 80).

Nutritional Facts (per tablespoon)
CALORIES: 23   CARBOHYDRATES: 0.6 G   CHOLESTEROL: 6 MG   FAT: 1.3 G   FIBER: 0.1 G
PROTEIN: 2 G   SODIUM: 86 MG   CALCIUM: 20 MG

Baked Clam Dip

YIELD: 3¼ CUPS

2 cans (10 ounces each) chopped clams, undrained
1 large round loaf sourdough bread
8-ounce block nonfat cream cheese

8-ounce block reduced-fat (Neufchâtel) cream cheese
2 tablespoons finely chopped onion
1 tablespoon lemon juice
2 teaspoons white wine Worcestershire sauce
Ground paprika

1. Drain the clams, reserving 2 tablespoons of the liquid. Set aside.
2. Cut the top from the bread loaf and set aside. Hollow out the bread, leaving a 1-inch-thick shell. Set aside.
3. Coat a baking sheet with nonstick cooking spray. Cut the removed bread into cubes, and arrange on the baking sheet. Bake at 350°F for 10 minutes, or until lightly toasted. Set aside.
4. Place the cream cheese, reserved clam juice, onion, lemon juice, and Worcestershire sauce in a large bowl, and beat with an electric mixer until smooth. Stir in the drained clams. Spread the mixture evenly in the hollowed-out loaf, cover with the bread top, and wrap in aluminum foil.
5. Bake the filled loaf at 350°F for about 1 hour and 10 minutes, or until the dip is hot and creamy. Place the loaf on a serving plate, remove and discard the top, and sprinkle the dip lightly with the paprika. Serve hot with whole-grain crackers and the toasted bread cubes.

Nutritional Facts (per tablespoon)
CALORIES: 21   CARBOHYDRATES: 0.5 G   CHOLESTEROL: 6 MG   FAT: 1.1 G   FIBER: 0 G
PROTEIN: 2 G   SODIUM: 44 MG   CALCIUM: 20 MG

Zippy Layered Bean Dip

YIELD: ABOUT 3 CUPS

1-pound can fat-free or low-fat refried beans
⅓ cup nonfat or light sour cream
1½ teaspoons chili powder
¾ cup shredded reduced-fat Cheddar cheese
¼ cup thinly sliced scallions
¼ cup sliced black olives
2 tablespoons finely chopped pickled jalapeño peppers

TOPPINGS
⅓ cup diced avocado (optional)
⅓ cup diced fresh tomatoes (optional)

1. Place the beans, sour cream, and chili powder in a medium-sized bowl, and stir to mix well. Spread the mixture over the bottom of a 9-inch glass pie pan. Top with the cheese, followed by the scallions, olives, and jalapeños.
2. Place the dish in a microwave oven and cook uncovered at high power for about 5 minutes, or until the edges are bubbly and the cheese is melted. Sprinkle the avocados and tomatoes over the top if desired, and serve hot with baked tortilla chips.

Nutritional Facts (per tablespoon)
CALORIES: 15 CARBOHYDRATES: 2 G CHOLESTEROL: 1 MG FAT: 0.3 G FIBER: 0.5 G
PROTEIN: 1.1 G SODIUM: 55 MG CALCIUM: 21 MG

Cold Stuff

Deviled Eggs

 *For the most nutrition, be sure to use omega-3-enriched eggs in this recipe.*

YIELD: 12 APPETIZERS

6 peeled hard-boiled eggs
¼ cup nonfat or light mayonnaise
1 tablespoon spicy brown or Dijon mustard
Pinch ground white pepper
2 to 3 teaspoons finely chopped fresh dill or chives or 2 tablespoons drained sweet pickle
    relish (optional)
Ground paprika

1. Cut the eggs in half lengthwise and remove the yolks. Place the yolks in a small bowl, and mash well. Add the mayonnaise, mustard, and pepper to the egg yolks, and stir until smooth. Stir in the herbs or relish if desired.

2. Spoon or pipe the yolk mixture into the hollowed-out eggs. Sprinkle some of the paprika over the top of each egg. Transfer to a serving platter and serve immediately, or cover and refrigerate until ready to serve.

Nutritional Facts (per appetizer)
CALORIES: 39   CARBOHYDRATES: 1 G   CHOLESTEROL: 107 MG   FAT: 2.3 G   FIBER: 0 G
PROTEIN: 3 G   SODIUM: 82 MG   CALCIUM: 39 MG

Shrimp with Spicy Cocktail Sauce

YIELD: 8 SERVINGS

1 pound peeled (tail-on) steamed shrimp

SAUCE
¾ cup ketchup or chili sauce
2 tablespoons prepared horseradish
1 tablespoon lemon juice
1 tablespoon Worcestershire sauce
6 to 8 drops hot pepper sauce (optional)

1. Combine all of the sauce ingredients, and stir to mix well. Cover and refrigerate for at least 1 hour.
2. Arrange the shrimp on a serving platter accompanied by the sauce.

Nutritional Facts (per serving)
CALORIES: 83   CARBOHYDRATES: 7 G   CHOLESTEROL: 110 MG   FAT: 0.7 G   FIBER: 0.4 G
PROTEIN: 12 G   SODIUM: 432 MG   CALCIUM: 83 MG

Stuffed Chicken Salad Sandwiches

✡ *For variety, substitute any of the other chicken or tuna spreads presented in this chapter for the Cranberry Chicken Spread.*

YIELD: 12 SERVINGS

1 recipe Cranberry Chicken Spread (page 74)
12 small whole wheat or sourdough dinner rolls

1. Slice the tops off the rolls and scoop out the centers, leaving a slightly less than ½-inch-thick shell.

2. Fill each hollowed-out roll with some of the spread. Replace the top, or leave the sandwiches open-faced. Serve immediately.

Nutritional Facts (per serving)
CALORIES: 123 CARBOHYDRATES: 16 G CHOLESTEROL: 15 MG FAT: 3.4 G FIBER: 2.2 G
PROTEIN: 8 G SODIUM: 198 MG CALCIUM: 33 MG

French Bread Finger Sandwiches

YIELD: 16 SERVINGS

1 cup chopped canned (drained) artichoke hearts
2 tablespoons bottled nonfat or reduced-fat Italian or
   balsamic vinaigrette salad dressing
1 long thin loaf (1 pound) sourdough French bread
¾ cup nonfat or light garlic-and-herb-flavored cream cheese
6 ounces thinly sliced roasted turkey breast, ham, or roast beef
2 ounces thinly sliced reduced-fat provolone or Swiss cheese
½ small red bell pepper, sliced into thin rings
2 thin slices red onion, separated into rings
12 leaves fresh spinach or arugula leaves

1. Combine the artichoke hearts and salad dressing in a small bowl, toss to mix well, and set aside.
2. Cut the loaf of bread in half lengthwise, and scoop out the centers of the bread halves, leaving a ½-inch-thick shell. Spread half of the cream cheese in the hollow of each bread half. Top the bottom half of the bread with the sliced turkey, ham, or roast beef; followed by the cheese; artichoke mixture; bell pepper rings; onion rings; and spinach or arugula.
3. Place the top half on the loaf, and cut the loaf into 1½-inch pieces. Secure each piece with a toothpick, and serve immediately.

Nutritional Facts (per appetizer)
CALORIES: 100 CARBOHYDRATES: 13 G CHOLESTEROL: 12 MG FAT: 1.5 G FIBER: 0.8 G
PROTEIN: 8 G SODIUM: 231 MG CALCIUM: 105 MG

High Rollers

6 flour tortillas (10-inch rounds), warmed to room temperature

1 cup plus 2 tablespoons nonfat or light garlic-and-herb or
    vegetable-flavored cream cheese

12 ounces thinly sliced roasted turkey breast

6 ounces thinly sliced reduced-fat Swiss or provolone cheese

12 Bibb or Boston lettuce leaves or 36 young, tender fresh spinach leaves

¼ cup plus 2 tablespoons finely chopped black olives

14-ounce can artichoke hearts, well drained and chopped

18 thin rings red bell pepper

1. Arrange the tortillas on a flat surface, and spread each with 3 tablespoons of the cream cheese, extending the cheese to the outer edges. Lay 2 ounces of sliced turkey over the *bottom half only* of each tortilla, leaving a 1-inch margin on each outer edge. Place 1 ounce of the cheese over the turkey. Arrange 2 lettuce or 6 spinach leaves over the cheese, and sprinkle with 1 tablespoon olives. Top the olive layer with a ¼ cup of the artichoke hearts and 3 red bell pepper rings.

2. Starting at the bottom, roll each tortilla up tightly. Cut a 1¼-inch piece off each end and discard. Slice the remainder of each tortilla into six 1¼-inch pieces. Arrange the rolls on a platter and serve immediately. Or leave the rolls intact, wrap in plastic wrap, and refrigerate for up to 8 hours before slicing and serving.

Nutritional Facts (per appetizer)
CALORIES: 53 CARBOHYDRATES: 6 G CHOLESTEROL: 9 MG FAT: 1 G FIBER: 0.8 G
PROTEIN: 4 G SODIUM: 142 MG CALCIUM: 52 MG

Variation:

Substitute ¾ cup grated carrot and 6 thin slices red onion, separated into rings, for the artichoke hearts and red bell pepper rings. Top the lettuce on each tortilla with 2 tablespoons of the carrots and several of the onion rings.

Ham and Cheese High Rollers

YIELD: 36 APPETIZERS

6 flour tortillas (10-inch rounds), warmed to room temperature
1 cup plus 2 tablespoons nonfat or light garlic-and-herb or
vegetable-flavored cream cheese
12 ounces thinly sliced ham (at least 97 percent lean)
6 ounces thinly sliced reduced-fat Cheddar cheese
12 Bibb or Boston lettuce leaves
18 thin slices plum tomato
12 thin rings green bell pepper

1. Arrange the tortillas on a flat surface, and spread each with 3 tablespoons of the cream cheese, extending the cheese to the outer edges. Lay 2 ounces of the ham over the *bottom half only* of each tortilla, leaving a 1-inch margin on each outer edge. Place 1 ounce of the cheese over the ham. Arrange 2 lettuce leaves over the cheese, and then top with 3 tomato slices and 2 green bell pepper rings.
2. Starting at the bottom, roll each tortilla up tightly. Cut a 1¼-inch piece off each end and discard. Slice the remainder of each tortilla into six 1¼-inch pieces. Arrange the rolls on a platter and serve immediately. Or leave the rolls intact, wrap in plastic wrap, and refrigerate for up to 8 hours before slicing and serving.

Nutritional Facts (per appetizer)
CALORIES: 53 CARBOHYDRATES: 5 G CHOLESTEROL: 9 MG FAT: 1.2 G FIBER: 0.4 G
PROTEIN: 4.2 G SODIUM: 173 MG CALCIUM: 48 MG

Spinach Pinwheels

YIELD: 32 APPETIZERS

10-ounce package frozen chopped spinach, thawed and squeezed dry
¼ cup grated carrots

¼ cup thinly sliced scallions

¼ cup chopped black olives

8-ounce block nonfat or reduced-fat (Neufchâtel) cream cheese, softened to room temperature

4 plain or spinach-flavored flour tortillas (10-inch rounds), warmed to room temperature

1. Place the spinach, carrots, scallions, olives, and cream cheese in a medium-sized bowl, and stir to mix well.
2. Arrange the tortillas on a flat surface, and spread each with a quarter of the cheese mixture, extending the mixture all the way to the top and bottom edges, but only to within 1 inch of the sides.
3. Starting at the bottom, roll each tortilla up tightly. Cut a 1¼-inch piece off each end, and discard. Slice the remainder of each tortilla into eight equal pieces. Arrange the rolls on a platter, and serve immediately. Or leave the rolls intact, wrap in plastic wrap, and refrigerate for up to 8 hours before slicing and serving.

Nutritional Facts (per appetizer)
CALORIES: 27 CARBOHYDRATES: 3.7 G CHOLESTEROL: 0 MG FAT: 0.5 G FIBER: 0.6 G PROTEIN: 1.9 G SODIUM: 70 MG CALCIUM: 33 MG

Fabulous Fruit Kebabs

YIELD: 16 APPETIZERS

16 medium whole fresh strawberries, rinsed and patted dry

16 one-inch cubes papaya or cantaloupe

16 one-inch cubes fresh pineapple

16 one-inch cubes honeydew melon

16 six-inch wooden skewers

HONEY-LIME DIP
1 cup nonfat or light sour cream
3 tablespoons honey
1½ tablespoons lime juice

1. Place all of the dip ingredients in a small bowl and stir to mix well. Cover and refrigerate until ready to serve.
2. Skewer 1 strawberry, papaya or cantaloupe piece, pineapple piece, and honeydew melon piece on each skewer. Serve the skewers accompanied by the honey-lime dip.

Nutritional Facts (per serving)
CALORIES: 46 CARBOHYDRATES: 11 G CHOLESTEROL: 0 MG FAT: 0.1 G FIBER: 1 G PROTEIN: 1.2 G SODIUM: 13 MG CALCIUM: 24 MG

Sensational Strawberries

YIELD: 24 PIECES

24 medium-sized strawberries with stems (about 1 pound)
⅓ cup sliced toasted almonds (page 30), coarsely crushed
2½ ounces semisweet baking chocolate

1. Rinse the berries with cool water (leave the stems on), and pat dry thoroughly with paper towels. Set aside. Place the almonds in a shallow dish and set aside.
2. Fill a 1-quart pot half full with water and bring to a boil over high heat. Reduce the heat to low to maintain the water at a low simmer. Chop the chocolate into pieces and put in a 1-cup glass measure. Place the measuring cup in the simmering water and stir frequently for several minutes or until the chocolate melts. Remove the pot from the heat, keeping the measuring cup containing the chocolate in the pot.
3. Insert a toothpick into the stem end of a strawberry and dip the berry into the melted chocolate to coat the lower two-thirds of the berry. Quickly roll the strawberry in the almonds, to cover the chocolate with a thin layer of almonds. Place the berry on a small baking sheet lined with wax paper. Refrigerate the berries for at least 30 minutes and up to 12 hours before serving.

Nutritional Facts (per piece)
CALORIES: 28 CARBOHYDRATES: 3 G CHOLESTEROL: 0 MG FAT: 1.9 G FIBER: 0.8 G PROTEIN: 0.7 G SODIUM: 0 MG CALCIUM: 7 MG

Honey-Glazed Pecans

YIELD: ABOUT 2¼ CUPS

¼ cup honey
3 tablespoons sugar
Pinch salt
2 cups pecan halves

1. Combine the honey, sugar, and salt in a medium bowl, and stir to mix well. Add the pecans, and toss to coat with the honey mixture.

2. Coat a large baking sheet with nonstick cooking spray, and spread the pecans in an even layer over the sheet. Bake at 350°F for about 15 to 20 minutes, stirring the pecans every 3 to 5 minutes, until they are deep golden brown and glazed. Watch the pecans closely during the last few minutes of baking to prevent them from becoming burned.

3. Coat a sheet of waxed paper or aluminum foil with nonstick cooking spray, and quickly spread the pecans in an even layer over the sheet. Use a fork to separate any pecans that are sticking together. Let the pecans cool completely and then transfer to an airtight container. To maintain freshness, refrigerate for up to 3 weeks or freeze for up to 3 months.

Nutritional Facts (per 2-tablespoon serving)
CALORIES: 102 CARBOHYDRATES: 6 G CHOLESTEROL: 0 MG FAT: 8.5 G FIBER: 1.1 G
PROTEIN: 1.1 G SODIUM: 7 MG CALCIUM: 8 MG

Cinnamon-Glazed Walnuts

YIELD: ABOUT 2⅓ CUPS

2 tablespoons evaporated skim milk or orange juice
¼ cup plus 2 tablespoons sugar
½ teaspoon ground cinnamon
Pinch salt

¼ teaspoon vanilla extract
2 cups walnut halves

1. Combine the milk or orange juice, sugar, cinnamon, salt, and vanilla extract in a medium-sized nonstick skillet, and stir to mix well. Place the skillet over medium heat, and cook for a minute or two, stirring frequently, or until the mixture comes to a boil and the sugar is dissolved. Add the walnuts, and toss to coat with the sugar mixture.
2. Cook, stirring constantly for several minutes, or until the sugar mixture coating the nuts is completely dry.
3. Quickly spread the walnuts in an even layer over a nonstick baking sheet. Use a fork to separate any nuts that are sticking together. Let the nuts cool completely and then transfer to an airtight container. To maintain freshness, refrigerate for up to 3 weeks or freeze for up to 3 months.

Nutritional Facts (per 2-tablespoon serving)
CALORIES: 90 CARBOHYDRATES: 6 G CHOLESTEROL: 0 MG FAT: 7.3 G FIBER: 0.7 G
PROTEIN: 1.8 G SODIUM: 10 MG CALCIUM: 17 MG

Black Bean Salsa Dip

YIELD: 1½ CUPS

15-ounce can black beans, rinsed and drained
½ cup bottled chunky-style salsa
2 to 3 tablespoons chopped fresh cilantro
¼ teaspoon ground cumin

1. Place all of the ingredients in a food processor, and process until smooth.
2. Serve immediately with baked tortilla chips, or cover and refrigerate until ready to serve.

Nutritional Facts (per tablespoon)
CALORIES: 13 CARBOHYDRATES: 2 G CHOLESTEROL: 0 MG FAT: 0.1 G FIBER: 1 G
PROTEIN: 1 G SODIUM: 52 MG CALCIUM: 6 MG

Sour Cream Salsa Dip

YIELD: 2¾ CUPS

16 ounces nonfat or light sour cream
1 cup bottled chunky-style salsa

1. Combine the sour cream and salsa in a medium-sized bowl, and stir to mix well.
2. Cover, and chill for at least 2 hours before serving. Serve with baked tortilla chips.

Nutritional Facts (per tablespoon)
CALORIES: 13   CARBOHYDRATES: 2.2 G   CHOLESTEROL: 0 MG   FAT: 0 G   FIBER: 0.1 G
PROTEIN: 0.6 G   SODIUM: 35 MG   CALCIUM: 13 MG

Great Guacamole

YIELD: 2¼ CUPS

3 cups diced peeled avocado (about 2 large or 3 small)
1 tablespoon lime juice
¼ cup finely chopped seeded plum tomato (about 1 large)
¼ cup finely chopped onion
2 tablespoons finely chopped fresh cilantro
1 tablespoon chopped pickled jalapeño pepper
1 teaspoon crushed garlic
¼ teaspoon salt

1. Place the avocado and lime juice in a large bowl, and use a potato masher to mash the flesh, leaving it slightly chunky. Add the remaining ingredients, and stir to mix well.
2. Serve immediately with baked tortilla chips. Or cover and refrigerate for up to 3 hours before serving. (Place a sheet of plastic wrap directly over the surface of the guacamole to prevent it from turning brown.)

Apple-Cheddar Spread

YIELD: ABOUT 2 CUPS

8-ounce block nonfat or reduced-fat (Neufchâtel) cream cheese,
    softened to room temperature
1 medium Granny Smith apple, peeled and finely chopped (about ¾ cup)
½ cup shredded nonfat or reduced-fat Cheddar cheese
¼ cup finely chopped dates
3 to 4 tablespoons finely chopped toasted pecans (page 30)

1. Place the cream cheese, apple, Cheddar cheese, and dates in a small bowl and stir to mix well. Spread the mixture into a small shallow dish and sprinkle the pecans over the top.
2. Serve immediately with whole-grain crackers, celery sticks, and apple wedges (dip the apple wedges in pineapple juice to prevent browning). Or cover and refrigerate until ready to serve, but let the spread come to room temperature before serving.

Cool Cucumber Dip

YIELD: 2 CUPS

1 medium-large cucumber, peeled, seeded, and cut into chunks
2 tablespoons finely chopped onion
¾ cup nonfat or light sour cream

¾ cup nonfat or light mayonnaise

1 tablespoon finely chopped fresh dill or parsley or 1 teaspoon dried dill or parsley

1. Place the cucumber in a food processor and process until finely chopped. Roll the cucumber in several layers of paper towels, and squeeze out the excess moisture. Place the chopped cucumber in a medium-sized bowl and stir in the remaining ingredients.
2. Transfer the dip to a serving dish, cover, and chill for at least 1 hour before serving. Serve with raw vegetables, whole-grain crackers, chunks of pumpernickel bread, and smoked salmon.

Nutritional Facts (per tablespoon)
CALORIES: 10 CARBOHYDRATES: 2 G CHOLESTEROL: 0 MG FAT: 0 G FIBER: 0 G
PROTEIN: 0.4 G SODIUM: 43 MG CALCIUM: 8 MG

Roasted Red Pepper Hummus

YIELD: 1½ CUPS

16-ounce can garbanzo beans (chickpeas), drained

½ cup diced roasted red bell pepper

¼ cup toasted sesame tahini (sesame butter)

2 teaspoons crushed garlic

2 teaspoons lemon juice

½ teaspoon ground cumin

⅛ teaspoon ground black pepper

2 teaspoons extra virgin olive oil (optional)

1. Combine all of the ingredients in the bowl of a food processor and process until smooth.
2. Serve immediately with wedges of whole-grain pita bread, whole-grain crackers, celery sticks, and carrot sticks. Or cover and refrigerate until ready to serve, but let the spread come to room temperature before serving.

Nutritional Facts (per tablespoon)
CALORIES: 29 CARBOHYDRATES: 3 G CHOLESTEROL: 0 MG FAT: 1.5 G FIBER: 0.9 G
PROTEIN: 1.2 G SODIUM: 50 MG CALCIUM: 16 MG

Zippy Artichoke Dip

YIELD: ABOUT 2¼ CUPS

14-ounce can artichoke hearts, drained and finely chopped
¾ cup light garlic-and-herb or vegetable-flavored cream cheese
¾ cup nonfat or light mayonnaise

1. Place the chopped artichoke hearts in a wire strainer and press out the excess liquid. Place the artichoke hearts, cream cheese, and mayonnaise in a medium-sized bowl, and stir to mix well.
2. Serve immediately or cover and chill for several hours before serving. Serve with raw vegetables, whole-grain crackers, and Parmesan Pita Crisps (page 80), or use as a filling for hollowed-out cherry tomatoes.

Nutritional Facts (per tablespoon)
CALORIES: 15 CARBOHYDRATES: 2 G CHOLESTEROL: 3 MG FAT: 0.7 G FIBER: 0.4 G
PROTEIN: 0.5 G SODIUM: 57 MG CALCIUM: 6 MG

Spinach Dip

YIELD: 4 CUPS

10-ounce package frozen chopped spinach, thawed and squeezed dry
16 ounces nonfat or light sour cream
½ cup nonfat or light mayonnaise
8-ounce can water chestnuts, drained and chopped
½ cup sliced scallions
1 package (1½ ounces) dry vegetable soup mix

1. Place all of the ingredients in a large bowl, and stir to mix well. Cover and refrigerate for several hours before serving.
2. Serve with raw vegetables and whole-grain crackers, or use as a filling for finger sandwiches and hollowed-out cherry tomatoes.

Nutritional Facts (per tablespoon)
CALORIES: 13   CARBOHYDRATES: 2.6 G   CHOLESTEROL: 0 MG   FAT: 0 G   FIBER: 0.2 G
PROTEIN: 0.7 G   SODIUM: 52 MG   CALCIUM: 14 MG

Spicy Mustard Dip

YIELD: 2¾ CUPS

2 cups nonfat or light sour cream
½ cup nonfat or light mayonnaise
3 tablespoons grainy-type spicy mustard
1 tablespoon honey

1. Place all of the ingredients in a medium bowl, and stir to mix well. Serve immediately or cover and refrigerate until ready to serve.
2. Serve with raw vegetables, rolled-up slices of lean ham, and cubes of light Cheddar and Swiss cheese.

Nutritional Facts (per tablespoon)
CALORIES: 15   CARBOHYDRATES: 2.8 G   CHOLESTEROL: 0 MG   FAT: 0 G   FIBER: 0 G
PROTEIN: 0.7 G   SODIUM: 40 MG   CALCIUM: 14 MG

Cranberry Chicken Spread

YIELD: 2½ CUPS

1½ cups finely chopped cooked chicken or turkey breast or
   2 cans (6 ounces each) chicken or turkey breast, drained
¼ cup dried sweetened cranberries
¼ cup chopped walnuts, almonds, or pecans
¼ cup finely chopped celery
¼ cup thinly sliced scallions
½ cup nonfat or light mayonnaise

1. Place the chicken or turkey, cranberries, nuts, celery, and scallions in a large bowl and toss to mix well. Add the mayonnaise, and stir to mix well. Add a little more mayonnaise if the mixture seems too dry.
2. Serve immediately, or cover and refrigerate until ready to serve. Serve with whole-grain crackers or use as a filling for celery sticks, endive leaves, or finger sandwiches.

Nutritional Facts (per tablespoon)
CALORIES: 18 CARBOHYDRATES: 1 G CHOLESTEROL: 7 MG FAT: 0.7 G FIBER: 0.1 G
PROTEIN: 1.8 G SODIUM: 25 MG CALCIUM: 2 MG

Almond Chicken Spread

YIELD: 2½ CUPS

1½ cups finely chopped cooked chicken or turkey breast or
    2 cans (6 ounces each) chicken or turkey breast, drained
⅓ cup slivered almonds
¼ cup grated carrots
¼ cup finely chopped celery
¼ cup thinly sliced scallions
½ cup nonfat or light mayonnaise
½ teaspoon dried dill or 1½ teaspoons finely chopped fresh dill (optional)

1. Place the chicken or turkey, almonds, carrots, celery, and scallions in a large bowl, and toss to mix well. Add the mayonnaise, and if desired, the dill, and stir to mix well. Add a little more mayonnaise if the mixture seems too dry.
2. Serve immediately, or cover and refrigerate until ready to serve. Serve with whole-grain crackers or use as a filling for celery sticks, endive leaves, or finger sandwiches.

Nutritional Facts (per tablespoon)
CALORIES: 16 CARBOHYDRATES: 0.8 G CHOLESTEROL: 5 MG FAT: 0.6 G FIBER: 0.1 G
PROTEIN: 1.9 G SODIUM: 26 MG CALCIUM: 3.6 MG

Sicilian Chicken Spread

YIELD: 2½ CUPS

1½ cups finely chopped cooked chicken or turkey breast or
    2 cans (6 ounces each) chicken or turkey breast, drained
¼ cup chopped black olives
¼ cup chopped walnuts
¼ cup finely chopped celery
¼ cup thinly sliced scallions
½ cup nonfat or light mayonnaise

1. Place the chicken or turkey, olives, walnuts, celery, and scallions in a large bowl, and toss to mix well. Add the mayonnaise, and stir to mix well. Add a little more mayonnaise if the mixture seems too dry.
2. Serve immediately, or cover and refrigerate until ready to serve. Use as a filling for celery sticks, endive leaves, hollowed-out cherry tomatoes, or finger sandwiches.

Nutritional Facts (per tablespoon)
CALORIES: 17 CARBOHYDRATES: 0.6 G CHOLESTEROL: 5 MG FAT: 0.7 G FIBER: 0.1 G
PROTEIN: 1.9 G SODIUM: 33 MG CALCIUM: 3 MG

Chutney Chicken Spread

YIELD: 2½ CUPS

1½ cups finely chopped cooked chicken or turkey breast or
    2 cans (6 ounces each) chicken or turkey breast, drained
¼ cup plus 2 tablespoons chopped roasted peanuts
¼ cup plus 2 tablespoons finely chopped celery
¼ cup thinly sliced scallions

DRESSING

¼ cup plus 2 tablespoons nonfat or light mayonnaise

2 tablespoons mango chutney

½ teaspoon curry paste or powder (optional)

1. Place the chicken or turkey, peanuts, celery, and scallions in a large bowl, and toss to mix well.
2. To make the dressing, place the mayonnaise, chutney, and if desired, the curry powder in a small bowl, and stir to mix well. Add the dressing to the chicken mixture, and toss to mix well. Add a little more mayonnaise if the mixture seems too dry.
3. Serve immediately, or cover and refrigerate until ready to serve. Use as a filling for celery sticks, endive leaves, or finger sandwiches.

Nutritional Facts (per tablespoon)
CALORIES: 19 CARBOHYDRATES: 1 G CHOLESTEROL: 5 MG FAT: 0.8 G FIBER: 0.1 G
PROTEIN: 2 G SODIUM: 21 MG CALCIUM: 3 MG

Cashew Crunch Chicken Spread

YIELD: 2½ CUPS

1½ cups finely chopped cooked chicken or turkey breast or
    2 cans (6 ounces each) chicken or turkey breast, drained

¼ cup plus 2 tablespoons chopped roasted cashews

¼ cup plus 2 tablespoons finely chopped celery

¼ cup thinly sliced scallions

½ cup nonfat or light mayonnaise

1. Place the chicken or turkey, cashews, celery, and scallions in a large bowl, and toss to mix well. Add the mayonnaise, and stir to mix well. Add a little more mayonnaise if the mixture seems too dry.
2. Serve immediately, or cover and refrigerate until ready to serve. Use as a filling for celery sticks, endive leaves, or finger sandwiches.

Nutritional Facts (per tablespoon)
CALORIES: 20 CARBOHYDRATES: 1 G CHOLESTEROL: 5 MG FAT: 0.9 G FIBER: 0.1 G
PROTEIN: 1.9 G SODIUM: 35 MG CALCIUM: 2 MG

Dilled Tuna Spread

✷ *For variety, substitute salmon for the tuna.*

YIELD: 2½ CUPS

2 cans (6 ounces each) albacore tuna in water, drained
¼ cup plus 2 tablespoons grated carrots
¼ cup plus 2 tablespoons finely chopped celery
¼ cup thinly sliced scallions
1 tablespoon finely chopped fresh dill or 1 teaspoon dried dill
½ cup nonfat or light mayonnaise

1. Place the tuna, carrots, celery, scallions, and dill in a large bowl and toss to mix well. Add the mayonnaise and stir to mix well. Add a little more mayonnaise if the mixture seems too dry.
2. Serve immediately, or cover and refrigerate until ready to serve. Use as a filling for celery sticks, endive leaves, hollowed-out cherry tomatoes, or finger sandwiches.

Nutritional Facts (per tablespoon)
CALORIES: 12 CARBOHYDRATES: 1 G CHOLESTEROL: 2 MG FAT: 0.1 G FIBER: 0.1 G
PROTEIN: 2 G SODIUM: 50 MG CALCIUM: 2 MG

Nut 'n' Honey Dip

YIELD: 1¾ CUPS

⅓ cup peanut butter
¼ to ⅓ cup honey

8-ounce block nonfat or reduced-fat (Neufchâtel) cream cheese,
    softened to room temperature
2 tablespooons skim or low-fat milk

1. Place the peanut butter and honey in a medium-sized bowl, and beat with an electric mixer to mix well. Beat in the cream cheese, and then the milk. Add a little more milk if the mixture seems too thick.
2. Serve immediately, or cover and refrigerate until ready to serve. Serve with sliced apples and pears, chunks of banana, whole fresh strawberries, and fresh pineapple spears. (Dip the apple slices, pear slices, and banana chunks in pineapple juice to prevent browning.)

Nutritional Facts (per tablespoon)
CALORIES: 35   CARBOHYDRATES: 3.7 G   CHOLESTEROL: 0 MG   FAT: 1.5 G   FIBER: 0.2 G
PROTEIN: 2 G   SODIUM: 54 MG   CALCIUM: 27 MG

Cinnamon-Raisin-Walnut Spread

YIELD: 1¼ CUPS

8-ounce block nonfat or reduced-fat (Neufchâtel) cream cheese,
    softened to room temperature
2 tablespoons maple syrup
½ teaspoon ground cinnamon
¼ cup dark raisins
3 tablespoons finely chopped walnuts

1. Place the cream cheese in a medium-sized bowl, and beat with an electric mixer until smooth. Add the maple syrup and cinnamon, and beat until smooth. Stir in the raisins and walnuts.
2. Cover and refrigerate for at least 2 hours before serving. Serve with whole-grain bagels.

Nutritional Facts (per tablespoon)
CALORIES: 28   CARBOHYDRATES: 3.6 G   CHOLESTEROL: 1 MG   FAT: 0.8 G   FIBER: 0.2 G
PROTEIN: 2 G   SODIUM: 55 MG   CALCIUM: 38 MG

Parmesan Pita Crisps

YIELD: 12 SERVINGS

6 whole wheat or oat-bran pita pockets (6-inch rounds)
¼ cup plus 2 tablespoons grated Parmesan cheese
1½ teaspoons dried parsley
Garlic-flavored or olive oil cooking spray

1. Using a sharp knife, cut each piece of pita bread around the entire outer edge to separate the bread into two rounds.
2. Arrange the pita rounds on a flat surface with the inside of the bread facing up. Sprinkle each round first with 1½ teaspoons of the Parmesan cheese, and then with ⅛ teaspoon of the parsley. Spray each pita round lightly with the cooking spray.
3. Cut each round into 6 wedges. Arrange the wedges in a single layer on a large ungreased baking sheet, and bake at 375°F for 4 to 6 minutes, or until lightly browned and crisp. Cool to room temperature.
4. Serve the crisps with dips and spreads.

Nutritional Facts (per 6 chips)
CALORIES: 79   CARBOHYDRATES: 15 G   CHOLESTEROL: 2 MG   FAT: 1.2 G   FIBER: 2 G
PROTEIN: 4.3 G   SODIUM: 208 MG   CALCIUM: 63 MG

Brews and Beverages

Light Eggnog

Yield: 10 servings

1 quart low-fat milk

1 cup fat-free egg substitute

¼ cup plus 2 tablespoons instant vanilla pudding mix

¼ to ⅓ cup sugar

1 tablespoon vanilla extract

¼ teaspoon ground nutmeg

1. Combine all of the ingredients in a blender, and blend for 1 minute or until well mixed. Transfer to a covered container and refrigerate for several hours.
2. Shake the eggnog well before serving.

Nutritional Facts (per ½-cup serving)
CALORIES: 94 CARBOHYDRATES: 16 G CHOLESTEROL: 4 MG FAT: 1 G FIBER: 0 G
PROTEIN: 5.6 G SODIUM: 180 MG CALCIUM: 133 MG

Frosty Fruit Punch

Yield: 16 servings

1 quart orange or pineapple sherbet

3 cups chilled cranberry juice cocktail (reduced-calorie or regular)

1½ cups chilled pineapple juice

1½ cups chilled orange juice

1 quart chilled ginger ale or lemon-lime soda
(sugar-free or regular)

1. Spoon rounded tablespoonfuls of the sherbet into a 4-quart punch bowl. Add the juices, and stir just until combined.
2. Slowly pour the ginger ale or lemon-lime soda down the side of the bowl, and stir gently to mix. Serve immediately.

Nutritional Facts (per ¾-cup serving)
CALORIES: 100 CARBOHYDRATES: 22 G CHOLESTEROL: 3 MG FAT: 0.9 G FIBER: 0.1 G
PROTEIN: 0.8 G SODIUM: 34 MG CALCIUM: 40 MG

Sparkling Fruit Punch

YIELD: 10 SERVINGS

3 cups chilled orange juice or apricot nectar

1 cup frozen cranberry juice cocktail concentrate
(reduced-calorie or regular), thawed

1½ cups chilled orange or pineapple juice

2 cups chilled club soda

10 lime slices (garnish)

1. Combine all of the ingredients except the lime slices in a large pitcher and stir well to blend.
2. Pour into ice-filled glasses, garnish each glass with a lime slice, and serve.

Nutritional Facts (per ¾-cup serving)
CALORIES: 73 CARBOHYDRATES: 17 G CHOLESTEROL: 0 MG FAT: 0 G FIBER: 0.2 G
PROTEIN: 0.6 G SODIUM: 14 MG CALCIUM: 26 MG

Mimosas

YIELD: 8 SERVINGS

3 cups chilled orange juice
750-milliliter bottle chilled champagne (about 3 cups)

1. Pour ¼ cup plus 2 tablespoons orange juice into each of eight 8-ounce champagne or wine-glasses.
2. Add ¼ cup plus 2 tablespoons champagne to each glass and serve immediately.

Nutritional Facts (per ¾-cup serving)
CALORIES: 102 CARBOHYDRATES: 10 G CHOLESTEROL: 0 MG FAT: 0 G FIBER: 0.2 G
PROTEIN: 0 G SODIUM: 5 MG CALCIUM: 18 MG

Hot Apple Cider

YIELD: 12 SERVINGS

2½ quarts unsweetened apple juice
3 sticks cinnamon
1 tablespoon whole cloves
½ teaspoon whole allspice

1. Place 2 cups of the apple juice and all of the spices in a 4-quart pot, and bring to a boil over high heat. Reduce the heat to low, and simmer covered for 10 minutes. Strain the mixture, discarding the spices, and return the juice to the pot.
2. Add the remaining apple juice to the pot, and simmer over medium-low heat until thoroughly heated. Serve warm in mugs.

Nutritional Facts (per ¾-cup serving)
CALORIES: 87 CARBOHYDRATES: 22 G CHOLESTEROL: 0 MG FAT: 0.2 G FIBER: 0.2 G
PROTEIN: 0.1 G SODIUM: 6 MG CALCIUM: 87 MG

Cinnamon Hot Chocolate

YIELD: 6 SERVINGS

¼ cup plus 2 tablespoons light brown sugar
¼ cup Dutch processed cocoa powder
½ cup instant nonfat dry milk powder
¾ teaspoon ground cinnamon
4½ cups skim or low-fat milk
1½ teaspoons vanilla extract

TOPPINGS:
¾ cup nonfat or light whipped topping
¼ teaspoon ground cinnamon

1. Place the sugar, cocoa powder, milk powder, and cinnamon in a 2½-quart pot, and stir to mix well. Add ½ cup of the milk, and whisk until smooth. Add the remaining milk, and whisk until smooth.
2. Place the pot over medium heat, and cook, whisking frequently, for about 5 minutes, or until the milk just begins to boil.
3. Remove the pot from the heat, and stir in the vanilla extract. Pour ¾ cup of the hot chocolate into each of eight 8-ounce mugs. Top each serving with 2 tablespoons of the whipped topping and a sprinkling of ground cinnamon. Serve immediately.

Nutritional Facts (per ¾-cup serving)
CALORIES: 168   CARBOHYDRATES: 31 G   CHOLESTEROL: 5 MG   FAT: 1.3 G   FIBER: 1.2 G
PROTEIN: 10 G   SODIUM: 150 MG   CALCIUM: 348 MG

PART THREE

Traditional Holiday Meals

WHENEVER WE THINK OF THANKSGIVING, Christmas, Hanukkah, Easter, Passover, and other traditional holidays, a flood of images comes to mind. Beautifully decorated fir trees, the flickering candle of a menorah, rainbow-colored eggs—these symbols are all inextricably linked with the holidays that brighten each calendar year. In fact, Christmas probably wouldn't seem like Christmas without an ornamented tree and gaily wrapped gifts. Just as strong as these images are those of the special foods that are traditionally served for each holiday. Thanksgiving turkey and stuffing, for instance, is a must for most of us. Thanksgiving just wouldn't be the same without it.

Yet, when we make the switch to a more healthful diet, we face a dilemma. How can we enjoy lavish meals of holiday favorites and still prepare low-fat high-nutrient dishes? Part Three answers this question with inventive menus that combine lighter traditional dishes with exciting new fare for festive meals that are sure to delight family and friends.

As you browse through the following menus and recipes to plan your next special-occasion get-together, you will notice that each menu provides more than one option for many of the dishes listed. This will allow you to create meals that best suit your family's tastes and your own style of entertaining. And don't hesitate to mix and match dishes from different menus throughout the book. For instance, pair a main dish from the Christmas menu with some of the side dishes from the Hanukkah or Easter menus. This way you can create an even greater variety of crowd-pleasing menus for many occasions throughout the year. Finally, don't forget that more holiday and party recipes can be found in Parts Two, Four, and Five.

Surviving the Season

November and December can be difficult months for those of us who are watching our weight. 'Tis the season for family feasts, office parties, and open houses. For almost two months, we are faced with every culinary temptation imaginable. To make matters worse, the hustle and bustle of the holidays increases stress levels and decreases the time available for exercise. Under situations like these, it's hard not to put on a few pounds! But take heart. With just a little forethought, you can enjoy all the festivities and still maintain a light and healthy lifestyle. The following strategies can help you retain some semblance of sanity this holiday season.

Plan ahead. *Make a list of all the holiday meals and parties you've been invited to, then mark them on your calendar. That way, you can work them into your daily meal plans. Save a third to a fourth of that day's calorie allotment for a cocktail party, and a third to a half of your allotment for a dinner party. Avoid going out to dinner after a cocktail party, as you will almost certainly overshoot your food limit for the day. Heavy hors d'oeuvres should be considered dinner.*

Don't go hungry. *If you go to a party feeling ravenous, you will most likely overeat. Don't starve yourself all day in anticipation of the goodies ahead. Instead, eat a light but balanced breakfast and lunch, and save some calories for the evening.*

Peruse and prioritize. *Before partaking of party foods, peruse the entire hors d'oeuvres table and prioritize your choices. Look for steamed seafood with cocktail sauce; smoked salmon; lean cold cuts like sliced turkey, lean ham, and roast beef; whole-grain crackers; and plenty of fresh vegetables and fruits. Avoid the high-fat dips, cheese balls, quiches, fatty meats, and fried hors d'oeuvres. And don't waste calories on ordinary junk foods like pretzels, and chips, and dips. Concentrate on foods that aren't usually available, and then enjoy them in moderation.*

Position yourself strategically. *At cocktail parties, make a conscious effort to position yourself away from the hors d'oeuvres table. Fill a small plate with food, and then go mingle. At dinner parties, put your napkin on your plate when you are comfortably full. This will prevent you from unconsciously nibbling any remaining food.*

Slow down to fill up. *By eating slowly, you will feel more satisfied with less food. (After twenty minutes of eating, the body signals a feeling of fullness to the brain.)*

Observe the law of diminishing returns. *The more you eat of something the less pleasure you receive. For example, that first bite of pecan pie is the best, because the taste is so new. As you continue to eat, the pleasure diminishes. So eat just a few bites, and receive 90 percent of the pleasure for only 10 percent of the calories!*

Balance the bubbly. *When it comes to calories, alcohol is second only to fat. Combine alcohol with creamy or sweet mixers, and you make matters worse. Alcohol also lowers your inhibitions, which can make you careless about food choices. What can you do? Sip a wine spritzer, or mix the liquor with water, soda, or a diet beverage. Then alternate alcoholic drinks with glasses of water. Or simply drink club soda or another nonalcoholic beverage, and spend more of your calorie budget on party foods.*

Prioritize exercise. *Though exercise often falls by the wayside during the busy holiday season, you must make every effort to keep it high on your list of priorities. Why? Not only does exercise help burn off those excess calories, it also relieves holiday stress. Make exercise a part of your holiday social activities. For instance, visit with relatives and friends during a leisurely walk—instead of over a piece of pie or a cup of eggnog. Just be sure not to exercise*

HOLIDAY FOOD (made with traditional high-calorie recipes)	MILES TO WALK TO BURN IT OFF*
EGGNOG (1 CUP)	3.6
PUMPKIN PIE (⅛ PIE)	3.2
PECAN PIE (⅛ PIE)	5.0
STUFFING (½ CUP)	2.0
SWEET POTATO CASSEROLE (½ CUP)	2.3
GREEN BEAN CASSEROLE (½ CUP)	1.5
BEEF BRISKET (3 OUNCES)	2.8

* Based on a body weight of 150 pounds. (A person weighing 150 pounds will burn about 100 calories per mile walked.)

too soon after eating a heavy meal. And, if you can manage it, try to exercise or just take a brisk walk shortly before *dinner. Why? Vigorous exercise actually suppresses the appetite for an hour or two immediately afterward. See the chart on page 89 to determine just how much exercise you must do to burn off that holiday treat.*

Don't let holiday stress be a saboteur. *Stress causes hormonal changes that increase appetite and fuel overeating in many people. Prioritize your holiday obligations, find ways to simplify, and learn how to say "no" when necessary. Be sure to schedule time for exercise, since this is one of the greatest stress reducers of all. And remember, it's no coincidence that* stressed *spelled backward is* desserts!

Set up a support system. *No one wants to put on excess pounds during the holidays, so enlist the help of friends, family, and coworkers. You'll then be able to help one another plan more healthful menus and eat within reason. And when you're the one hosting a party, offer plenty of light and healthy options. People will appreciate this more than you know.*

Thanksgiving

T hanksgiving kicks off the holiday season into full swing. For many people, the season brings to mind fond memories of festive feasts—and not-so-fond memories of the resulting extra pounds. Fortunately, it is possible to lighten up these foods and still make them every bit as enjoyable as ever. The proof is in the traditional Thanksgiving dinner that follows.

When aiming for light and healthy fare, it's hard to go wrong with turkey as a main course. The stuffing and gravy, however, are usually loaded with fat. Here you will find a variety of flavorful stuffings that contain just a fraction of the usual fat. And don't be afraid to pour on Foolproof Fat-Free Gravy. Simple to make and guilt-free, it is delicious over turkey and stuffing.

Accompany the main course with Thanksgiving favorites like Waldorf Salad, Pineapple Sweet Potato Casserole, Sour Cream and Chive Mashed Potatoes, and Glorious Green Bean Casserole. If you are crazy for cranberries, you will be delighted with the array of sauces and relishes offered here. What's for dessert? Try some Deep-Dish Pumpkin or Apple Streusel Pie—both are substantially lighter than traditional versions.

Although Thanksgiving dinner is an extravagant meal, the preparations for it need not be overwhelming. Only two dishes must be fully prepared right before serving: the turkey and the mashed potatoes. However, once the turkey is placed in the oven to roast, it requires very little attention. And, of course, the mashed potatoes are quite easy to make at the last minute.

Thanksgiving Dinner

SERVES 10 TO 12

Savory Roast Turkey (page 93) with choice of stuffing (pages 98-101)

Foolproof Fat-Free Gravy (page 94)

Waldorf Salad (page 103)
or Festive Fruit Salad (page 110)

Glorious Green Bean Casserole (page 96)
or Green Beans with Bacon and Onions (page 97)

Sour Cream and Chive Mashed Potatoes (page 101)

Pineapple Sweet Potato Casserole (page 102)
or Citrus-Glazed Sweet Potatoes (page 102)

Choice of Cranberry Sauce (pages 104-110)

Deep-Dish Pumpkin Pie (page 111)
Apple Streusel Pie (page 112)

Savory Roast Turkey

YIELD: ABOUT 12 SERVINGS

12- to 14-pound turkey, fresh or defrosted
½ cup water
½ cup medium-dry sherry

BASTING SAUCE
1 tablespoon frozen apple juice concentrate, thawed
1 tablespoon Dijon mustard
2 teaspoons lemon pepper
½ teaspoon garlic powder

1. Remove the packet containing the giblets and neck from the cavities of the turkey. (You may have to release the legs from a wire or plastic lock in order to do this.) Rinse the turkey inside and out, and dry it with paper towels. Trim away any excess fat.
2. Transfer the turkey to a rack in a large roasting pan. Return the legs to the wire or plastic lock, or loosely tie them together with sturdy string. Fold the wings back and underneath the bird.
3. Pour the water and sherry into the bottom of the roasting pan. Combine the basting sauce ingredients in a small bowl, and stir to mix well. Brush the sauce over the skin of the bird. Cover the pan with aluminum foil, crimping the foil around the edges of the pan to seal it tightly.
4. Bake at 325°F for 2½ hours. Carefully remove the foil (steam will escape), and cook for an additional 30 minutes, basting occasionally with the pan juices, until the turkey is nicely browned, the drumsticks move easily in the sockets, and a thermometer inserted in the thigh (not touching the bone) reads 180° to 185°F. (Note: if you are using a regular meat thermometer instead of an instant-read type, insert it after you remove the foil.) Remove the turkey from the oven, and let sit loosely covered with foil for 20 minutes before carving.

Nutritional Facts (per 3-ounce serving, skinless white meat)
CALORIES: 114   CARBOHYDRATES: 0 G   CHOLESTEROL: 70 MG   FAT: 0.6 G   FIBER: 0 G
PROTEIN: 26 G   SODIUM: 44 MG   CALCIUM: 10 MG

Nutritional Facts (per 3-ounce serving, skinless dark meat)
CALORIES: 163   CARBOHYDRATES: 0 G   CHOLESTEROL: 68 MG   FAT: 6.6 G   FIBER: 0 G
PROTEIN: 24 G   SODIUM: 64 MG   CALCIUM: 25 MG

Foolproof Fat-Free Gravy

YIELD: 3 CUPS

Drippings from Savory Roast Turkey (page 93)
Pinch ground white pepper
¼ teaspoon poultry seasoning
2 teaspoons chicken bouillon granules
¼ cup plus 2 tablespoons unbleached flour
⅔ cup skim or low-fat milk (for a richer gravy use evaporated skim or low-fat milk)

Turkey Tips

If you have never cooked a turkey before, it may seem like an overwhelming project. However, as the recipe on page 93 shows, cooking a turkey can really be quite easy, and once you put it in the oven, the turkey requires very little attention. Here are some tips to keep in mind when cooking a turkey.

◆ *How big should your bird be? For turkeys weighing 12 pounds or less, purchase ¾ to 1 pound per person. For turkeys over 12 pounds, purchase ½ to ¾ pounds per person. Purchase a bigger turkey if you desire plenty of leftovers.*

◆ *Thaw your turkey properly. Never thaw a turkey on the counter, because it provides the ideal breeding ground for bacterial growth. Instead, thaw it safely in the refrigerator, microwave, or submerged under cool water—changing the water every 30 minutes. When thawing a turkey in the refrigerator, place it in its original wrapper in a large pan on the bottom shelf. This will prevent the juices from contaminating other foods in the refrigerator. Allow approximately 24 hours per 5 pounds of turkey. After thawing, cook the turkey within 1 to 2 days.*

◆ *Use a meat thermometer to judge doneness. This is the only reliable way to be sure that your bird is cooked to the temperature that destroys harmful bacteria. Read the instructions that come with your thermometer to make sure you are using it properly. Insert the tip of the thermometer into the thickest part of the thigh next to the body. The turkey is done when the thermometer registers at least 180°F. If the turkey is stuffed, you must also be sure that the stuffing has reached a temperature of at least 165°F to be safe.*

◆ *Store leftovers safely. Remove any stuffing and carve the meat off the bones within 2 hours of roasting. Place leftovers in shallow containers (so they will cool quickly) and use within 3 days or wrap well and freeze for up to 2 months.*

1. Defat the turkey drippings by placing them in a fat-separator cup. (If you don't have a fat-separator cup, pour the drippings into a bowl, add a few ice cubes, and skim off the fat once it hardens.) Pour 2⅓ cups of the defatted drippings into a 1½-quart pot and add the pepper, poultry seasoning, and bouillon granules. Bring the mixture to a boil over high heat, then reduce the heat to low and simmer covered for 3 minutes.

2. Combine the flour and milk in a jar with a tight-fitting lid, and shake until smooth. Slowly add the milk mixture to the simmering broth, stirring constantly with a wire whisk. Continue to cook and stir for a minute or two, or until the gravy is thick and bubbly. Serve hot.

Nutritional Facts (per ¼-cup serving)
CALORIES: 25 CARBOHYDRATES: 3.7 G CHOLESTEROL: 0 MG FAT: 0.1 G FIBER: 0.2 G
PROTEIN: 2.1 G SODIUM: 136 MG CALCIUM: 19 MG

Glorious Green Bean Casserole

YIELD: 12 SERVINGS

1 tablespoon skim or low-fat milk
2 teaspoons cornstarch
¾ cup nonfat or light sour cream
10¾-ounce can condensed reduced-fat and -sodium cream of mushroom soup, undiluted
2 packages (1 pound each) frozen French-cut or regular-cut green beans, cooked until tender and well drained
8-ounce can sliced mushrooms, drained
⅓ cup slivered almonds
1 medium yellow onion, very thinly sliced
½ cup grated Parmesan cheese
Butter-flavored nonstick cooking spray

1. Place the milk and cornstarch in a small bowl and stir to dissolve the cornstarch. Add the sour cream and condensed soup and stir to mix well. Set aside.
2. Place the green beans, mushrooms, and almonds in a large bowl, add the sour cream mixture and stir to mix well. Coat a 9-by-13-inch baking dish with the cooking spray, and spread the green bean mixture evenly in the dish. Spread the onions in an even layer over the green beans, and then sprinkle the cheese over the top. Spray the top of the casserole lightly with the cooking spray.
3. Bake at 350°F for about 30 minutes, or until the edges are bubbly and the top is lightly browned. Remove the dish from the oven, and let sit for 5 minutes before serving.

Nutritional Facts (per ⅔-cup serving)
CALORIES: 98   CARBOHYDRATES: 12 G   CHOLESTEROL: 5 MG   FAT: 3.4 G   FIBER: 2.9 G
PROTEIN: 5 G   SODIUM: 232 MG   CALCIUM: 138 MG

Green Beans with Bacon and Onions

YIELD: 12 SERVINGS

8 cups 1½-inch pieces fresh green beans (about 2 pounds)
2 tablespoons extra virgin olive oil
2 medium yellow onions, thinly sliced
1 teaspoon dried thyme
½ teaspoon salt
¼ teaspoon ground black pepper
2 teaspoons light brown sugar
1 tablespoon balsamic vinegar
3 slices extra-lean turkey bacon, cooked, drained, and crumbled

1. Fill a 6-quart pot half full with water and bring to a boil over high heat. Add the green beans and allow the pot to return to a boil. Cook the beans for about 4 minutes, or until just tender. Drain the beans well and return them to the pot. Cover to keep warm, and set aside.

2. While the green beans are cooking, coat a large nonstick skillet with the olive oil, and preheat over medium heat. Add the onions, thyme, salt, and pepper, and sauté for about 5 minutes, or until the onions are wilted and beginning to brown. Cover the skillet periodically if it becomes too dry. (The steam released from the cooking onions will moisten the skillet.) Add the brown sugar, and sauté for another minute. Add the vinegar, stir to mix well, and remove the skillet from the heat.

3. Add the onions and bacon to the green beans and toss to mix well. Serve hot.

Nutritional Facts (per ¾-cup serving)
CALORIES: 59   CARBOHYDRATES: 8 G   CHOLESTEROL: 5 MG   FAT: 2.4 G   FIBER: 1.2 G
PROTEIN: 2.4 G   SODIUM: 134 MG   CALCIUM: 33 MG

Savory Stuffings

Stuffing is the ultimate comfort food, and nearly every family has its favorite stuffing recipe. The problem is, whether your stuffing is savory with sage or sweet with apples and raisins, it's probably also loaded with unnecessary fat and calories. But as you will see, all that extra fat is not necessary. Although the following stuffing recipes are substantially lighter than most, they remain flavorful and moist.

For safety's sake, it is best to cook the stuffing outside the bird. Why? Stuffing, improperly handled, is a perfect breeding ground for the harmful bacteria sometimes found in poultry. For this reason, the following stuffing recipes are baked in a casserole dish. If you choose to bake your stuffing inside the bird, reduce the amount of broth used in the following recipe by half, as the juices from the bird will make the extra liquid unnecessary. Always stuff the bird right before roasting, and be sure to stuff it loosely, leaving a little space at the end for expansion. After spooning in the stuffing, secure the turkey's legs and wings, as explained in the turkey recipe (page 93), and cook thoroughly. The internal temperature of the stuffing should reach 165°F. Remove the stuffing from the bird directly after roasting, and enjoy!

SAVORY SAGE AND HERB STUFFING

Yield: 12 servings

1 pound stale oatmeal, multigrain, whole wheat, or sourdough bread,
    or any combination (about 14 to 16 slices)
2 tablespoons reduced-fat margarine or light butter
1½ cups chopped onion
1½ cups chopped celery (include the leaves)
2 teaspoons dried sage
1 teaspoon dried thyme
1 teaspoon dried marjoram
¼ teaspoon ground black pepper
10¾-ounce can condensed reduced-fat and -sodium cream
    of mushroom, celery, or chicken soup, undiluted

1½ cups low-sodium chicken broth (plus additional broth if needed)
¼ cup plus 2 tablespoons fat-free egg substitute

1. Tear 3 of the bread slices into pieces, place in the bowl of a food processor, and process for a few seconds, or until the bread is a mixture of coarse crumbs with some small (¼- to ½-inch) pieces mixed in. Place the processed bread in a large bowl, and set aside. Process the remaining bread slices in the same manner, and add them to the bowl. There should be 11 cups of bread crumbs and pieces. Adjust the amount if necessary.

2. Spread the processed bread evenly over 2 large baking sheets. Bake at 350°F for 10 minutes, stir the bread on each sheet, and switch the positions of the pans in the oven. Bake for 10 additional minutes, or until the bread is lightly browned and crisp. Remove the pans from the oven and set aside to cool. (Note: You can prepare the bread up to 2 days in advance and store the crumbs in an airtight container until ready to prepare the stuffing.)

3. Place the margarine or butter, onion, celery, sage, thyme, marjoram, and pepper in a large nonstick skillet. Cover the skillet and cook over medium heat for about 6 to 8 minutes, stirring occasionally, until the vegetables are tender. Add a little broth to the skillet if it becomes too dry.

4. Add the cooked vegetables to the bread and toss to mix well. Combine the undiluted soup, broth, and egg substitute in a small bowl, and stir with a wire whisk to mix well. Slowly add the broth mixture to the bread mixture, while tossing gently. The mixture should be moist and should hold together nicely. Add a little more broth if the mixture seems too dry.

5. Coat a 9-by-13-inch baking dish with nonstick cooking spray, and spoon the stuffing lightly into the dish. Cover the dish with aluminum foil, and bake at 325°F for 30 minutes. Remove the dish from the oven, and let sit covered for 10 minutes before serving.

Nutritional Facts (per ¾-cup serving)
CALORIES: 138 CARBOHYDRATES: 22 G CHOLESTEROL: 0 MG FAT: 3.2 G FIBER: 2.1 G
PROTEIN: 4.5 G SODIUM: 373 MG CALCIUM: 42 MG

Variations:

To make **Mushroom and Herb Stuffing,** sauté 2½ cups chopped fresh mushrooms along with the onion and celery.

> *Nutritional Facts (per ¾-cup serving)*
> CALORIES: 142 CARBOHYDRATES: 23 G CHOLESTEROL: 0 MG FAT: 3.2 G FIBER: 2.3 G
> PROTEIN: 4.9 G SODIUM: 373 MG CALCIUM: 42 MG

To Make **Garden Herb Stuffing,** sauté ¾ cup chopped green bell peppers and ¾ cup shredded carrots along with the onion and celery.

> *Nutritional Facts (per ¾-cup serving)*
> CALORIES: 144 CARBOHYDRATES: 23 G CHOLESTEROL: 0 MG FAT: 3.2 G FIBER: 2.5 G
> PROTEIN: 4.5 G SODIUM: 373 MG CALCIUM: 42 MG

To make **Savory Apple Stuffing,** sauté 2 cups chopped peeled Granny Smith apple along with the onion and celery. If desired, add ¼ cup plus 2 tablespoons dark or golden raisins or dried cranberries to the stuffing mixture.

> *Nutritional Facts (per ¾-cup serving)*
> CALORIES: 148 CARBOHYDRATES: 25 G CHOLESTEROL: 0 MG FAT: 3.2 G FIBER: 2.5 G
> PROTEIN: 4.5 G SODIUM: 373 MG CALCIUM: 42 MG

To make **Festive Fruit Stuffing,** add an 8-ounce can of undrained crushed pineapple, ¼ cup plus 2 tablespoons golden raisins, and an 8-ounce can of chopped, drained water chestnuts or ½ cup chopped toasted pecans (page 30) to the stuffing mixture along with the celery and onion. Reduce the broth to ¾ cup.

> *Nutritional Facts (per ¾-cup serving)*
> CALORIES: 159 CARBOHYDRATES: 29 G CHOLESTEROL: 0 MG FAT: 3 G FIBER: 3.1 G
> PROTEIN: 4.5 G SODIUM: 373 MG CALCIUM: 44 MG

To make **Savory Sausage Stuffing,** add ½ pound cooked, crumbled ground turkey breakfast sausage or Italian sausage to the stuffing mixture.

> *Nutritional Facts (per ¾-cup serving)*
> CALORIES: 155 CARBOHYDRATES: 21 G CHOLESTEROL: 15 MG FAT: 4.5 G FIBER: 1.9 G
> PROTEIN: 7 G SODIUM: 398 MG CALCIUM: 41 MG

To make **Shortcut Stuffing,** substitute 5½ cups (about 11 ounces) of packaged dried and crumbled herb-seasoned stuffing (regular or cornbread) for the made-from-scratch dried bread in any of the above recipes. Omit the sage, thyme, marjoram, and black pepper when you sauté the vegetable mixture. (Nutritional Facts are based on the basic recipe.)

Nutritional Facts (per ¾-cup serving)
CALORIES: 139 CARBOHYDRATES: 25 G CHOLESTEROL: 0 MG FAT: 2.3 G FIBER: 2.7 G
PROTEIN: 4.4 G SODIUM: 510 MG CALCIUM: 57 MG

Sour Cream and Chive Mashed Potatoes

YIELD: 12 SERVINGS

3¾ pounds Yukon Gold potatoes (about 10 medium)
1 cup plus 2 tablespoons nonfat or light sour cream
1 tablespoon plus 1½ teaspoons dried chives
¾ teaspoon salt
⅛ teaspoon ground white pepper

1. Peel the potatoes and cut them into chunks. Place the potatoes in a 4-quart pot, add water just to cover, and bring to a boil over high heat. Reduce the heat to medium, cover, and cook for about 12 minutes, or until soft.
2. Drain the potatoes, reserving ½ cup of the cooking liquid. Return the potatoes to the pot and stir in the sour cream, chives, salt, pepper, and ¼ cup plus 2 tablespoons of the cooking liquid.
3. Mash the potatoes with a potato masher or beat with an electric mixer until smooth. If the potatoes are too stiff, add enough of the reserved cooking liquid to achieve the desired consistency. Serve hot.

Nutritional Facts (per ¾-cup serving)
CALORIES: 130 CARBOHYDRATES: 29 G CHOLESTEROL: 0 MG FAT: 0.1 G FIBER: 2.3 G
PROTEIN: 3.5 G SODIUM: 166 MG CALCIUM: 36 MG

Pineapple Sweet Potato Casserole

YIELD: 12 SERVINGS

2 cans (29 ounces each) cut sweet potatoes in water or light syrup, drained

2 cans (8 ounces each) crushed pineapple in juice, undrained

2 tablespoons light brown sugar

½ cup chopped toasted pecans (page 30)

¼ cup dried sweetened cranberries or chopped dates (optional)

3 cups mini marshmallows

1. Place the potatoes in a large bowl and cut into 1-inch pieces. Combine the pineapple and brown sugar, stir to dissolve the sugar, and add to the sweet potatoes. Add the pecans and, if desired, the cranberries or dates to the sweet potatoes, and toss to mix well.

2. Coat a 9-by-13-inch baking dish with nonstick cooking spray, and spread the sweet potato mixture evenly in the dish. Sprinkle the marshmallows over the top of the casserole.

3. Bake at 350°F for about 40 minutes, or until the edges are bubbly and the topping is lightly browned. Serve hot.

Nutritional Facts (per ⅔-cup serving)
CALORIES: 179 CARBOHYDRATES: 36 G CHOLESTEROL: 0 MG FAT: 3.8 G FIBER: 2.3 G
PROTEIN: 2.2 G SODIUM: 52 MG CALCIUM: 30 MG

Citrus-Glazed Sweet Potatoes

✿ *For variety, substitute apple juice and apple jelly for the orange juice and marmalade.*

YIELD: 12 SERVINGS

3½ pounds sweet potatoes peeled and cut in ¾-inch chunks (about 8½ cups)

¼ cup reduced-fat margarine or light butter

¼ cup light brown sugar

¼ cup orange marmalade

½ cup orange juice

¼ teaspoon ground ginger

¼ teaspoon ground cinnamon

1. Place the potatoes in a 4-quart pot and cover with water. Bring the potatoes to a boil, then reduce the heat to medium. Cover and cook for about 10 minutes, or until the potatoes are just tender (do not overcook). Drain well.
2. Coat a 9-by-13-inch baking dish with nonstick cooking spray, and spread the potatoes over the bottom of the dish.
3. Combine the margarine or butter, brown sugar, marmalade, orange juice, ginger, and cinnamon in a 1-quart pot, and stir to mix well. Bring the mixture to a boil over medium-high heat, then pour over the potatoes.
4. Bake at 350°F for 20 minutes. Stir the potatoes, and cook for an additional 20 minutes, or until most of the liquid has evaporated and the potatoes are glazed. Serve hot.

Nutritional Facts (per ⅔-cup serving)
CALORIES: 136   CARBOHYDRATES: 29 G   CHOLESTEROL: 0 MG   FAT: 1.8 G   FIBER: 2.5 G
PROTEIN: 1.5 G   SODIUM: 47 MG   CALCIUM: 30 MG

Waldorf Salad

YIELD: 10 SERVINGS

4½ cups diced unpeeled Red Delicious, Gala, or Empire apples (about 6 medium)

1½ cups sliced celery

½ cup plus 1 tablespoon dark raisins or dried sweetened cranberries

½ cup chopped walnuts or toasted pecans (page 30)

DRESSING

¼ cup plus 2 tablespoons nonfat or light mayonnaise

¼ cup plus 2 tablespoons nonfat or light sour cream

1. Place the apples, celery, raisins or cranberries, and walnuts or pecans in a large bowl, and toss to mix well. Place the dressing ingredients in a small bowl, and stir to mix well.
2. Add the dressing to the apple mixture and toss to mix well. Cover the salad and chill for at least 2 hours before serving.

Nutritional Facts (per ⅔-cup serving)
Calories: 108   Carbohydrates: 16 g   Cholesterol: 0 mg   Fat: 4.5 g   Fiber: 2.6 g
Protein: 1.4 g   Sodium: 85 mg   Calcium: 36 mg

Cranberries Any Way You Like Them

Cranberry recipes are as varied as stuffing recipes. Perhaps you like your cranberries made into sauce enlivened with orange juice and rind. Or perhaps you prefer your cranberries in a festive mold. Whatever your preferences may be, you're sure to find a dish that will please both you and your guests among the recipes presented below.

CITRUS CRANBERRY SAUCE

Yield: 12 servings

1 cup orange juice
½ tablespoon freshly grated orange rind or ½ teaspoon dried orange rind
½ to ⅔ cup light brown sugar
12 ounces (3 cups) fresh or frozen cranberries

1. Combine the orange juice, orange rind, and brown sugar in a 2-quart pot, and stir to mix well. Place over medium-high heat and bring to a boil.
2. Add the cranberries to the pot and stir to mix. Reduce the heat to medium and boil gently with the cover on the pot slightly ajar for 7 to 10 minutes, or until the cranberry skins pop open and the mixture is thick. Stir occasionally to prevent the mixture from boiling over.

3. Allow the mixture to cool to room temperature; then cover and refrigerate for at least 4 hours before serving.

Nutritional Facts (per 3-tablespoon serving)
CALORIES: 57 CARBOHYDRATES: 14 G CHOLESTEROL: 0 MG FAT: 0 G FIBER: 1.2 G
PROTEIN: 0 G SODIUM: 3 MG CALCIUM: 12 MG

CRANBERRY-APRICOT SAUCE

✸ *For variety, substitute canned peaches for the apricots.*

YIELD: 13 SERVINGS

1-pound can apricots in juice or light syrup, undrained
½ cup light brown sugar
¼ teaspoon ground ginger
12 ounces (3 cups) fresh or frozen cranberries, stemmed

1. Place the apricots and their juice in a blender and blend until coarsely chopped.
2. Combine the apricots, brown sugar, and ginger in a 2½-quart pot and stir to mix well. Place over medium-high heat and bring to a boil.
3. Add the cranberries to the pot and stir to mix. Reduce the heat to medium and boil gently with the cover on the pot slightly ajar for 7 to 10 minutes, or until the cranberry skins pop open and the mixture is thick. Stir occasionally to prevent the mixture from boiling over.
4. Allow the mixture to cool to room temperature; then cover and refrigerate for at least 4 hours before serving.

Nutritional Facts (per ¼-cup serving)
CALORIES: 59 CARBOHYDRATES: 15 G CHOLESTEROL: 0 MG FAT: 0 G FIBER: 1.6 G
PROTEIN: 0.3 G SODIUM: 4 MG CALCIUM: 10 MG

CRANBERRY-PEAR CONSERVE

YIELD: 12 SERVINGS

3 cups diced peeled fresh pears (about 3 large)
2 cups fresh or frozen cranberries, stemmed
¾ cup pear nectar
¼ cup light brown sugar
¼ cup golden raisins
¼ teaspoon ground cinnamon
¼ teaspoon ground nutmeg
¼ teaspoon ground ginger

1. Combine all of the ingredients in a 2½-quart pot and stir to mix well. Place over medium-high heat and bring to a boil.
2. Reduce the heat to medium-low and boil gently with the cover on the pot slightly ajar for about 10 minutes, or until the cranberry skins pop open and the mixture is thick. Stir occasionally to prevent the mixture from boiling over.
3. Allow the mixture to cool to room temperature, then cover and refrigerate for at least 4 hours before serving.

Nutritional Facts (per ¼-cup serving)
CALORIES: 69   CARBOHYDRATES: 18 G   CHOLESTEROL: 0 MG   FAT: 0 G   FIBER: 2 G
PROTEIN: 0.4 G   SODIUM: 3 MG   CALCIUM: 12 MG

FRESH CRANBERRY-APPLE RELISH

YIELD: 16 SERVINGS

12 ounces (3 cups) fresh or frozen cranberries
1½ cups coarsely chopped unpeeled red apples
½ cup chopped walnuts
½ to ⅔ cup sugar

1. Place the cranberries and apples in the bowl of a food processor, and process until finely chopped. (Note that depending on the size of your food processor, you may have to do this in two batches.)
2. Transfer the mixture to a covered container and stir in the walnuts and sugar. Cover and refrigerate for several hours or overnight before serving.

Nutritional Facts (per 3-tablespoon serving)
CALORIES: 63 CARBOHYDRATES: 10 G CHOLESTEROL: 0 MG FAT: 2.5 G FIBER: 1.3 G
PROTEIN: 0.7 G SODIUM: 0 MG CALCIUM: 6 MG

FRESH CRANBERRY-ORANGE RELISH

YIELD: 16 SERVINGS

1 medium orange
12 ounces (3 cups) fresh or frozen (unthawed) cranberries
½ cup chopped pecans
½ to ⅔ cup sugar

1. Slice the orange, discarding the ends. Peel the slices, reserving one quarter of the rind, and remove the seeds.
2. Place the orange slices, the reserved orange rind, and the cranberries in the bowl of a food processor, and process until finely chopped. (Note that depending on the size of your food processor, you may have to do this in two batches.)
3. Transfer the mixture to a covered container, and stir in the pecans and sugar. Cover and refrigerate for several hours or overnight before serving.

Nutritional Facts (per 3-tablespoon serving)
CALORIES: 63 CARBOHYDRATES: 9 G CHOLESTEROL: 0 MG FAT: 2.7 G FIBER: 1.3 G
PROTEIN: 0.5 G SODIUM: 0 MG CALCIUM: 7 MG

CRANBERRY FLUFF

YIELD: 12 SERVINGS

2 cups fresh or frozen cranberries
½ cup sugar
2 cans (8 ounces each) crushed pineapple in juice, well drained
1 cup finely chopped peeled apple
1½ cups mini marshmallows
½ cup chopped pecans (optional)
3 cups nonfat or light whipped topping

1. Place the cranberries and sugar in the bowl of a food processor and process until the cranberries are finely chopped.
2. Transfer the cranberry mixture to a large bowl, and stir in the drained pineapple, apple, marshmallows, and, if desired, the pecans. Cover and refrigerate for several hours or overnight.
3. Fold in the whipped topping just before serving.

Nutritional Facts (per ½-cup serving)
CALORIES: 107 CARBOHYDRATES: 26 G CHOLESTEROL: 0 MG FAT: 0.7 G FIBER: 1.2 G
PROTEIN: 0.2 G SODIUM: 15 MG CALCIUM: 2 MG

MOLDED CRANBERRY-APPLE RELISH

YIELD: 8 SERVINGS

1 package (4-serving size) sugar-free cranberry or raspberry gelatin mix
¼ cup sugar
¾ cup boiling water
¾ cup cold water
1¼ cups fresh or frozen cranberries, finely chopped
  (use a food processor for best results)

1 medium apple, peeled and finely chopped

¼ cup finely chopped celery

¼ cup finely chopped walnuts

1. Place the gelatin mix and sugar in a large heat-proof bowl, add the boiling water, and stir for 2 minutes, or until the gelatin mix is completely dissolved. Add the cold water to the gelatin mixture, and stir again.

2. Place the gelatin mixture in the refrigerator and chill for about 30 minutes, or until the gelatin is the consistency of raw egg whites. Stir the cranberries, apple, celery, and walnuts into the gelatin. Spread the mixture evenly into a 4-cup gelatin mold lightly coated with nonstick cooking spray.

3. Cover the gelatin and refrigerate for at least 6 hours, or until firm. Unmold* the gelatin onto a lettuce-lined serving plate. Slice and serve chilled.

Nutritional Facts (per serving)
CALORIES: 63 CARBOHYDRATES: 10 G CHOLESTEROL: 0 MG FAT: 2.5 G FIBER: 1.1 G
PROTEIN: 1.4 G SODIUM: 30 MG CALCIUM: 7 MG

To unmold the ring, loosen the edges of the gelatin with a knife. Place a serving platter upside down over the mold, and invert the mold onto the platter. It should slide out easily. If it does not, dip the mold in warm (not hot) water for 5 to 10 seconds before unmolding.

MOLDED CRANBERRY-PINEAPPLE RELISH

YIELD: 8 SERVINGS

1 package (4-serving size) sugar-free cranberry gelatin mix

¼ cup light brown sugar

¾ cup boiling water

8-ounce can crushed pineapple in juice

1¼ cups fresh or frozen cranberries, finely chopped
  (use a food processor for best results)

¼ cup finely chopped celery

¼ cup finely chopped toasted pecans (page 30) or walnuts (optional)

1. Place the gelatin mix and brown sugar in a large heat-proof bowl, add the boiling water, and stir for 2 minutes, or until the gelatin mix is completely dissolved. Drain the pineapple juice into a 1-cup measure, and add enough ice water to bring the volume to ¾ cup. Add the juice–ice water mixture to the gelatin mixture, and stir again.

2. Place the gelatin mixture in the refrigerator and chill for about 30 minutes, or until the gelatin is the consistency of raw egg whites. Stir the cranberries, drained pineapple, celery, and, if desired, the pecans or walnuts into the gelatin. Spread the mixture evenly into a 4-cup gelatin mold lightly coated with nonstick cooking spray.

3. Cover the gelatin and refrigerate for at least 6 hours, or until firm. Unmold* the gelatin onto a lettuce-lined serving plate. Slice and serve chilled.

Nutritional Facts (per serving)
CALORIES: 55 CARBOHYDRATES: 13 G CHOLESTEROL: 0 MG FAT: 0.1 G FIBER: 1 G
PROTEIN: 0.8 G SODIUM: 35 MG CALCIUM: 9 MG

*To unmold the ring, loosen the edges of the gelatin with a knife. Place a serving platter upside down over the mold, and invert the mold onto the platter. It should slide out easily. If it does not, dip the mold in warm (not hot) water for 5 to 10 seconds before unmolding.

Festive Fruit Salad

YIELD: 10 SERVINGS

4 large navel oranges

1-pound can pineapple chunks in juice, undrained

½ cup shredded sweetened coconut

¼ cup sliced toasted almonds or chopped toasted pecans (page 30) (optional)

2 medium bananas, peeled and sliced
⅔ cup mini marshmallows

1. Peel the oranges, cutting down to the flesh. Cut the orange segments away from the membranes, and place the orange segments and the juices that have accumulated in a large bowl.
2. Add the undrained pineapple chunks, coconut, and, if desired, the almonds or pecans to the oranges and toss to mix well. Cover the mixture and refrigerate for at least 2 hours. Add the bananas and marshmallows to the salad 30 to 60 minutes before serving.

Nutritional Facts (per ⅔-cup serving)
CALORIES: 108 CARBOHYDRATES: 23 G CHOLESTEROL: 0 MG FAT: 1.9 G FIBER: 2.5 G
PROTEIN: 1.2 G SODIUM: 15 MG CALCIUM: 31 MG

Deep-Dish Pumpkin Pie

YIELD: 8 SERVINGS

1 unbaked Pat-In Pie Crust (page 301) or 1 frozen 9-inch deep-dish pie crust
1 cup nonfat or light whipped topping (optional)

FILLING
1½ cups canned pumpkin
¾ cup light brown sugar
2½ teaspoons pumpkin pie spice
1½ teaspoons vanilla extract
12-ounce can evaporated skim or low-fat milk
½ cup fat-free egg substitute

1. To make the filling, place the pumpkin, brown sugar, pie spice, and vanilla extract in a large bowl and stir with a wire whisk to mix well. Slowly whisk in the evaporated milk and the egg substitute.

2. Pour the filling into the crust, and bake uncovered at 400°F for 15 minutes. Reduce the heat to 350°F, and bake for 45 additional minutes, or until a sharp knife inserted near the center of the pie comes out clean.

3. Allow the pie to cool to room temperature before cutting into wedges and serving. Top each serving with some of the whipped topping if desired. Refrigerate leftovers.

Nutritional Facts (per serving)
CALORIES: 220 CARBOHYDRATES: 39 G CHOLESTEROL: 2 MG FAT: 4 G FIBER: 2.2 G
PROTEIN: 7.3 G SODIUM: 129 MG CALCIUM: 166 MG

Apple Streusel Pie

YIELD: 8 SERVINGS

1 unbaked Pat-In Pie Crust (page 301) or 1 frozen 9-inch deep-dish pie crust

FILLING
¼ cup light brown sugar
1 tablespoon plus 2 teaspoons cornstarch
½ teaspoon ground cinnamon
¼ teaspoon ground nutmeg
¼ cup plus 1 tablespoon apple juice
6 cups peeled sliced Golden Delicious apples
¼ cup dark raisins, dried sweetened cranberries, or pitted dried sweet cherries

TOPPING
⅓ cup honey crunch wheat germ, or chopped pecans or walnuts
⅓ cup light brown sugar
¼ cup whole wheat pastry flour or unbleached flour
1 tablespoon reduced-fat margarine or light butter,
*   softened to room temperature*

1. To make the filling, place the brown sugar, cornstarch, cinnamon, and nutmeg in a 4-quart pot and stir to mix well. Add the apple juice and stir to mix well. Place the pot over medium heat and cook, stirring constantly, until the mixture comes to a boil. Add the apples and the raisins, cranberries, or cherries and cook, stirring constantly, for another minute or two, or until the fruit is coated with a thick glaze.

2. Spread the filling evenly in the crust. Cover the pie loosely with a piece of aluminum foil (spray the underside of the foil with nonstick cooking spray), and bake at 400°F for 25 minutes, or until the apples begin to soften and release their juices.

3. While the pie is baking, prepare the topping by placing the wheat germ or nuts, brown sugar, and flour in a small bowl. Stir to mix well. Add the margarine or butter and stir until the mixture is moist and crumbly. Add a little more margarine or butter if the mixture seems too dry.

4. Remove the pie from the oven, and sprinkle the topping over the pie. Reduce the oven temperature to 375°F, and bake uncovered for an additional 30 minutes, or until the topping is nicely browned and the filling is bubbly around the edges. Cover loosely with aluminum foil during the last few minutes of baking if the topping starts to brown too quickly.

5. Allow the pie to cool at room temperature for at least 1 hour before cutting into wedges and serving. Serve warm or at room temperature.

Nutritional Facts (per serving)
CALORIES: 256 CARBOHYDRATES: 51 G CHOLESTEROL: 0 MG FAT: 5.2 G FIBER: 4.4 G
PROTEIN: 4.1 G SODIUM: 59 MG CALCIUM: 32 MG

Christmas

As visions of sugarplums dance in our heads, so perhaps do less-pleasant visions of heavy, diet-busting holiday roasts, side dishes, and desserts. Ready for a change of pace? Then delight guests with one of these two deliciously light Christmas dinners.

The first menu features a flavorful twist on the Thanksgiving turkey dinner. Begin with a glorious salad of mixed baby greens topped with roasted pears and a sprinkling of dried cranberries and pecans. Then present the impressive main course—Herb-Roasted Turkey Breast accompanied by savory, citrus-laced gravy. On the side, dishes like Cranberry Wild Rice Pilaf, Orange Whipped Sweet Potatoes, and Celery Crunch Casserole add a pleasing contrast of colors and textures. Last, but not least, is your choice of creamy Cran-Raspberry Trifle or show-stopping Triple Fudge Torte. Either of these delectable desserts will bring an easy but elegant conclusion to this delightful meal.

If you're all "turkeyed-out" after Thanksgiving, the second Christmas menu may be just what you're looking for. A crowd-pleasing lean baked ham coated with a spiced apple glaze takes center stage. Since this entrée starts with a precooked ham, it is as easy to make as it is delicious. Accompany the ham with dishes like Maple-Glazed Acorn Squash, Nutty Green Beans, and Mandarin-Cranberry Ring. And for dessert, wow guests with deceptively decadent Black Forest Cake or comforting Cranberry-Apple Rice Pudding. Either choice would bring a memorably sweet ending to this delightful holiday dinner.

Christmas Dinner

MENU ONE

SERVES 8 TO 10

Glorious Green Salad (page 116)

Herb-Roasted Turkey Breast (page 117)
with Savory Gravy (page 118)

Cranberry Wild Rice Pilaf (page 119)

Orange Whipped Sweet Potatoes (page 120)
or Citrus-Glazed Carrots (page 121)

Broccoli Casserole (page 121)
or Celery Crunch Casserole (page 122)

Flaxseed Dinner Rolls (page 123)
or Multigrain Dinner Rolls

Cran-Raspberry Trifle (page 125)
or Triple Fudge Torte (page 126)

ADVANCE PLANNING TIPS

◆ Roast the pears for Glorious Green Salad a day in advance. Prepare the Honey-Glazed Pecans that top the salad well in advance and refrigerate or freeze until needed.

◆ Cook the rice for Cranberry Wild Rice Pilaf a day in advance. Chop the vegetables for the pilaf the day before and store in a covered container in the refrigerator until ready to prepare the dish. Or prepare the entire dish the day before, place in a 2-quart casserole dish, and refrigerate. Cover the dish with aluminum foil, and reheat in 350°F oven for about 25 minutes. (Remove from the refrigerator 30 to 60 minutes before placing in the oven.)

◆ Thaw the broccoli for Broccoli Casserole the day before, squeeze dry, and refrigerate until ready to assemble the casserole and bake. If making Celery Crunch Casserole, cook the celery the day before, cover, and refrigerate until ready to assemble the casserole and bake.

◆ Flaxseed Dinner Rolls can be prepared the day before and reheated just before serving. Place the rolls on a large microwave-safe plate, cover with damp paper towels, and heat at medium-high power for a minute or two, or just until heated through.

◆ Prepare Cran-Raspberry Trifle the morning of your dinner, since it should chill for several hours before serving. Prepare Triple Fudge Torte a full day in advance, since it becomes moister and more delicious with time.

Glorious Green Salad

YIELD: 10 SERVINGS

8 ounces mixed baby salad greens with fresh herbs (about 15 cups loosely packed)

½ cup plus 2 tablespoons dried sweetened cranberries

½ cup plus 2 tablespoons nonfat or reduced-fat feta cheese

½ cup plus 2 tablespoons chopped Honey-Glazed Pecans (page 68) or chopped toasted pecans (page 30)

½ cup plus 2 tablespoons bottled light balsamic vinaigrette salad dressing

ROASTED PEARS

5 medium-small firm but ripe pears

2 tablespoons frozen orange juice concentrate, thawed

1 tablespoon balsamic vinegar

Butter-flavored nonstick cooking spray

1. To make the roasted pears, peel the pears and cut each one in half lengthwise. Use a spoon or melon baller to scoop out the core and the fibrous line leading from the core to the stem end. Combine the orange juice concentrate and balsamic vinegar in a small bowl, stir to mix well, and brush some of the mixture over all sides of the pears.

2. Coat a large baking sheet with the cooking spray and arrange the pears on the sheet with the centers facing down. Spray the pears lightly with the cooking spray and bake at 400°F for 10 minutes. Turn the pears over, spray again with the cooking spray, and bake for an additional 10 minutes. Turn the pears once more and bake for 3 additional minutes, or until they are nicely browned and tender. Let the pears cool to room temperature, then place in a covered container and refrigerate until ready to assemble the salads.

3. To assemble the salads, place 1½ cups of the salad greens on each of 10 serving plates. Top the greens on each plate with a roasted pear half and a tablespoon each of the cranberries, feta cheese, and pecans. Drizzle some of the dressing over each salad, and serve immediately.

Nutritional Facts (per serving)
CALORIES: 163   CARBOHYDRATES: 24 G   CHOLESTEROL: 1 MG   FAT: 7.3 G   FIBER: 3.6 G
PROTEIN: 3 G   SODIUM: 290 MG   CALCIUM: 58 MG

Herb-Roasted Turkey Breast

YIELD: 12 SERVINGS

7-pound bone-in turkey breast

⅓ cup medium-dry sherry

⅓ cup orange juice

⅔ cup chicken broth

¼ teaspoon fines herbes or dried thyme
Pinch ground white pepper

BASTING SAUCE
1 tablespoon frozen orange juice concentrate, thawed
2 teaspoons Dijon mustard
1 teaspoon fines herbes, or ¼ teaspoon each dried thyme, marjoram, sage, and rosemary
1 teaspoon lemon pepper
¼ teaspoon garlic powder

1. Remove any excess skin from the turkey breast, leaving only enough to cover the top and sides. Rinse the turkey with cool water and pat dry with paper towels. Place on a rack in a roasting pan.
2. Combine the basting sauce ingredients in a small bowl, and brush over the top and sides of the turkey breast. Pour the sherry, orange juice, and broth into the bottom of the pan and then stir in the herbs and white pepper. Cover the pan with aluminum foil, crimping the foil around the edges of the pan to seal.
3. Bake at 325°F for 2 hours. Carefully remove the foil (steam will escape), and bake uncovered for an additional 30 minutes, basting occasionally with the pan juices, until the skin is golden brown and a thermometer inserted in the thickest part of the breast registers 170°F.
4. Transfer the turkey to a serving platter. Cover the turkey loosely with aluminum foil and let sit for 15 minutes before slicing. Serve with Savory Gravy (below).

Nutritional Facts (per 3-ounce skinless serving)
CALORIES: 125   CARBOHYDRATES: 3 G   CHOLESTEROL: 73 MG   FAT: 1 G   FIBER: 0 G
PROTEIN: 26 G   SODIUM: 86 MG   CALCIUM: 12 MG

Savory Gravy

YIELD: 2¼ CUPS

¼ cup unbleached flour
½ cup skim or low-fat milk

Roast turkey drippings

1 teaspoon chicken bouillon granules

1. Combine the flour and milk in a jar with a tight-fitting lid, and shake until smooth. Set aside.
2. Pour the drippings from the roast turkey into a fat-separator cup. (If you don't have a fat-separator cup, pour the drippings into a bowl, add a few ice cubes, and skim off the fat once it hardens.) Pour the defatted drippings into a 2-cup measure and add water if necessary to bring the volume to 1¾ cups.
3. Pour the drippings mixture into a 1-quart saucepan, and add the bouillon granules. Bring the mixture to a boil over medium heat. Slowly stir the flour mixture into the gravy and continue to cook and stir for another minute or two, or until the gravy is thickened and bubbly. Transfer the gravy to a gravy boat, and serve hot.

Nutritional Facts (per ¼-cup serving)
CALORIES: 27   CARBOHYDRATES: 4 G   CHOLESTEROL: 0 MG   FAT: 0 G   FIBER: 0 G
PROTEIN: 1 G   SODIUM: 126 MG   CALCIUM: 21 MG

Cranberry Wild Rice Pilaf

YIELD: 10 SERVINGS

1¼ cups long-grain or basmati brown rice

½ cup plus 2 tablespoons wild rice

4¼ cups water

½ teaspoon salt

2 tablespoons plus 1½ teaspoons reduced-fat margarine or light butter

½ cup plus 2 tablespoons chopped onion

½ cup plus 2 tablespoons thinly sliced celery

½ cup dried sweetened cranberries

¾ teaspoon fines herbes or dried thyme

1. Place the brown rice, wild rice, water, and salt in a 3-quart nonstick pot and bring to a boil over high heat. Reduce the heat to low, cover, and simmer without stirring for 45 to 50 minutes, or until the rice is tender. Remove the rice from the heat, and set aside.

2. Melt the margarine or butter in a large nonstick skillet over medium heat. Add the onion, celery, cranberries, and fines herbes or thyme. Cover the skillet and cook, stirring occasionally, for about 4 minutes, or until the vegetables are tender. Add a little water to the skillet if it becomes too dry.

3. Add the rice to the skillet mixture, and toss to mix well. Serve hot.

Nutritional Facts (per ⅔-cup serving)
CALORIES: 153 CARBOHYDRATES: 30 G CHOLESTEROL: 0 MG FAT: 2.1 G FIBER: 2 G
PROTEIN: 3.5 G SODIUM: 107 MG CALCIUM: 12 MG

Orange Whipped Sweet Potatoes

YIELD: 10 SERVINGS

3 pounds fresh sweet potatoes (about 4 medium-large)
¼ cup light brown sugar
¼ cup reduced-fat margarine or light butter
2 tablespoons frozen orange juice concentrate, thawed
⅜ teaspoon ground ginger
⅜ teaspoon ground nutmeg

1. Peel the potatoes and cut into ¾-inch chunks. Place the potatoes in a 4-quart pot and add water to barely cover. Bring to a boil over high heat, then reduce the heat to medium-low, cover, and simmer for 10 to 12 minutes, or until the potatoes are soft.

2. Drain the potatoes and return them to the pot. Add the remaining ingredients and mash with a potato masher or beat with an electric mixer until smooth. Serve hot.

Nutritional Facts (per ½-cup serving)
CALORIES: 159 CARBOHYDRATES: 34 G CHOLESTEROL: 0 MG FAT: 2.1 G FIBER: 3.4 G
PROTEIN: 2 G SODIUM: 53 MG CALCIUM: 37 MG

Citrus-Glazed Carrots

YIELD: 10 SERVINGS

2 pounds baby carrots (about 7 cups)
1 cup water
¼ teaspoon salt
¼ cup reduced-fat margarine or light butter
¼ cup orange marmalade
¼ to ½ teaspoon ground ginger

1. Place the carrots, water, and salt in a large, deep nonstick skillet and bring to a boil over medium-high heat. Reduce the heat to medium, cover, and cook for 5 to 7 minutes, or until just tender. Add a little more water during cooking if the skillet becomes too dry, but only enough to prevent scorching.
2. Add the margarine or butter, marmalade, and ginger, and raise the heat to medium-high. Cook, stirring frequently, for another minute or two, or until most of the liquid evaporates and the carrots are coated with the glaze. Serve hot.

Nutritional Facts (per ⅔-cup serving)
CALORIES: 72   CARBOHYDRATES: 13 G   CHOLESTEROL: 0 MG   FAT: 2.5 G   FIBER: 1.7 G
PROTEIN: 0.8 G   SODIUM: 104 MG   CALCIUM: 24 MG

Broccoli Casserole

YIELD: 10 SERVINGS

2 packages (10 ounces each) frozen chopped broccoli, thawed and squeezed dry
10¾-ounce can condensed reduced-fat cream of mushroom soup, undiluted
1 cup shredded reduced-fat Cheddar cheese
¼ cup nonfat or light mayonnaise
¼ cup fat-free egg substitute

¼ cup coarsely crushed cornflake crumbs
Butter-flavored nonstick cooking spray

1. Place the broccoli, soup, cheese, mayonnaise, and egg substitute in a large bowl and stir to mix well. Coat an 8-by-8-inch (2-quart) casserole dish with the cooking spray, and spread the broccoli mixture evenly in the dish. Sprinkle the cornflake crumbs over the top of the casserole and spray the top lightly with the cooking spray.
2. Bake at 350°F for about 35 minutes, or until the edges are bubbly and the top is nicely browned. Remove the casserole from the oven and let sit for 5 minutes before serving.

Nutritional Facts (per ⅔-cup serving)
CALORIES: 77 CARBOHYDRATES: 8 G CHOLESTEROL: 7 MG FAT: 2.3 G FIBER: 1.7 G
PROTEIN: 5.8 G SODIUM: 267 MG CALCIUM: 94 MG

Celery Crunch Casserole

YIELD: 10 SERVINGS

3 cups thinly sliced celery
1 tablespoon skim or low-fat milk
2 teaspoons cornstarch
¾ cup nonfat or light sour cream
10¾-ounce can condensed reduced-fat and -sodium cream of mushroom soup, undiluted
8-ounce can sliced water chestnuts, drained
4-ounce can sliced mushrooms, drained
¼ cup slivered almonds
¼ cup grated Parmesan cheese
1 tablespoon plus 1½ teaspoons dried seasoned bread crumbs
Butter-flavored nonstick cooking spray

1. Place the celery and 1 tablespoon of water in a large nonstick skillet. Cover and cook over medium heat, stirring occasionally, for about 5 minutes, or until the celery is crisp-tender.

(Add a little more water if the skillet becomes too dry, but only enough to prevent scorching.) Drain off any excess liquid.

2. Place the milk and the cornstarch in a small bowl and stir to dissolve the cornstarch. Whisk in the sour cream and the undiluted soup.

3. Add the water chestnuts, mushrooms, and almonds to the celery, and toss to mix well. Add the soup mixture and stir to mix well. Coat an 8-by-8-inch (2-quart) baking dish with the cooking spray and spread the celery mixture evenly in the dish.

4. Combine the Parmesan cheese and bread crumbs in a small bowl and stir to mix well. Sprinkle the topping over the celery mixture and spray the top lightly with the cooking spray. Bake at 350°F for about 25 to 30 minutes, or until the edges are bubbly and the top is lightly browned. Remove the dish from the oven and let sit for 5 minutes before serving.

Nutritional Facts (per ½-cup serving)
CALORIES: 89 CARBOHYDRATES: 11 G CHOLESTEROL: 4 MG FAT: 2.9 G FIBER: 2.3 G
PROTEIN: 4 G SODIUM: 290 MG CALCIUM: 105 MG

Flaxseed Dinner Rolls

YIELD: 12 ROLLS

2¼ cups wheat blend or regular bread flour
¼ cup whole flaxseeds
¼ cup instant buttermilk powder or nonfat dry milk powder
1½ teaspoons rapid-rising yeast
1 tablespoon plus 1 teaspoon sugar
½ teaspoon salt
¾ cup plus 2 tablespoons water
1 tablespoon lecithin granules* or canola oil
Butter-flavored nonstick cooking spray

1. Place all of the ingredients except for ¼ cup of the flour in the pan of a bread machine. Set the machine to "rise," "dough," "manual," or equivalent setting so that the machine will mix

and knead the dough and let it rise once. Check the mixture 5 minutes after the machine has started. It should form a soft, satiny dough. If the dough seems too sticky, add a little more flour, a tablespoonful at a time. (Be careful not to make the dough too stiff, or it will be hard to shape.)

2. When the dough is ready, remove it from the machine, pinch it into 12 pieces, and roll each piece into a ball. Coat a medium-sized baking sheet with the cooking spray and arrange the dough balls, spacing them 2 inches apart, on the sheet. Cover the balls with a clean kitchen towel and let rise in a warm place for about 35 minutes, or until doubled in size.

3. Spray the tops of the rolls lightly with the cooking spray, and bake at 350°F for about 18 minutes, or until lightly browned. Serve hot.

> *Nutritional Facts (per roll)*
> CALORIES: 99 CARBOHYDRATES: 17 G CHOLESTEROL: 0 MG FAT: 2.1 G FIBER: 2 G
> PROTEIN: 3.7 G SODIUM: 112 MG CALCIUM: 25 MG

> *Lecithin granules, a nutritious product derived from soybeans, condition the dough and make it rise better. They can be purchased in most natural foods stores.*

To make the dough by hand:

1. Place 1½ cups of the flour and all of the flaxseeds, milk powder, yeast, sugar, and salt in a large bowl, and stir to mix well. Place the water and the lecithin granules or canola oil in a small saucepan and heat until very warm (125° to 130° F). Add the warm-water mixture to the flour mixture, and stir for 1 minute. Stir in enough of the remaining flour, 2 tablespoons at a time, to form a soft dough that does not stick to the bowl.

2. Sprinkle 2 tablespoons of the remaining flour over a flat surface and turn the dough onto the surface. Knead the dough for 5 minutes, gradually adding enough of the remaining flour to form a satiny ball that is smooth and elastic. (Be careful not to make the dough too stiff, or it will be hard to shape.)

3. Coat a large bowl with the cooking spray and place the ball of dough in the bowl. Cover the bowl with a clean kitchen towel, and let the dough rise in a warm place for about 35 minutes, or until doubled in size.

4. When the dough has risen, punch it down and proceed as directed in steps 2 and 3 above.

Cran-Raspberry Trifle

✿ *For variety, substitute chocolate cake and pudding mix for the vanilla cake and pudding mix.*

YIELD: 10 SERVINGS

10 (½-inch) slices fat-free vanilla loaf cake or low-fat pound cake
1 cup whole-berry cranberry sauce
2 cups fresh raspberries or fresh sliced strawberries or 1 cup each

PUDDING MIXTURE
2½ cups skim or low-fat milk
6 serving-size package cook-and-serve or instant vanilla pudding mix
   (sugar-free or regular)

TOPPING
1¾ cups nonfat or light whipped topping
½ cup nonfat or low-fat vanilla yogurt (sugar-free or regular)
3 tablespoons sliced toasted almonds (page 30)

1. Use the milk to prepare the pudding according to package directions. Transfer to a covered container and refrigerate until well chilled.
2. To assemble the trifle, spread about 1½ tablespoons of the cranberry sauce over each of the cake slices, and arrange half of the cake slices over the bottom of a 2½-quart glass bowl. Top the cake slices with half of the raspberries or strawberries, and then half of the pudding. Repeat the layers.
3. To make the topping, place the whipped topping in a medium-sized bowl, and gently fold in the yogurt. Swirl the mixture over the top of the trifle, cover, and chill for 3 to 6 hours before serving. Just before serving, sprinkle with the almonds.

Nutritional Facts (per serving)
CALORIES: 201 CARBOHYDRATES: 43 G CHOLESTEROL: 1 MG FAT: 1.7 G FIBER: 2.6 G
PROTEIN: 4.4 G SODIUM: 209 MG CALCIUM: 116 MG

Triple Fudge Torte

YIELD: 10 SERVINGS

1 package (4-serving size) instant chocolate pudding mix
1 cup plus 2 tablespoons skim or low-fat milk
1 ready-made fat-free or low-fat chocolate loaf cake (15 ounces) or
   1 Light Chocolate Loaf Cake (page 127)
¼ cup coffee liqueur

GLAZE
¾ cup powdered sugar
2 tablespoons Dutch processed cocoa powder
⅛ teaspoon ground cinnamon
1 tablespoon skim or low-fat milk
3 tablespoons sliced almonds

1. Place the pudding mix and milk in a medium-sized bowl and whisk for 2 minutes, or until well mixed. Place the pudding in the refrigerator for about 10 minutes, or until very thick.
2. Using a bread knife, slice the cake horizontally into 3 layers. Place the layers on a flat surface and sprinkle each of the bottom two layers with 2 tablespoons of the liqueur. Set aside.
3. To assemble the cake, place the bottom cake layer on a serving plate and spread half of the pudding over the cake layer. Top with the middle cake layer and the remaining pudding. Place the top layer on the cake. Cover the cake with plastic wrap or aluminum foil and refrigerate for at least 12 hours (preferably for 24 hours).
4. To make the glaze, place the sugar, cocoa, and cinnamon in a small bowl and stir to mix well. Stir in the milk, adding a little more if necessary, to make a thick glaze. If using a microwave oven, place the glaze in a microwave-safe bowl, and heat at high power for 45 seconds, or until hot and runny. If using a conventional stove top, place the glaze in a small pot and, stirring constantly, cook over medium heat for 45 seconds, or until hot and runny.
5. Spread the glaze over the top of the chilled cake, allowing some of the mixture to drip down the sides. Sprinkle the almonds over the top. Allow the glaze to cool for 5 minutes before slicing and serving, or return the cake to the refrigerator and chill until ready to serve.

Nutritional Facts (per serving)
CALORIES: 223 CARBOHYDRATES: 48 G CHOLESTEROL: 0 MG FAT: 1.1 G FIBER: 1.4 G
PROTEIN: 4 G SODIUM: 350 MG CALCIUM: 48 MG

Light Chocolate Loaf Cake

✤ *For variety, fold 1 cup of finely ground almonds, hazelnuts, or walnuts into the batter.*

YIELD: 2 CAKES (8 SLICES EACH)

1 box (1 pound, 2.25 ounces) chocolate fudge cake mix
¾ cup nonfat or low-fat vanilla yogurt
¾ cup water or room temperature coffee
½ cup plus 1 tablespoon fat-free egg substitute

1. Place the cake mix in a large bowl, add the yogurt, water or coffee, and egg substitute, and beat with an electric mixer for 1 minute, or until well mixed. Set the batter aside for 15 minutes, then beat for an additional minute.

2. Coat two 8-by-4-inch loaf pans with nonstick cooking spray, and divide the batter evenly between the pans. Bake at 350°F for about 40 minutes, or just until the top springs back when lightly touched and a wooden toothpick inserted in the center of the cake comes out clean. Be careful not to overbake.

3. Allow the cake to cool in the pan for 40 minutes. Then invert onto a serving platter and cool to room temperature before slicing and serving.

Nutritional Facts (per serving)
CALORIES: 142 CARBOHYDRATES: 28 G CHOLESTEROL: 0 MG FAT: 1.9 G FIBER: 0.8 G
PROTEIN: 2.9 G SODIUM: 265 MG CALCIUM: 53 MG

Christmas Dinner

Menu Two

Serves 8 to 10

Spiced Apple-Glazed Ham (page 129)

Macaroni with Three Cheeses (page 130)

Maple-Glazed Acorn Squash (page 132)
or Savory Rutabaga (page 133)

Nutty Green Beans (page 134)
or Country-Style Collard Greens (page 134)

Mandarin-Cranberry Ring (page 135)
or Cran-Raspberry Ring (page 136)

Yogurt Drop Biscuits (page 137)
or Multigrain Dinner Rolls

Black Forest Cake (page 138)
or Cranberry-Apple Rice Pudding (page 140)

◆ Slice and clean the acorn squash or peel and dice the rutabaga the day before. Place in a zip-type bag and refrigerate until you are ready to prepare the dish.

◆ Clean and cut the green beans the day before. Place in a zip-type bag and refrigerate until you are ready to cook the beans. If you are making Country-Style Collard Greens, look for prewashed chopped greens in the fresh produce section of your grocery store. Or clean and chop your own greens and refrigerate in a zip-type bag until ready to cook.

◆ Prepare Mandarin-Cranberry Ring or Cran-Raspberry Ring the day before, as they require at least 6 hours of refrigeration before serving.

◆ Mix the dry ingredients for Yogurt Drop Biscuits, cover, and set aside until ready to stir in the liquid ingredients and bake.

◆ Prepare Black Forest Cake the day before. It becomes moister and more delicious if allowed to refrigerate for 24 hours before serving. If you are making Cranberry-Apple Rice Pudding, cook it the day before and refrigerate, as it can be served either cold or warm. If you prefer your rice pudding warm, it can be quickly reheated in a microwave oven.

Spiced Apple-Glazed Ham

YIELD: ABOUT 12 SERVINGS

5- to 7-pound lean bone-in fully cooked ham

GLAZE
¼ cup apple jelly
1 tablespoon dry or medium sherry
2 teaspoons Dijon mustard

⅛ teaspoon ground cinnamon
⅛ teaspoon ground cloves

1. To make the glaze, place all of the glaze ingredients in a small pot and stir to mix well. Place the pot over medium heat and cook, stirring frequently, for a minute or two, or until the jelly melts and the mixture is smooth. Remove the pot from the heat and set aside.
2. If desired, score the top of the ham in a diamond pattern, making cuts about ¼-inch deep. (If using a spiral-sliced ham, do not score.) Coat a 9-by-13-inch pan with nonstick cooking spray, and place the ham cut side down in the pan. Cover loosely with a foil tent and bake at 350°F for about 1¼ to 1¾ hours (about 1¾ to 2¼ hours for a 7-pound ham), or until a thermometer inserted in the center of the ham (not touching the bone) registers just under 140°F.
3. Remove the foil and brush some of the glaze over the ham. Bake for an additional 15 to 20 minutes, basting several times, or until the ham is nicely glazed and the thermometer registers at least 140°F.
4. Remove the ham from the oven, cover loosely with foil, and let sit for 10 minutes before slicing and serving.

Nutritional Facts (per 3-ounce serving)
CALORIES: 152 CARBOHYDRATES: 7 G CHOLESTEROL: 50 MG FAT: 7 G FIBER: 0 G
PROTEIN: 15 G SODIUM: 820 MG CALCIUM: 5 MG

Variation:

To make **Orange-Ginger Glazed Ham,** combine ¼ cup orange marmalade or apricot fruit spread, 1 tablespoon dry sherry, 2 teaspoons Dijon mustard, and ¼ teaspoon ground ginger in a small bowl and stir to mix well. Substitute for the apple glaze in the above recipe.

Macaroni with Three Cheeses

YIELD: 12 SERVINGS

12 ounces elbow macaroni (about 3 cups)
¼ cup plus 1 tablespoon unbleached flour

Choosing Your Holiday Ham

A holiday ham is always a crowd pleaser. If you have never prepared a ham, you will be happy to know that most hams available in supermarkets today are already fully cooked and require only heating before serving. Some, like spiral-sliced hams, are also presliced, making them a natural for fuss-free entertaining. Here are some tips for choosing your holiday ham.

◆ *Be sure to read the Nutrition Facts label, as hams vary in fat content from about 5 grams per 3-ounce cooked serving to over 15 grams. Some brands of lower-sodium hams are also available.*

◆ *To heat a fully cooked ham, place the ham in a large roasting pan, cover loosely with a foil tent, and bake at 350°F for about 15 to 20 minutes per pound, or until the internal temperature of the ham reaches 140°F. Add a festive touch by basting your ham with a flavorful glaze and cooking uncovered during the last 15 to 20 minutes of baking. (Note that some hams are pre-glazed, making this step unnecessary.)*

◆ *How much will you need? A boneless ham will yield 4 to 5 servings per pound. A bone-in ham will yield 2 to 3 servings per pound. Purchase a larger ham if you desire plenty of leftovers.*

1½ teaspoons dry mustard
½ teaspoon dried sage, finely crumbled
¼ teaspoon ground black pepper
4 cups skim or low-fat milk
2 cups diced reduced-fat process Cheddar cheese (like Velveeta Light)
1 cup shredded reduced-fat white Cheddar cheese
¼ cup grated Parmesan cheese
3 tablespoons dried seasoned Italian bread crumbs
Butter-flavored nonstick cooking spray

1. Cook the macaroni al dente according to package directions. Drain well, return to the pot, and set aside.

2. To make the sauce, combine the flour, mustard, sage, and pepper in a 3-quart microwave-safe bowl. Add about ¼ cup of the milk and whisk until the mixture is smooth and no lumps of flour remain. Slowly whisk in the remaining milk. Microwave the milk mixture at high power for 6 minutes, whisking every 2 minutes. Then microwave for an additional 3 to 5 minutes, whisking every 45 to 60 seconds, or until the mixture is bubbly and thickens slightly. Add the cheeses and microwave for an additional minute, whisking every 30 seconds, or until the cheese is melted.

3. Pour the cheese sauce over the macaroni and toss to mix well. Coat a 9-by-13-inch baking dish with the cooking spray, and spread the macaroni mixture evenly in the pan. Sprinkle the bread crumbs over the macaroni mixture, then spray the top lightly with the cooking spray.

4. Bake uncovered at 350° F for about 30 minutes, or until the edges are bubbly and the topping is lightly browned. Remove the dish from the oven and let sit for 10 minutes before serving.

Nutritional Facts (per ¾-cup serving)
CALORIES: 230 CARBOHYDRATES: 31 G CHOLESTEROL: 16 MG FAT: 4.6 G FIBER: 0.9 G
PROTEIN: 14.5 G SODIUM: 507 MG CALCIUM: 323 MG

Maple-Glazed Acorn Squash

YIELD: 10 SERVINGS

15 rings (each ¾-inch thick) fresh acorn squash (about 4 medium)
¼ cup maple syrup or honey
¼ cup reduced-fat margarine or light butter
2 tablespoons apple or orange juice concentrate, thawed
¼ to ½ teaspoon dried thyme, rosemary, or ginger

1. Remove the seeds from the squash rings, and cut each ring in half to make 30 semicircles. Coat a large nonstick baking sheet with nonstick cooking spray and arrange the squash in a single layer in the pan.

2. Combine the maple syrup or honey, margarine or butter, juice concentrate, and thyme, rosemary, or ginger in a small microwave-safe bowl. Microwave at high power for about 45 seconds, or until the margarine or butter is melted. Stir the mixture and drizzle over the squash.

3. Cover the pan with aluminum foil and bake at 400°F for 20 minutes. Carefully remove the foil (steam will escape), and brush the pan juices over the squash. Bake for an additional 10 minutes, basting occasionally, until the squash is tender, most of the liquid has evaporated, and the squash is nicely glazed. Serve hot.

Nutritional Facts (per serving)
CALORIES: 79 CARBOHYDRATES: 16 G CHOLESTEROL: 0 MG FAT: 2.1 G FIBER: 1.4 G
PROTEIN: 0.7 G SODIUM: 44 MG CALCIUM: 34 MG

Savory Rutabaga

YIELD: 10 SERVINGS

2 large rutabagas (about 1½ pounds each)
2 cups water
1 tablespoon ham, chicken, or vegetable bouillon granules
2 tablespoons light brown sugar
1 teaspoon dry mustard

1. Peel the rutabagas, and cut into ⅝-inch chunks (there should be about 8 cups). Place the rutabaga chunks and the remaining ingredients in a large, deep nonstick skillet or a 4-quart pot and bring to a boil over high heat.
2. Reduce the heat to low, cover, and simmer for about 20 minutes, stirring occasionally, or until the rutabaga is tender.
3. Raise the heat under the pot to medium-high and cook uncovered, stirring frequently, for about 5 minutes more, or until most of the liquid has evaporated. Serve hot.

Nutritional Facts (per ⅔-cup serving)
CALORIES: 52 CARBOHYDRATES: 11 G CHOLESTEROL: 0 MG FAT: 0.2 G FIBER: 2.8 G
PROTEIN: 1.3 G SODIUM: 214 MG CALCIUM: 54 MG

Nutty Green Beans

YIELD: 10 SERVINGS

8 cups 1-inch pieces fresh green beans (about 2 pounds)
3 tablespoons reduced-fat margarine or light butter
½ teaspoon fines herbes or dried thyme
¼ teaspoon salt
⅓ cup sliced toasted almonds (page 30) or chopped walnuts

1. Fill a 6-quart pot half full with water and bring to a boil over high heat. Add the green beans and allow the pot to return to a boil. Cook the beans for about 4 minutes, or just until tender.
2. Drain the beans well and return them to the pot. Add the margarine or butter, fines herbes or thyme, and salt. Cook over low heat, tossing to mix, for a minute or two or until the margarine or butter is melted. Toss in the almonds or walnuts and serve hot.

Nutritional Facts (per ⅔-cup serving)
CALORIES: 61 CARBOHYDRATES: 7 G CHOLESTEROL: 0 MG FAT: 3.4 G FIBER: 3.4 G
PROTEIN: 2.4 G SODIUM: 94 MG CALCIUM: 40 MG

Country-Style Collard Greens

✻ *For variety, substitute turnip greens for the collards.*

YIELD: 10 SERVINGS

2 pounds prewashed cut fresh collard greens,
    or 2 pounds frozen cut collard greens
1½ cups water
1 cup diced lean ham

1½ teaspoons dry mustard

1 teaspoon ham or chicken bouillon granules

1. Place all of the ingredients in a 6-quart pot, and bring to a boil over high heat. Stir to mix well, reduce the heat to medium-low, and cover.
2. Cook the greens, stirring occasionally, for about 20 minutes, or until tender. Serve hot.

Nutritional Facts (per ⅔-cup serving)
CALORIES: 43 CARBOHYDRATES: 6 G CHOLESTEROL: 4 MG FAT: 0.8 G FIBER: 3.3 G
PROTEIN: 4.8 G SODIUM: 216 MG CALCIUM: 131 MG

Mandarin-Cranberry Ring

YIELD: 10 SERVINGS

2 packages (4-serving size) sugar-free cranberry or raspberry gelatin mix

1¼ cups boiling water

2 cans (11 ounces each) mandarin oranges in juice or light syrup

1-pound can whole-berry cranberry sauce

½ cup chopped walnuts

1. Place the gelatin mix in a large heatproof bowl, add the boiling water, and stir for 2 minutes, or until the gelatin mix is completely dissolved. Set aside.
2. Drain the juice from the oranges into a 2-cup measure, and add enough cold water to bring the volume to 1¼ cups. Add the juice-water mixture to the hot gelatin mixture, and stir to mix well.
3. Place the gelatin mixture in the refrigerator and chill for about 40 minutes, or until the gelatin is the consistency of raw egg whites. Stir the drained oranges, cranberry sauce, and walnuts into the gelatin. Spread the mixture evenly into a 6-cup ring mold or bundt pan lightly coated with nonstick cooking spray.
4. Cover the gelatin and refrigerate for at least 6 hours, or until firm. Unmold* the gelatin onto

a serving plate. Slice and serve chilled. Alternatively, pour the gelatin into an 8-inch square dish, chill until firm, and cut into squares to serve.

Nutritional Facts (per serving)
CALORIES: 150 CARBOHYDRATES: 28 G CHOLESTEROL: 0 MG FAT: 3.9 G FIBER: 1.1 G
PROTEIN: 2 G SODIUM: 58 MG CALCIUM: 6 MG

*To unmold the ring, loosen the edges of the gelatin with a knife. Place a serving platter upside down over the mold, and invert the mold onto the platter. It should slide out easily. If it does not, dip the mold in warm (not hot) water for 5 to 10 seconds before unmolding.

Cran-Raspberry Ring

YIELD: 10 SERVINGS

2 packages (4-serving size) sugar-free raspberry gelatin mix
1¼ cups boiling water
1 cup frozen raspberries, thawed and crushed
1 cup whole-berry cranberry sauce
⅓ cup chopped walnuts (optional)
1 cup nonfat or light sour cream, or 8 ounces nonfat or reduced-fat
    (Neufchâtel) cream cheese, softened to room temperature
1 pound seedless green grapes (optional)

1. Place the gelatin mix in a medium heatproof bowl, add the boiling water, and stir for 2 minutes, or until the gelatin mix is completely dissolved.
2. Pour the juice that has accumulated from the thawed raspberries into a 2-cup measure, and add enough cold water to bring the volume to 1½ cups. Add the juice-water mixture to the hot gelatin mixture, and stir to mix well.
3. Pour 1 cup of the gelatin mixture into a small bowl and set aside at room temperature. Refrigerate the remaining 1¾ cups of gelatin mixture for about 40 minutes, or until the gelatin is the consistency of raw egg whites. Whisk the raspberries, cranberry sauce, and, if desired,

the walnuts into the thickened gelatin, then spoon the mixture into a 6-cup ring mold or bundt pan lightly coated with nonstick cooking spray. Refrigerate for about 1 hour, or until the gelatin is set but still sticky to the touch.

4. Slowly add the reserved 1 cup of gelatin mixture to the sour cream or cream cheese, and stir with a wire whisk or beat with an electric mixer until smooth. Pour over the gelatin-fruit mixture in the mold. Cover, and refrigerate for at least 6 hours, or until firm. Unmold* the gelatin onto a serving plate. If desired, arrange some of the grapes in the center of the ring and the rest around the outer edges of the ring. Slice and serve chilled. Alternatively, layer the gelatin into an 8-inch (2-quart) square dish, chill until firm, and cut into squares to serve.

Nutritional Facts (per serving)
CALORIES: 78 CARBOHYDRATES: 17 G CHOLESTEROL: 0 MG FAT: 0 G FIBER: 1.2 G
PROTEIN: 2.6 G SODIUM: 67 MG CALCIUM: 31 MG

To unmold the ring, loosen the edges of the gelatin with a knife. Place a serving platter upside down over the mold, and invert the mold onto the platter. It should slide out easily. If it does not, dip the mold in warm (not hot) water for 5 to 10 seconds before unmolding.

Yogurt Drop Biscuits

YIELD: 12 BISCUITS

2 cups unbleached flour
2 tablespoons sugar
1 tablespoon baking powder
¼ teaspoon salt
½ cup plus 2 tablespoons plain nonfat or low-fat yogurt
½ cup skim or low-fat milk
2 tablespoons canola oil

1. Place the flour, sugar, baking powder, and salt in a medium bowl and stir to mix well.
2. Combine the yogurt, milk, and oil in a small bowl and stir to mix well. Add the yogurt

mixture to the flour mixture and stir just until the dry ingredients are moistened. Add a little more milk, if necessary, to form a moderately thick batter.

3. Coat a medium-sized baking sheet with nonstick cooking spray, and drop heaping table-spoonfuls of the batter onto the sheet. For crusty biscuits, space the biscuits 1 inch apart. For soft biscuits, space the biscuits so that they are barely touching.

4. Bake at 375°F for about 12 minutes, or until the tops are just beginning to brown. Be careful not to overbake. Serve hot.

Nutritional Facts (per biscuit)
CALORIES: 106 CARBOHYDRATES: 18 G CHOLESTEROL: 0 MG FAT: 2.3 G FIBER: 0.4 G
PROTEIN: 3.1 G SODIUM: 226 MG CALCIUM: 128 MG

Variations:

To make **Whole Wheat Drop Biscuits,** substitute whole wheat pastry flour for half of the unbleached flour.

Nutritional Facts (per biscuit)
CALORIES: 109 CARBOHYDRATES: 18 G CHOLESTEROL: 0 MG FAT: 2.5 G FIBER: 1.5 G
PROTEIN: 3.4 G SODIUM: 226 MG CALCIUM: 128 MG

To make **Oat-Bran Drop Biscuits,** substitute oat bran for ½ cup of the unbleached flour.

Nutritional Facts (per biscuit)
CALORIES: 99 CARBOHYDRATES: 17 G CHOLESTEROL: 0 MG FAT: 2.6 G FIBER: 1 G
PROTEIN: 3.3 G SODIUM: 226 MG CALCIUM: 130 MG

Black Forest Cake

YIELD: 16 SERVINGS

1 box (1 pound, 2.25 ounces) chocolate fudge cake mix
¼ teaspoon baking soda
¾ cup room temperature coffee

½ cup unsweetened applesauce

½ cup fat-free egg substitute

FILLING

1 (4-serving size) package instant white chocolate, dark chocolate,
  or pistachio pudding mix (sugar-free or regular)

1¼ cups skim or low-fat milk

20-ounce can light (reduced-sugar) cherry pie filling

FROSTING

2½ cups nonfat or light whipped topping

2 tablespoons sliced toasted almonds (page 30)

2 tablespoons shaved dark chocolate

1. Place the cake mix and baking soda in a large bowl and stir to mix well. Add the coffee, applesauce, and egg substitute, and beat with an electric mixer for 2 minutes.

2. Coat two 9-inch round cake pans with nonstick cooking spray, then lightly flour the bottom of each pan. Spread the batter evenly in the pans. Bake at 350°F for about 23 minutes, or just until the top springs back when lightly touched and a wooden toothpick inserted in the center of the cakes comes out clean. Be careful not to overbake. Remove the cakes from the oven and cool in the pans on wire racks for 30 minutes. Remove the cakes from the pans and place on wire racks to cool completely.

3. To make the filling, place the pudding mix and milk in a medium-sized bowl and stir with a wire whisk for about 2 minutes, or until well mixed and thickened. Remove ½ cup of the pudding (to use in the frosting), and set aside.

4. Invert one cake layer onto a large cutting board. Using a bread knife, cut through the layer to separate it into two layers. Repeat this procedure with the second cake layer to make a total of four layers.

5. Place one cake layer, cut side up, on a serving plate and spread it with half of the cherry pie filling, extending the filling all the way to the edges. Place another layer, cut side up, over the first layer and spread it with the pudding. Place the third layer, cut side up, over the second layer and spread it with the remaining cherry pie filling. Place the top layer on the cake, right side up, and set aside.

6. To make the frosting, combine the whipped topping and the reserved ½ cup of pudding in a medium-sized bowl, and gently fold the two ingredients together. Spread the frosting over the sides and top of the cake, swirling with a knife. Sprinkle the almonds and shaved chocolate over the top. Cover the cake and refrigerate for at least 12 hours (preferably for 24 hours) before slicing and serving.

Nutritional Facts (per serving)
CALORIES: 198   CARBOHYDRATES: 39 G   CHOLESTEROL: 0 MG   FAT: 2.9 G   FIBER: 1.4 G
PROTEIN: 3.3 G   SODIUM: 330 MG   CALCIUM: 62 MG

Cranberry-Apple Rice Pudding

✱ *For variety, substitute dark or golden raisins for the dried cranberries.*

YIELD: 10 SERVINGS

2 tablespoons reduced-fat margarine or light butter
1½ cups finely chopped peeled Golden Delicious apples
   (about 2 medium)
4½ cups skim or low-fat milk
1 cup basmati or long-grain white rice
Pinch salt
½ cup dried sweetened cranberries
½ cup plus 2 tablespoons sugar
2 tablespoons instant nonfat dry milk powder
½ cup plus 2 tablespoons fat-free egg substitute
1 teaspoon vanilla extract

1. Put the margarine or butter and the apples in a 1-quart nonstick pot, and place over medium heat. Cover and cook for 2 minutes, stirring a couple of times. Reduce the heat to low and cook for an additional 3 minutes, or until the apples are soft (do not let the apples brown). Add a little water during cooking if the pot begins to dry out. Set aside.
2. Place 4 cups of the milk and all of the rice and salt in a nonstick 4-quart pot and place over

medium heat. Cook, stirring frequently, until the mixture just begins to bubble around the edges. Reduce the heat to low, cover, and simmer, stirring occasionally, for about 25 minutes, or until the rice is tender and most of the milk has been absorbed.

3. Add the dried cranberries to the rice mixture, cover, and cook for about 2 minutes, or until the cranberries start to soften.

4. Place the sugar and milk powder in a small bowl and stir to mix well. Add the remaining ½ cup milk and stir to mix well. Add the egg substitute and vanilla extract, and stir to mix well. Slowly stir the milk mixture into the rice mixture. Cook, stirring constantly for 3 to 5 minutes, or until the mixture thickens slightly.

5. Remove the pot from the heat, stir in the apples, and allow the pudding to cool for 20 minutes. Stir the pudding, and add a little more milk if the mixture seems too thick. Spoon into dessert dishes and serve warm, or refrigerate and serve chilled. To reheat the pudding after chilling, microwave at high power for about 4 minutes, stirring after each minute, just until warmed through.

Nutritional Facts (per ⅔-cup serving)
CALORIES: 207 CARBOHYDRATES: 40 G CHOLESTEROL: 2 MG FAT: 1.5 G FIBER: 0.9 G
PROTEIN: 7.5 G SODIUM: 136 MG CALCIUM: 180 MG

Hanukkah

Eight days of Hanukkah means lots of friends, family, and good food. The two Hanukkah menus presented here provide something for everyone with both traditional holiday treats and some new dishes, all made with a lighter touch.

The first menu features easy but elegant Lemon-Herb Salmon Steaks served with a creamy horseradish-dill sauce. Of course, latkes are a must, and this menu features a truly fuss-free version of this Hanukkah favorite. Choose from other side dishes such as Slim Caesar Salad, a cheesy Spinach-Noodle Kugel, and Sweet and Sour Cabbage. What's for dessert? Choose from Winter Wonder Parfaits—layers of angel food cake, low-fat vanilla ice cream, and a festive berry sauce—or a homemade Upside-Down Pear Cake. Both are as beautiful as they are delicious.

The second Hanukkah menu is a delight to the eye as well as the taste buds. Garlic and Herb Roasted Chicken makes a striking appearance. Side dishes like Crimson Cabbage Salad, Provincial Green Beans, and Sweet Potato Latkes add a delightful contrast of colors and flavors. Dessert options include Winter Fruit Crumble—a combination of apricots and pears topped with a crunchy oat-pecan topping—or a warm brandy- and honey-laced fruit compote. Either of these light and delicious desserts would bring the perfect conclusion to this hearty meal.

Hanukkah Dinner

MENU ONE

SERVES 8 TO 10

Lemon-Herb Salmon Steaks (page 144)

Slim Caesar Salad (page 145)
or Dilled Cucumber Salad (page 146)

Light and Easy Potato Latkes (page 147)
with Applesauce or Light Sour Cream

Spinach-Noodle Kugel (page 148)
or Broccoli-Corn Casserole (page 149)

Sweet and Sour Cabbage (page 150)

Pumpernickel Dinner Rolls

Winter Wonder Parfaits (page 151)
or Upside-Down Pear Cake (page 152)

Lemon-Herb Salmon Steaks

YIELD: 10 SERVINGS

10 salmon steaks or fillets (5 ounces each)
2½ tablespoons finely chopped fresh dill or 2½ teaspoons dried dill
2 tablespoons lemon pepper
2½ teaspoons crushed garlic
Olive oil nonstick cooking spray

SAUCE

⅔ cup nonfat or light sour cream

⅔ cup nonfat or light mayonnaise

1½ tablespoon finely chopped fresh dill or 1½ teaspoons dried dill

2 teaspoons prepared horseradish

1. Combine all of the sauce ingredients in a small bowl and stir to mix well. Cover and refrigerate until ready to serve.

2. Rinse the salmon and pat dry with paper towels. Combine the dill, lemon pepper, and garlic in a small bowl and stir to mix well. Rub some of the herb mixture over both sides of the salmon.

3. Coat a large baking sheet with the cooking spray and arrange the steaks or fillets on the sheet, spacing them a couple of inches apart. Spray the tops of the steaks with the cooking spray. Bake at 400°F for about 10 to 12 minutes, or until the salmon flakes easily with a fork. Serve hot, accompanied by the sauce.

Nutritional Facts (per serving)
CALORIES: 233   CARBOHYDRATES: 5 G   CHOLESTEROL: 79 MG   FAT: 9.2 G   FIBER: 0.1 G
PROTEIN: 29 G   SODIUM: 315 MG   CALCIUM: 38 MG

Slim Caesar Salad

YIELD: 10 SERVINGS

12 cups torn romaine lettuce

1½ cups ready-made low-fat Caesar or sourdough croutons

3 tablespoons grated Parmesan cheese

DRESSING

½ cup nonfat or light mayonnaise

3 tablespoons grated Parmesan cheese

2 tablespoons extra virgin olive oil

1 tablespoon plus 1 teaspoon lemon juice

1 teaspoon crushed garlic

¾ teaspoon anchovy paste

½ teaspoon coarsely ground black pepper

1. Place all of the dressing ingredients in a small bowl and stir to mix well.
2. Place the lettuce in a large salad bowl. Pour the dressing over the lettuce and toss to mix well. Add the croutons and Parmesan cheese and toss again. Serve immediately.

Nutritional Facts (per 1⅓-cup serving)
CALORIES: 95 CARBOHYDRATES: 9 G CHOLESTEROL: 3 MG FAT: 4.4 G FIBER: 1.2 G
PROTEIN: 3.7 G SODIUM: 254 MG CALCIUM: 76 MG

Dilled Cucumber Salad

YIELD: 10 SERVINGS

4 medium cucumbers, peeled and thinly sliced

1 medium onion, very thinly sliced and separated into rings

DRESSING

¼ cup plus 2 tablespoons white wine vinegar

¼ cup water

2 tablespoons sugar

½ teaspoon salt

⅛ teaspoon ground white pepper

1½ tablespoons finely chopped fresh dill, or 1½ teaspoons dried dill

1. Place the cucumbers and onion rings in a shallow dish. Combine the dressing ingredients in a small bowl, and pour over the vegetables. Toss to mix well.
2. Cover the salad and refrigerate for several hours or overnight, stirring occasionally, before serving.

Light and Easy Potato Latkes

YIELD: 10 SERVINGS

1½ pounds (about 9 cups) frozen shredded hash brown potatoes, thawed or 1½ pounds
  refrigerated shredded hash brown potatoes (about 5 cups lightly packed)
1 cup finely chopped onion
2 tablespoons matzo meal
½ teaspoon salt (omit if the hash browns already contain salt)
¼ teaspoon ground black pepper
¼ cup plus 2 tablespoons fat-free egg substitute
1 teaspoon dried dill, parsley, or chives (optional)
Butter-flavored nonstick cooking spray

1. Place all of the ingredients except for the cooking spray in a large bowl, and stir to mix well. (Note: The batter can be made a day in advance and refrigerated until ready to use.)

2. Coat 2 large nonstick baking sheets with the cooking spray. For each pancake, spoon ¼ cup batter onto the sheet and form into a 3-inch pancake. Spray the tops of the pancakes with the cooking spray.

3. Bake at 425°F for 10 minutes, turn the pancakes with a spatula, spray again, and switch the positions of the pans in the oven. Bake for an additional 8 to 10 minutes, or until golden brown. If desired, spray the latkes once again with a light coating of the cooking spray just before serving to give them a pan-fried appearance. Serve hot, topped with nonfat or light sour cream or unsweetened applesauce if desired.

Variation:

To make a healthier version of traditional fried potato latkes, coat a large nonstick skillet with 1 tablespoon of canola oil and preheat over medium-high heat until a drop of water sizzles when added to the skillet. For each pancake, spoon ¼ cup batter into the skillet and spread to form a 3½-inch pancake. Fry 4 pancakes at a time for about 3 minutes on each side, or until golden brown. Drain on paper towels, and serve hot topped with light sour cream or applesauce. Add more oil to the pan between batches, and be sure the oil is preheated before adding additional pancakes to the skillet.

> **Nutritional Facts (per 2 pancakes)**
> CALORIES: 119 CARBOHYDRATES: 14 G CHOLESTEROL: 0 MG FAT: 5.5 G FIBER: 1 G
> PROTEIN: 2 G SODIUM: 142 MG CALCIUM: 8 MG

Spinach-Noodle Kugel

YIELD: 10 SERVINGS

6 ounces wide yolk-free egg noodles (about 3¾ cups)
10-ounces frozen chopped spinach, thawed and squeezed dry
4-ounce can sliced mushrooms, drained
1 cup nonfat or low-fat cottage cheese
1½ cups shredded reduced-fat Swiss cheese
1 teaspoon dried dill
¼ teaspoon ground black pepper
1 cup fat-free egg substitute
¾ cup evaporated skim or low-fat milk
¼ cup grated Parmesan cheese
Butter-flavored nonstick cooking spray

1. Cook the noodles al dente according to package directions. Drain well and return to the pot.
2. Add the spinach, mushrooms, cottage cheese, Swiss cheese, dill, and black pepper and toss to mix well.

3. Coat an 8-by-12-inch baking dish with the cooking spray, and spread the noodle mixture evenly in the dish. Place the egg substitute and evaporated milk in a small bowl, stir to mix well, and pour over the noodle mixture. Sprinkle the Parmesan cheese over the top, and then spray the top lightly with the cooking spray.

4. Cover the dish with aluminum foil and bake at 350°F for 30 minutes. Remove the foil and bake for an additional 10 minutes, or until the top is lightly browned and a sharp knife inserted in the center of the dish comes out clean.

5. Remove the dish from the oven and let sit for 10 minutes before cutting into squares and serving.

> *Nutritional Facts (per serving)*
> CALORIES: 170 CARBOHYDRATES: 18 G CHOLESTEROL: 11 MG FAT: 3.3 G FIBER: 1.5 G
> PROTEIN: 17 G SODIUM: 343 MG CALCIUM: 298 MG

Variation:

To make **Broccoli-Noodle Kugel,** substitute 10 ounces frozen chopped broccoli, thawed and well drained, for the spinach.

> *Nutritional Facts (per serving)*
> CALORIES: 170 CARBOHYDRATES: 18 G CHOLESTEROL: 11 MG FAT: 3.3 G FIBER: 1.5 G
> PROTEIN: 17 G SODIUM: 329 MG CALCIUM: 282 MG

Broccoli-Corn Casserole

YIELD: 10 SERVINGS

*2 packages (10 ounces each) frozen chopped broccoli,
    thawed and squeezed dry*
16-ounce can creamed corn
*¾ cup garlic-and-herb or chive-and-onion-flavored light cream cheese
    softened to room temperature*
¼ cup plus 2 tablespoons fat-free egg substitute

¼ cup plus 1 tablespoon coarsely crushed cornflake crumbs
Butter-flavored nonstick cooking spray

1. Combine the broccoli, corn, cream cheese, and egg substitute in a large bowl and stir to mix well. Coat an 8-by-8-inch (2-quart) casserole dish with the cooking spray, and spread the broccoli mixture evenly in the dish. Sprinkle the cornflake crumbs over the top of the casserole and spray the top lightly with the cooking spray.

2. Bake at 350°F for about 35 minutes, or until the edges are bubbly and the top is nicely browned. Remove the casserole from the oven, and let sit for 5 minutes before serving.

Nutritional Facts (per ½-cup serving)
CALORIES: 95 CARBOHYDRATES: 15 G CHOLESTEROL: 12 MG FAT: 2.7 G FIBER: 2.5 G
PROTEIN: 4.6 G SODIUM: 224 MG CALCIUM: 39 MG

Sweet and Sour Cabbage

YIELD: 10 SERVINGS

1 tablespoon plus 1½ teaspoons walnut or canola oil
1 medium yellow onion, very thinly sliced
2¼ cups peeled and chopped Granny Smith apple
*   (about 3 medium-small)*
8 cups coarsely shredded red cabbage
*   (about 1 medium head)*
½ cup vegetable or chicken broth
3 tablespoons apple cider vinegar
¼ to ⅓ cup apple jelly
½ teaspoon salt
¼ to ½ teaspoon caraway seeds (optional)
⅛ teaspoon ground black pepper

1. Coat a 6-quart nonstick pot with the oil, and place over medium heat. Add the onions, cover, and cook, stirring occasionally, for about 3 minutes, or until the onions start to soften.

2. Add the remaining ingredients to the skillet, and stir to mix well. Cover and cook, stirring occasionally, for about 12 to 15 minutes, or until the cabbage is tender. Add a little more broth during cooking if the skillet becomes too dry. But keep only enough liquid in the skillet to prevent scorching. If there is excess liquid at the end of cooking, remove the lid, and cook, stirring frequently, for a minute to two or until most of the liquid evaporates. Serve hot.

Nutritional Facts (per ⅔-cup serving)
CALORIES: 83   CARBOHYDRATES: 16 G   CHOLESTEROL: 0 MG   FAT: 2.3 G   FIBER: 2.2 G
PROTEIN: 1.1 G   SODIUM: 134 MG   CALCIUM: 35 MG

Winter Wonder Parfaits

YIELD: 10 SERVINGS

6⅔ cups low-fat vanilla ice cream
10 slices (½-inch thick) angel food cake or fat-free
    vanilla loaf cake (about 7 ounces)
⅓ cup Glazed Almonds (page 322) (optional)

SAUCE
½ cup orange juice
½ cup sugar
1½ cups fresh or frozen cranberries
2½ cups sliced fresh or frozen strawberries

1. To make the sauce, combine the orange juice, sugar, and cranberries in a 2-quart pot, and bring to a boil over medium-high heat. Reduce the heat to medium-low, cover, and cook for about 5 minutes, or until the cranberry skins pop open and the mixture has thickened. Stir occasionally to prevent the mixture from boiling over.
2. Add the strawberries to the cranberry mixture, and again bring to a boil. Reduce the heat to medium-low, and cook covered for an additional 2 minutes, stirring occasionally, or just until the strawberries begin to break down. Remove the sauce from the heat and refrigerate until needed.

3. When ready to assemble the parfaits, place 1½ teaspoons of the sauce in the bottom of each of ten 10-ounce balloon wineglasses or parfait glasses. Crumble 1 slice of the cake, and place half of the slice over the sauce. Top with ⅓ cup of the ice cream and a rounded tablespoon of the sauce. Repeat the cake, ice cream, and sauce layers. Top each parfait with a sprinkling of the almonds if desired, and serve immediately.

Nutritional Facts (per serving)
CALORIES: 274 CARBOHYDRATES: 56 G CHOLESTEROL: 6 MG FAT: 3.1 G FIBER: 3.3 G
PROTEIN: 4.7 G SODIUM: 216 MG CALCIUM: 181 MG

Upside-Down Pear Cake

YIELD: 8 SERVINGS

1 cup unbleached flour
1½ teaspoons baking powder
3 tablespoons margarine or butter,
   softened to room temperature
½ cup plus 2 tablespoons sugar
¼ cup plus 2 tablespoons fat-free egg substitute or
   2 large eggs, lightly beaten
½ cup nonfat or low-fat buttermilk
1 teaspoon vanilla extract

TOPPING
1 tablespoon plus 1 teaspoon frozen orange juice concentrate, thawed
¼ cup plus 2 tablespoons light or dark brown sugar
2½ cups peeled pear slices (about 2½ large)

1. To make the topping, coat a 10-inch ovenproof nonstick skillet with nonstick cooking spray, and spread the juice concentrate over the bottom of the skillet. Sprinkle the brown sugar over the bottom of the skillet. Arrange the pears in concentric circles over the bottom of the skillet. Set aside.

2. Place the flour and baking powder in a small bowl, and stir to mix well. Set aside. Place the margarine or butter, sugar, and 2 tablespoons of the egg substitute or 1 egg in a medium-sized bowl, and beat with an electric mixer until smooth. Add the flour mixture, buttermilk, vanilla extract, and the remaining egg or egg substitute to the margarine or butter mixture, and beat at low speed just enough to mix well.

3. Spread the batter over the fruit, and bake at 350°F for about 40 minutes, or just until the top springs back when lightly touched and a wooden toothpick inserted in the center of the cake comes out clean.

4. Remove the cake from the oven, and let sit for 5 minutes. Run a knife around the edges of the pan to loosen the sides of the cake, then invert the cake onto a serving platter. Let the cake sit for at least 25 minutes before cutting into wedges and serving.

> *Nutritional Facts (per serving)*
> CALORIES: 230 CARBOHYDRATES: 46 G CHOLESTEROL: 0 MG FAT: 4.1 G FIBER: 1.6 G
> PROTEIN: 3.4 G SODIUM: 135 MG CALCIUM: 88 MG

For Variety:

◆ Substitute fresh apple or peach slices for the pears.

◆ Substitute 1 pound of canned drained apricot halves for the pear slices. Arrange the apricot halves over the bottom of the skillet with the cut sides down. Fill in the spaces between the apricot halves with pecan halves or maraschino cherries if desired.

◆ Substitute 1 pound of canned drained pineapple rings for the pear slices. Arrange the slices over the bottom of the skillet, and fill in the spaces with pecan halves or maraschino cherry halves if desired.

◆ Substitute 1½ cups of fresh or frozen (partially thawed) blueberries or halved pitted sweet cherries for the pears. Add ¼ teaspoon dried lemon rind to the cake batter along with the flour.

Hanukkah Dinner

Menu Two

SERVES 8 TO 10

Garlic and Herb Roasted Chicken (page 155)
with Pan Gravy (page 156)

Crimson Cabbage Salad (page 157)
or Orange-Onion Salad (page 158) with
Cranberry Vinaigrette Salad Dressing (page 159)

Provincial Green Beans (page 159)
or Green Peas with Pearl Onions (page 160)

Sweet Potato Latkes (page 161)

Cranberry-Pear Conserve (page 106)

Multigrain Dinner Rolls

Winter Fruit Crumble (page 162)
or Fast and Fabulous Fruit Compote (page 163)

ADVANCE PLANNING TIPS:

◆ *Prepare Crimson Cabbage Salad the day before, as it needs time to marinate. If you are making Orange-Onion Salad instead, prepare the dressing the day before.*

◆ *If you are making Provincial Green Beans, rinse and cut the beans the day before, dry thoroughly, and store in a zip-type bag until ready to cook.*

◆ *Prepare the batter for Sweet Potato Latkes the day before and refrigerate until ready to use.*

◆ *Prepare Cranberry-Pear Conserve the day before and refrigerate until ready to serve.*

◆ *Prepare Winter Fruit Crumble to the point of adding the topping up to a day in advance and refrigerate. Prepare the topping and refrigerate in a separate container. Remove from the refrigerator 30 to 60 minutes before ready to assemble and bake. If you are making Fast and Fabulous Fruit Compote instead, prepare it the day before, and rewarm just before serving.*

Garlic and Herb Roasted Chicken

YIELD: 10 SERVINGS

2 roasting chickens (5 pounds each)

2 teaspoons lemon pepper

2 teaspoons dried rosemary

1 teaspoon dried thyme or marjoram

2 to 3 teaspoons crushed garlic or ½ to ¾ teaspoon garlic powder

½ teaspoon salt

Olive oil nonstick cooking spray

½ cup medium-dry sherry or white wine

½ cup water

1. Trim the excess skin and fat away from the cavities of the chickens, and remove and discard the giblets. Rinse the chickens with cool water and pat dry with paper towels.

2. Combine the lemon pepper, rosemary, thyme or marjoram, garlic, and salt in a small bowl and stir to mix well. Using your fingers, loosen the skin and spread the herb mixture over the meat of the breast, thighs, and drumsticks. Spray the skin of the birds lightly with the cooking spray.

3. Place each chicken on a rack in its own 9-by-13-inch roasting pan. Fold the wings back and underneath the birds, and tie the legs together with a piece of string. Pour half of the sherry or wine and water into the bottom of each pan. Cover the pans with aluminum foil, crimping the foil around the edges of the pan to seal tightly.

4. Bake at 375°F for 45 minutes. Carefully remove the foil (steam will escape), and bake for an additional 30 to 45 minutes, basting the birds occasionally with the pan juices, until the chickens are nicely browned, the drumsticks move easily in the sockets, and a thermometer inserted in the thigh (not touching the bone) reads 180° to 185°F. Remove the chickens from the oven, and let sit loosely covered with foil for 15 minutes before carving.

Nutritional Facts (per 3-ounce serving, skinless white meat)
CALORIES: 140   CARBOHYDRATES: 0 G   CHOLESTEROL: 72 MG   FAT: 3 G   FIBER: 0 G
PROTEIN: 26 G   SODIUM: 115 MG   CALCIUM: 13 MG

Nutritional Facts (per 3-ounce serving, skinless dark meat)
CALORIES: 162   CARBOHYDRATES: 0 G   CHOLESTEROL: 79 MG   FAT: 7.2 G   FIBER: 0 G
PROTEIN: 23 G   SODIUM: 100 MG   CALCIUM: 10 MG

Pan Gravy

YIELD: 2 CUPS

Drippings from Garlic and Herb Roasted Chicken (page 155)
⅛ teaspoon ground white pepper
1½ teaspoons chicken bouillon granules
3 tablespoons plus 1½ teaspoons unbleached flour
½ cup water

1. Defat the chicken drippings by placing them in a fat-separator cup. Pour the defatted drippings into a 2-cup measure, and add water, if necessary, to bring the volume to 1½ cups. Place the defatted drippings in a 1-quart pot, and add the pepper and bouillon granules. Bring the mixture to a boil over high heat, then reduce the heat to low, and simmer covered for 1 minute.

2. Combine the flour and ½ cup of water in a jar with a tight-fitting lid, and shake until smooth. Slowly add the flour mixture to the simmering broth, stirring constantly with a wire whisk. Continue to cook and stir for a minute or two, or until the gravy is thick and bubbly. Serve hot.

Nutritional Facts (per 2-tablespoon serving)
CALORIES: 13 CARBOHYDRATES: 1 G CHOLESTEROL: 0 MG FAT: 0 G FIBER: 0 G
PROTEIN: 0.5 G SODIUM: 109 MG CALCIUM: 1 MG

Crimson Cabbage Salad

YIELD: 10 SERVINGS

6 medium (2½-inch diameter) beets without leaves (about 1½ pounds)*
7 cups coarsely shredded red cabbage (about ¾ medium head)
½ red onion, very thinly sliced

DRESSING
⅓ cup white wine vinegar
¼ cup sugar
3 tablespoons walnut oil
1 tablespoon Dijon mustard
1 tablespoon finely chopped fresh dill or 1 teaspoon dried dill
½ teaspoon salt
¼ teaspoon ground black pepper

1. Leave the rootlets and 1 inch of the stems on the beets, and scrub well. Wrap the beets together in aluminum foil, and place the wrapped beets on a medium-sized baking sheet. Bake at 400°F for about 1 hour, or until the beets are easily pierced with a toothpick. Open the foil,

and allow the beets to cool to room temperature. Peel the cooled beets and then coarsely grate them. You should have about 2 cups of packed grated beets.

2. Combine the beets, cabbage, and onion in a large bowl, and toss to mix well. Combine all of the dressing ingredients in a small bowl, and stir to mix well. Pour the dressing over the salad, and toss to mix well.

3. Cover the salad, and refrigerate for at least 8 hours or overnight, stirring occasionally, before serving.

Nutritional Facts (per ¾-cup serving)
CALORIES: 87   CARBOHYDRATES: 12 G   CHOLESTEROL: 0 MG   FAT: 4.4 G   FIBER: 1.9 G
PROTEIN: 1.5 G   SODIUM: 187 MG   CALCIUM: 38 MG

Wear plastic gloves when handling beets to prevent the juices from staining your hands.

Orange-Onion Salad

YIELD: 10 SERVINGS

8 ounces prewashed mixed baby salad greens or spinach (about 15 cups loosely packed)
2 cups fresh orange segments or 2 cans (11 ounces each) mandarin oranges, drained
10 thin slices red onion, separated into rings
⅓ cup chopped walnuts or pine nuts
½ cup plus 2 tablespoons Cranberry Vinaigrette Salad Dressing (page 159) or bottled
    light raspberry or balsamic vinaigrette salad dressing

1. Place 1½ cups of the salad greens or spinach on each of 10 serving plates. Top the greens on each plate with a scant quarter-cup of the orange sections, a few onion rings, and a sprinkling of walnuts or pine nuts.

2. Drizzle some of the dressing over each salad, and serve immediately.

Nutritional Facts (per serving)
CALORIES: 103   CARBOHYDRATES: 12 G   CHOLESTEROL: 0 MG   FAT: 5.8 G   FIBER: 3.9 G
PROTEIN: 2.2 G   SODIUM: 81 MG   CALCIUM: 56 MG

Cranberry Vinaigrette Salad Dressing

YIELD: 1⅛ CUPS

½ cup whole-berry cranberry sauce

¼ cup white wine vinegar

¼ cup extra virgin olive oil or walnut oil

2 tablespoons orange juice

½ teaspoon crushed garlic

½ teaspoon salt

¼ teaspoon ground black pepper

¼ teaspoon dried thyme

1. Place all of the ingredients in a blender and blend until smooth.
2. Cover and refrigerate for at least 2 hours before serving. Let the dressing sit at room temperature for a minute or two to liquefy the oil.

Nutritional Facts (per tablespoon)
CALORIES: 37   CARBOHYDRATES: 2.6 G   CHOLESTEROL: 0 MG   FAT: 3 G   FIBER: 0.9 G
PROTEIN: 0 G   SODIUM: 66 MG   CALCIUM: 0 MG

Provincial Green Beans

YIELD: 10 SERVINGS

8 cups 1-inch pieces fresh green beans (about 2 pounds)

2 tablespoons extra virgin olive oil

1½ teaspoons crushed garlic

2 cups sliced fresh mushrooms

¼ teaspoon dried thyme or fines herbes

¼ teaspoon salt

⅛ teaspoon ground black pepper

1. Place a large pot of water over high heat, and bring to boil. Add the green beans, and allow the pot to return to a boil. Cook the beans for about 4 minutes, or just until tender. Drain the beans, and return to the pot. Cover to keep warm.

2. Place the olive oil in a large deep nonstick skillet and preheat over medium-high heat. Add the garlic, mushrooms, and thyme or fines herbes, and cook, stirring frequently, for several minutes, or until the mushrooms are tender. Periodically place a lid over the skillet if it begins to dry out. (The steam released from the cooking mushrooms will moisten the skillet.)

3. Add the green beans, salt, and pepper to the mushrooms, and reduce the heat to low. Toss the green beans and mushrooms together for a minute or two over low heat, and serve immediately.

Nutritional Facts (per ¾-cup serving)
CALORIES: 52 CARBOHYDRATES: 6 G CHOLESTEROL: 0 MG FAT: 2.8 G FIBER: 1 G
PROTEIN: 1.9 G SODIUM: 63 MG CALCIUM: 30 MG

Green Peas with Pearl Onions

YIELD: 10 SERVINGS

2 cups frozen pearl onions (10 ounces)
3 tablespoons reduced-fat margarine or light butter
¼ cup medium-dry sherry
¼ teaspoon dried thyme
2 packages (10 ounces each) frozen green peas
¼ teaspoon salt
⅛ teaspoon ground black pepper

1. Combine the onions, margarine or butter, sherry, and thyme in a large nonstick skillet and bring to a boil over medium-high heat. Reduce the heat to medium and cook, stirring occasionally, for 2 minutes, or until the onions are thawed.

2. Add the peas to the skillet mixture and raise the heat to bring the mixture to a boil. Reduce the heat to low and simmer covered for an additional 3 to 5 minutes, stirring occasionally, or until the onions and peas are tender. Stir in the salt and pepper and serve hot.

Sweet Potato Latkes

YIELD: 10 SERVINGS

1½ pounds sweet potatoes (about 3 medium), peeled and
    coarsely shredded (to make about 5 cups lightly packed)
¾ cup finely chopped onion
3 tablespoons matzo meal
½ teaspoon salt
¼ teaspoon ground black pepper
¼ cup plus 2 tablespoons fat-free egg substitute
1 tablespoon finely chopped fresh parsley, dill, or chives or 1 teaspoon dried
Butter-flavored nonstick cooking spray

1. Place all of the ingredients except for the cooking spray in a large bowl, and stir to mix well. (Note: The batter can be prepared a day in advance and refrigerated until ready to use.) Coat 2 large nonstick baking sheets with the cooking spray. For each pancake spoon ¼ cup batter onto the sheet and form into a 3-inch pancake. Spray the tops of the pancakes with the cooking spray.

2. Bake at 425°F for 10 minutes, turn the pancakes with a spatula, spray again, and switch the positions of the pans in the oven. Bake for an additional 7 to 10 minutes, or until golden brown. If desired, spray the latkes once again with a light coating of the cooking spray just before serving to give them a pan-fried appearance. Serve hot, topped with unsweetened applesauce if desired.

Nutritional Facts (per 2 pancakes)
CALORIES: 81 CARBOHYDRATES: 18 G CHOLESTEROL: 0 MG FAT: 0.8 G FIBER: 2.3 G
PROTEIN: 2.4 G SODIUM: 144 MG CALCIUM: 21 MG

Winter Fruit Crumble

YIELD: 10 SERVINGS

2 cans (1 pound each) apricot halves in juice or light syrup
2 cans (1 pound each) pear slices in juice or light syrup
2 tablespoons sugar
2 teaspoons cornstarch

TOPPING
¾ cup old-fashioned (5-minute) rolled oats
⅓ cup whole wheat pastry flour or unbleached flour
½ cup light brown sugar
½ teaspoon ground cinnamon
¼ teaspoon ground ginger
3 tablespoons chilled margarine or butter, cut into small pieces
1 tablespoon frozen white grape juice concentrate, thawed
½ cup chopped toasted pecans (page 30)

1. Drain the apricots and pears, reserving ¼ cup of the combined juices. Place the apricots and pears in a large bowl and set aside. Place the sugar and cornstarch in a small bowl and stir to mix well. Add the reserved ¼ cup of juice to the sugar mixture and stir to mix well. Pour the sugar mixture over the fruit, and toss to mix well. Coat an 8-by-12-inch baking dish or a shallow 2½-quart casserole dish with nonstick cooking spray and spread the fruit mixture in the dish.

2. To make the topping, combine the oats, flour, brown sugar, cinnamon, and ginger in a medium-sized bowl and stir to mix well. Using a pastry cutter or two knives, cut in the margarine or butter until the mixture is crumbly. Add the grape juice concentrate and stir lightly until the mixture is moist and crumbly. Add a little more juice concentrate if the mixture seems too dry. Add the pecans and toss lightly to mix.

3. Spread the oat mixture over the fruit and bake at 375°F for about 35 minutes or until the fruit is bubbly around the edges and the topping is golden brown. Cover the dish loosely with foil during the last few minutes of baking if the topping starts to brown too quickly. Remove the dish from the oven and let sit for 20 minutes before serving warm.

Nutritional Facts (per serving)
CALORIES: 202 CARBOHYDRATES: 33 G CHOLESTEROL: 0 MG FAT: 7.5 G FIBER: 3.4 G
PROTEIN: 2.8 G SODIUM: 41 MG CALCIUM: 28 MG

Fast and Fabulous Fruit Compote

YIELD: 10 SERVINGS

1¼ cups dried apricots (about 30)

1¼ cups pitted prunes (about 30)

1¼ cups halved dried pears or peaches (about 12)

¾ cup dried sweetened cranberries or pitted dried sweet cherries

2 cups orange juice or pear nectar

2 cups water

2 to 4 tablespoons honey

¼ cup brandy

1 teaspoon dried orange rind

1. Place all of the ingredients in a 3-quart nonstick pot and bring to a boil over medium-high heat. Reduce the heat to low, cover, and simmer for 15 minutes, stirring occasionally, or until the fruit is soft. Remove the lid and simmer uncovered for an additional 5 to 10 minutes, stirring occasionally, or until the juices are thick and syrupy.

2. Remove the pot from the heat and let sit for 15 minutes before serving warm. Or cover and refrigerate, and reheat just before serving. This compote is also delicious served over a scoop of low-fat vanilla ice cream.

Nutritional Facts (per ½-cup serving)
CALORIES: 223 CARBOHYDRATES: 54 G CHOLESTEROL: 0 MG FAT: 0.5 G FIBER: 5.5 G
PROTEIN: 1.6 G SODIUM: 6 MG CALCIUM: 29 MG

Passover ✡

atzo—a crackerlike unleavened bread—takes center stage during the week of Passover. Fortunately, matzo has always been fat-free and is wonderfully versatile as well. In the two Seder menus presented in this section, you'll find this and other traditional Passover foods married with a variety of light and healthy ingredients to make untraditionally light and delicious holiday dishes.

In the first Seder menu, clear chicken soup brimming with light and tender matzo balls begins the meal. The main course, Baked Chicken Paprika, starts with skinless chicken, and is well seasoned with garlic, onions, tomato juice, and paprika. Side dishes like Sweet Potato and Carrot Tzimmes, Colorful Coleslaw, and Nutty Brussels Sprouts round out the meal. For dessert, delight guests with a show-stopping Pavolva—crisp meringue shells brimming with fresh berries—or opt for simple but elegant plums poached in a citrus- and spice-laced syrup.

The second Passover menu offers another collection of crowd-pleasing dishes that are perfect for a healthy and satisfying holiday dinner. Like the first menu, this one begins with a Passover must—matzo ball soup. This version features a golden broth enriched with sweet potatoes. The soup course is followed by a hearty main dish of Spiced Beef Brisket with Carrots and Prunes. On the side are dishes like Asparagus Vinaigrette, Glazed Onions, and fresh spinach sautéed with apples, raisins, and pine nuts. For dessert, enjoy stunning Almond-Crusted Fruit Tart. Or serve Crisp Hazelnut Cookies. These lightly sweet cookies are perfect paired with a cup of after-dinner coffee. For a beautiful presentation, serve with a platter of fresh whole strawberries.

Passover Seder

Menu One

Serves 6 to 8

Chicken Soup with Matzo Balls (page 166)

Baked Chicken Paprika (page 168)

Sweet Potato and Carrot Tzimmes (page 169)
or Roasted Potatoes and Onions (page 170)

Colorful Coleslaw (page 171)
or Mixed Green Salad with Apples,
Cranberries, and Pecans (page 172)
with Citrus Vinaigrette Salad Dressing (page 173)

Nutty Brussels Sprouts (page 173)
or Fresh Roasted Asparagus (page 174)

Pavlova with Raspberries (page 175)
or Spiced Poached Plums (page 176)

◆ *Prepare Chicken Soup with Matzo Balls a day or two in advance. Refrigerate and reheat just before serving.*

◆ *If you purchase preskinned chicken for making Baked Chicken Paprika, the dish can be quickly assembled and popped into the oven shortly before dinner is served. If desired, this dish can also be assembled to the point of baking the day before, and refrigerated. Remove the dish from the refrigerator 30 to 60 minutes before baking.*

◆ *Sweet Potato and Carrot Tzimmes can be fully prepared the day before, if desired, and re-heated in just 20 minutes. Or cut up the sweet potatoes, carrots, and prunes the day be-fore, and assemble and bake the dish on the day of your dinner.*

◆ *Colorful Coleslaw should be made the day before, so that it has time to marinade. If you are making Mixed Green Salad with Apples, Cranberries, and Pecans, prepare the dress-ing the day before, and purchase prewashed salad greens.*

◆ *Rinse and cut the Brussels sprouts or asparagus the day before, dry with paper towels, and store in a zip-type plastic bag until ready to cook.*

◆ *Prepare the Pavlova shells a day or two in advance and store in an airtight container. If you are making Spiced Poached Plums, do so the day before, so the dessert has plenty of time to chill and develop its full flavors.*

Chicken Soup with Matzo Balls

YIELD: 8 SERVINGS

6 cups unsalted chicken broth
¾ cup chopped onion
½ cup sliced celery
⅓ cup chopped carrot

1 tablespoon chicken bouillon granules

⅛ teaspoon ground white pepper

⅛ teaspoon ground nutmeg

2 tablespoons finely chopped fresh parsley, or 2 teaspoons dried parsley

1 recipe Fluffy Fat-Free Matzo Balls (below)

1. Place the chicken broth, onion, celery, carrot, bouillon granules, pepper, and nutmeg in a 3-quart pot, and bring to a boil over high heat. Reduce the heat to low, cover, and simmer for 20 minutes or until the vegetables are soft.

2. Use a slotted spoon to transfer the vegetables from the pot to a blender. Add 1 cup of the hot broth, and carefully blend at low speed with the lid slightly ajar (to allow steam to escape) for 30 seconds or until the mixture is smooth. Return the blended mixture to the pot.

3. Add the parsley and matzo balls to the soup and simmer, covered, for 5 to 10 minutes. Ladle the soup into individual serving bowls, placing 3 matzo balls in each bowl, and serve hot.

Nutritional Facts (per ¾-cup broth with 3 matzo balls)
CALORIES: 87 CARBOHYDRATES: 13 G CHOLESTEROL: 3 MG FAT: 1.3 G FIBER: 1 G
PROTEIN: 6.2 G SODIUM: 551 MG CALCIUM: 23 MG

Fluffy Fat-Free Matzo Balls

YIELD: 8 SERVINGS

6 large egg whites, warmed to room temperature

½ teaspoon salt

Pinch ground white pepper

1 cup plus 2 tablespoons matzo meal

2 teaspoons chicken bouillon granules

1. Place the egg whites in the bowl of an electric mixer and sprinkle with the salt. Beat at high speed until stiff peaks form when the beaters are removed. Stir the white pepper into the matzo meal, then gently stir the matzo meal into the beaten egg whites, 3 tablespoons at a time. Set the mixture aside for 10 minutes.

2. Half-fill a 6-quart pot with water and bring to a rapid boil over high heat. Add the chicken bouillon granules. Coat your hands lightly with nonstick cooking spray and gently shape the matzo meal mixture into 24 (1-inch) balls. Drop the balls into the boiling water, reduce the heat to medium-low, and simmer, covered, for 20 minutes, or until the matzo balls are cooked through.

3. Remove the matzo balls with a slotted spoon, and immediately add them to your chicken soup. Or transfer to a covered container, and refrigerate for 1 to 2 days.

Nutritional Facts (per 3 matzo balls)
CALORIES: 54 CARBOHYDRATES: 8 G CHOLESTEROL: 0 MG FAT: 0.1 G FIBER: 0.5 G
PROTEIN: 3.7 G SODIUM: 221 MG CALCIUM: 4 MG

For variety, stir any of the following into the matzo meal along with the white pepper:

◆ 1 tablespoon finely chopped fresh dill, parsley, or chives (or 1 teaspoon dried herbs)

◆ ⅛ teaspoon garlic powder, ½ teaspoon onion powder, and 1 teaspoon finely crumbled dried parsley

◆ 1 teaspoon curry powder plus 1 tablespoon finely chopped fresh parsley (or 1 teaspoon dried parsley)

Baked Chicken Paprika

YIELD: 8 SERVINGS

4 pounds bone-in skinless chicken breasts, thighs, and drumsticks
½ teaspoon salt
½ teaspoon coarsely ground black pepper
1 teaspoon garlic powder
Olive oil nonstick cooking spray
2 medium yellow onions, thinly sliced and separated into rings
1 cup tomato juice
1 tablespoon plus 1 teaspoon ground paprika
2 tablespoons finely chopped fresh parsley

1. Rinse the chicken and pat dry with paper towels. Sprinkle the pieces with the salt, pepper, and garlic powder.
2. Coat a large nonstick skillet with the cooking spray and place over medium-high heat. Place the chicken in the skillet, 3 to 4 pieces at a time, and cook for about 2 minutes, or until nicely browned on the bottom. Spray the tops of the chicken lightly with the cooking spray, turn, and cook for another couple of minutes, or until nicely browned on both sides.
3. Coat an 11-by-13-inch roasting pan (or the bottom of a broiler pan) with the cooking spray, and arrange half of the onion rings over the bottom of the pan. Pour the tomato juice in the pan, and lay the chicken in a single layer over the onions and tomato juice. Sprinkle the paprika over the chicken, and cover with the remaining onion rings.
4. Cover the pan tightly with aluminum foil and bake at 400°F for 30 minutes. Carefully remove the foil (steam will escape), baste the chicken with the pan juices, and bake for an additional 20 to 25 minutes, or until the chicken is tender and no longer pink inside. Transfer the chicken to a serving platter, drizzle the pan juices over the top, and sprinkle with the parsley. Serve hot.

Nutritional Facts (per 3-ounce serving, skinless white meat)
CALORIES: 169   CARBOHYDRATES: 6 G   CHOLESTEROL: 72 MG   FAT: 3.4 G   FIBER: 1.4 G
PROTEIN: 27 G   SODIUM: 265 MG   CALCIUM: 29 MG

Nutritional Facts (per 3-ounce serving, skinless dark meat)
CALORIES: 191   CARBOHYDRATES: 6 G   CHOLESTEROL: 80 MG   FAT: 7.4 G   FIBER: 1.4 G
PROTEIN: 24 G   SODIUM: 280 MG   CALCIUM: 27 MG

Sweet Potato and Carrot Tzimmes

YIELD: 8 SERVINGS

4 cups ¼-inch-thick slices peeled sweet potatoes (about 3 medium)
4 cups ½-inch-thick slices peeled Granny Smith apples (about 5 medium)
1 cup ¼-inch-thick slices carrots (about 2 medium)
¾ cup pitted prunes, halved
1½ teaspoons potato starch
2 tablespoons orange juice

2 tablespoons honey

2 tablespoons light brown sugar

1½ teaspoons dried grated orange rind, or 1½ tablespoons fresh grated orange rind

1. Coat a 9-by-13-inch baking dish with nonstick cooking spray. Spread half of the potatoes over the bottom of the dish. Top with half of the apples, half of the carrots, and finally half of the prunes. Repeat the layers.

2. Combine the potato starch and orange juice in a small bowl, and stir to dissolve the potato starch. Add the honey, brown sugar, and orange rind, and stir to mix well. Pour the orange juice mixture over the tzimmes. Cover the pan with aluminum foil and cut six 1-inch slits in the foil to allow steam to escape.

3. Bake at 350°F for 1 hour and 15 minutes, or until the layers are tender. Serve hot.

Nutritional Facts (per ¾-cup serving)
CALORIES: 178   CARBOHYDRATES: 44 G   CHOLESTEROL: 0 MG   FAT: 0.5 G   FIBER: 4.7 G
PROTEIN: 1.8 G   SODIUM: 16 MG   CALCIUM: 33 MG

Roasted Potatoes and Onions

YIELD: 8 SERVINGS

2 pounds new potatoes (about 24 medium)

¼ teaspoon garlic powder

½ teaspoon salt

⅛ teaspoon ground black pepper

2 tablespoons extra virgin olive oil

2 medium yellow onions, sliced ½ inch thick

1. Scrub the potatoes, and cut into 1-inch chunks. (There should be about 6 cups of potatoes.)

2. Place the potatoes, garlic powder, salt, and pepper in a large bowl, and toss to mix well. Drizzle the olive oil over the potato mixture and toss again.

3. Coat an 11-by-13-inch roasting pan (or the bottom of a broiler pan) with nonstick cooking spray, and spread the mixture in a single layer in the pan.

4. Cover the pan with aluminum foil, and bake at 400°F for 25 minutes. Remove the foil, stir in the onions, and bake for an additional 20 minutes, turning with a spatula every 7 minutes, or until the potatoes and onions are tender and nicely browned. Serve hot.

Nutritional Facts (per ¾-cup serving)
CALORIES: 142   CARBOHYDRATES: 26 G   CHOLESTEROL: 0 MG   FAT: 3.6 G   FIBER: 2.8 G
PROTEIN: 2.5 G   SODIUM: 153 MG   CALCIUM: 16 MG

Variations:

To make **Paprika Roasted Potatoes,** add 2 teaspoons ground paprika along with the garlic powder, salt, and pepper.

To make **Roasted Potatoes Dijon,** add 1 tablespoon Dijon mustard and 1 teaspoon dried rosemary along with the garlic, salt, and pepper.

Colorful Coleslaw

YIELD: 10 SERVINGS

4 cups coarsely shredded green cabbage (about ½ medium head)
4 cups coarsely shredded red cabbage (about ½ medium head)
2 cups shredded carrot
1 small yellow onion, halved lengthwise and very thinly sliced

DRESSING
⅓ cup white wine vinegar
2 tablespoons sugar
3 tablespoons extra virgin olive oil
1 tablespoon Dijon mustard
1 tablespoon finely chopped fresh dill or 1 teaspoon dried dill
½ teaspoon salt
¼ teaspoon ground black pepper
⅛ teaspoon celery seed

1. Combine the cabbage, carrots, and onion in a large bowl, and toss to mix well. Combine all of the dressing ingredients in a small bowl, and stir to mix well. Pour the dressing over the salad, and toss to mix well.

2. Cover the salad, and refrigerate for at least 8 hours or overnight, stirring occasionally, before serving.

Nutritional Facts (per ¾-cup serving)
CALORIES: 73 CARBOHYDRATES: 8 G CHOLESTEROL: 0 MG FAT: 4.3 G FIBER: 2 G
PROTEIN: 1.2 G SODIUM: 170 MG CALCIUM: 37 MG

Mixed Green Salad with Apples, Cranberries, and Pecans

YIELD: 8 SERVINGS

6 ounces prewashed mixed baby salad greens (about 12 cups loosely packed)
2 cups matchstick-sized pieces peeled Granny Smith apples (about 2 large)
¼ cup plus 2 tablespoons dried sweetened cranberries
¼ cup plus 2 tablespoons chopped Honey-Glazed Pecans (page 68)
  or sliced toasted almonds (page 30) (optional)
¼ cup Citrus Vinaigrette Salad Dressing (page 173)

1. Combine the salad greens, apples, cranberries, and if desired, the nuts in a large bowl.

2. Pour the dressing over the salad, and toss to mix well. Add a little more dressing if the mixture seems too dry. Serve immediately.

Nutritional Facts (per 1½-cup serving)
CALORIES: 78 CARBOHYDRATES: 12 G CHOLESTEROL: 0 MG FAT: 3.6 G FIBER: 1.3 G
PROTEIN: 0.5 G SODIUM: 78 MG CALCIUM: 85 MG

Citrus Vinaigrette Salad Dressing

YIELD: ½ CUP

¼ cup extra virgin olive oil

2 tablespoons white wine vinegar

1 tablespoon frozen orange juice concentrate, thawed

1 tablespoon honey

½ teaspoon salt

¼ teaspoon dried thyme

⅛ teaspoon ground black pepper

1. Combine all of the dressing ingredients in a blender and blend for about 1 minute.
2. Cover and refrigerate for at least 1 hour before serving. Let the chilled dressing sit at room temperature for a few minutes to liquefy the olive oil.

Nutritional Facts (per tablespoon)
CALORIES: 71 CARBOHYDRATES: 3 G CHOLESTEROL: 0 MG FAT: 6.7 G FIBER: 0 G
PROTEIN: 0 G SODIUM: 145 MG CALCIUM: 1 MG

Nutty Brussels Sprouts

YIELD: 8 SERVINGS

2 pounds fresh Brussels sprouts

1 tablespoon plus 1 teaspoon walnut oil

¼ teaspoon salt

¼ teaspoon ground black pepper

3 tablespoons finely chopped walnuts

1. Trim a small sliver off the bottom of each Brussels sprout and remove the loose outer leaves. Rinse the sprouts and cut each one in half from top to bottom. (There should be about 8 cups of sprouts.) Set aside.

2. Fill a 6-quart pot half full with water and bring to a boil over high heat. Add the sprouts and allow the pot to return to a boil. Cook the sprouts for 4 to 7 minutes, or until tender. Drain well and toss with the walnut oil, salt, and pepper.

3. Transfer to a serving dish and sprinkle the walnuts over the top. Serve immediately.

Nutritional Facts (per ¾-cup serving)
CALORIES: 76 CARBOHYDRATES: 8 G CHOLESTEROL: 0 MG FAT: 4.3 G FIBER: 3.5 G
PROTEIN: 3.4 G SODIUM: 167 MG CALCIUM: 40 MG

Fresh Roasted Asparagus

YIELD: 8 SERVINGS

2½ pounds fresh asparagus spears
Nonstick olive oil cooking spray
½ teaspoon salt
¼ teaspoon ground black pepper

1. Rinse the asparagus spears with cool water and snap off and discard the tough stem ends. Pat the asparagus dry with paper towels. Coat 2 large baking sheets with the cooking spray, and arrange the spears in a single layer on the sheets.

2. Spray the spears lightly with the cooking spray and sprinkle with the salt and pepper. Bake at 450°F for 6 minutes, switch the positions of the pans in the oven, and bake for an additional 5 minutes, or just until the spears are tender. Serve hot.

Nutritional Facts (per serving)
CALORIES: 30 CARBOHYDRATES: 5 G CHOLESTEROL: 0 MG FAT: 0.5 G FIBER: 2.4 G
PROTEIN: 2.4 G SODIUM: 145 MG CALCIUM: 24 MG

Pavlova with Raspberries

✺ *For best results, make the shells on a nonhumid day, and make sure there are no traces of egg yolk mixed in with the whites.*

YIELD: 8 SERVINGS

3 large egg whites, brought to room temperature
¼ teaspoon cream of tartar
⅛ teaspoon salt
¾ cup sugar
¾ teaspoon vanilla extract

FILLINGS
4 cups raspberry or chocolate sorbet
2⅔ cups fresh raspberries
⅓ cup chocolate syrup
⅓ cup sliced toasted almonds (page 30)
   or Glazed Almonds (page 322)

1. Place the egg whites, cream of tartar, and salt in a medium-sized bowl and beat with an electric mixer until soft peaks form when the beaters are removed.
2. Gradually add the sugar, a tablespoon at a time, while beating continuously, until all of the sugar has been incorporated, the mixture is glossy, and stiff peaks form when the beaters are removed. Beat in the vanilla extract.
3. Place a sheet of aluminum foil over the bottom of a large baking sheet and drop the meringue onto the sheet in 8 mounds, spacing the mounds about 4 inches apart. Using the back of a spoon, spread each mound into a 3½-inch circle, creating a center that is about ½ inch thick and building up the sides to about 1¼ inches in height.
4. Bake at 250°F for 1 hour, or until the shells are creamy white and firm to the touch. Turn the oven off, and allow the shells to cool in the oven for 1 hour with the door ajar, then carefully peel the shells from the foil. (Note: The shells can be made up to 3 days in advance and stored in an airtight container until ready to use.)
5. To assemble the desserts, place a ½-cup scoop of sorbet in the center of each pavlova, and top

with ⅓ cup of the berries. Drizzle the chocolate syrup over the top of each pavlova and sprinkle with the almonds. Serve immediately.

Nutritional Facts (per serving)
CALORIES: 278 CARBOHYDRATES: 62 G CHOLESTEROL: 0 MG FAT: 2.6 G FIBER: 5.6 G
PROTEIN: 3 G SODIUM: 65 MG CALCIUM: 21 MG

Variations:

This recipe can be easily varied to suit other menus and occasions. Here are some ideas:

◆ Fold ⅓ to ½ cup finely ground toasted almonds or hazelnuts into the whipped egg white mixture.

◆ Sift 1 to 2 tablespoons of cocoa powder and ⅛ teaspoon cinnamon over the whipped egg white mixture, and then gently fold in.

◆ Fill each shell with a dollop of light whipped topping and some fresh raspberries or sliced strawberries. Drizzle a little chocolate syrup or melted seedless raspberry jam over the top.

◆ Fill the shells with a scoop of low-fat strawberry or peach ice cream and top with fresh sliced strawberries or diced peaches.

◆ Fill the shells with a couple of tablespoons of lemon curd and top with fresh fruit.

Spiced Poached Plums

YIELD: 8 SERVINGS

1 cup dry red wine
1 cup orange juice
⅔ cup sugar
4 whole cloves
3 cinnamon sticks, 2 inches long
12 medium unpeeled plums, pitted and quartered

1. Place the wine, orange juice, and sugar in a large nonstick skillet. Place the skillet over medium-high heat, and cook, stirring frequently, until the sugar dissolves and the mixture comes to a boil.
2. Add the cloves, cinnamon sticks, and plums to the skillet and return the mixture to a boil. Reduce the heat to low, cover, and simmer for 3 minutes. Turn the plums over and simmer for 2 additional minutes, or just until the plums are tender.
3. Using a slotted spoon, transfer the plums to a medium-sized bowl. Increase the heat under the skillet to medium, and cook, stirring frequently, for about 5 minutes, or until the wine mixture is reduced by half and is slightly syrupy.
4. Pour the syrup over the plums, cover, and refrigerate for several hours, or overnight, so that the plums are well chilled. Remove and discard the cinnamon sticks and cloves, and spoon the plums into 8 serving dishes, pouring some of the syrup over each serving. Serve chilled.

Nutritional Facts (per serving)
CALORIES: 167 CARBOHYDRATES: 36 G CHOLESTEROL: 0 MG FAT: 0.8 G FIBER: 1.6 G
PROTEIN: 1 G SODIUM: 2 MG CALCIUM: 6 MG

Passover Seder

MENU TWO

SERVES 6 TO 8

Golden Matzo Ball Soup (page 179)

Spiced Beef Brisket with Carrots and Prunes (page 180)

Asparagus Vinaigrette (page 182)
or Springtime Squash Salad (page 183)

Glazed Onions (page 183)

Sweet and Savory Spinach (page 184)
or Spinach-Stuffed Tomatoes (page 185)

Almond-Crusted Fruit Tart (page 186)
or Crisp Hazelnut Cookies (page 188) with Fresh Strawberries

ADVANCE PLANNING TIPS:

◆ *Prepare Golden Matzo Ball Soup a day in advance. Refrigerate and reheat just before serving.*

◆ *Spiced Beef Brisket with Carrots and Prunes can be easily assembled in the hours before guests arrive, and then placed in the oven, where it will require little attention until it's time to make the sauce. Or if you choose, make this dish the day before your dinner, and reheat it right before serving.*

◆ *Asparagus Vinaigrette and Springtime Squash Salad are perfect make-ahead dishes, as they should be fully prepared the day before to allow the flavors to blend.*

◆ *Spinach-Stuffed Tomatoes can be prepared to the point of baking a day in advance, covered and refrigerated. Remove from the refrigerator 30 to 60 minutes before baking.*

◆ *The crust and glaze for Almond-Crusted Fruit Tart can both be made a day in advance so that you can quickly assemble the tart up to 5 hours before serving. If you are making Crisp Hazelnut Cookies, you can bake them the day before your dinner and store in an airtight container until ready to serve.*

Golden Matzo Ball Soup

YIELD: 8 SERVINGS

5½ cups unsalted vegetable or chicken broth

1¼ cups peeled and diced sweet potato or butternut squash

¾ cup chopped onion

½ cup sliced celery

1 tablespoon vegetable or chicken bouillon granules

⅛ teaspoon ground white pepper

⅛ teaspoon ground nutmeg or ginger

1 recipe Fluffy Fat-Free Matzo Balls (page 167)

1. Place the broth, potato or squash, onion, celery, bouillon granules, pepper, and nutmeg or ginger in a 3-quart pot, and bring to a boil over high heat. Reduce the heat to low, cover, and simmer for 20 minutes or until the vegetables are soft.

2. Use a slotted spoon to transfer the vegetables from the pot to a blender. Add 1 cup of the hot broth, and carefully blend at low speed with the lid slightly ajar (to allow steam to escape) for 30 seconds or until the mixture is smooth. Return the blended mixture to the pot.

3. Add the matzo balls to the soup and simmer, covered, for 10 minutes. Ladle the soup into individual serving bowls, placing 3 matzo balls in each bowl, and serve hot.

Nutritional Facts (per ¾-cup broth with 3 matzo balls)
CALORIES: 103 CARBOHYDRATES: 18 G CHOLESTEROL: 3 MG FAT: 1.2 G FIBER: 1.5 G
PROTEIN: 6.2 G SODIUM: 538 MG CALCIUM: 24 MG

Spiced Beef Brisket with Carrots and Prunes

YIELD: 8 SERVINGS

2½ to 3-pound well-trimmed flat half boneless beef brisket
½ teaspoon coarsely ground black pepper
¼ teaspoon garlic powder
1 cup chopped onion
½ cup beef broth
3 tablespoons light or dark brown sugar
½ teaspoon salt
½ teaspoon ground cinnamon
¼ teaspoon ground ginger
1 tablespoon lemon juice
1 pound baby carrots
1 cup pitted prunes

1. Rinse the meat with cool water and pat dry with paper towels. Sprinkle both sides with the pepper and garlic powder.

2. Coat a large ovenproof nonstick skillet with nonstick cooking spray and preheat over medium-high heat. Place the brisket in the skillet and cook for about 2 minutes on each side or until nicely browned. Remove the skillet from the heat and spread the onions over the meat. Pour the broth into the bottom of the skillet, cover tightly with aluminum foil, and bake at 325°F for 2 hours.

3. Remove the skillet from the oven, and carefully remove the foil (steam will escape). Stir the brown sugar, salt, cinnamon, ginger, and lemon juice into the pan juices and arrange the carrots around the brisket. Re-cover the skillet, and return it to the oven for an additional 30 minutes, or until the meat and carrots are tender. Transfer the meat and carrots to a serving platter, and cover to keep warm.

4. To make the sauce, pour the pan juices into a fat-separator cup, and then pour the defatted drippings back into the skillet. Add the prunes and cook over medium-high heat, stirring frequently, for about 5 minutes, or until the prunes are plumped and the pan juices are reduced to about 1 cup. Using a slotted spoon, transfer the prunes to the serving platter along with the brisket and carrots. Pour the pan juices into a warmed gravy boat. Slice the brisket thinly across the grain, and serve hot with the carrots, prunes, and pan juices.

Nutritional Facts (per serving)
CALORIES: 264   CARBOHYDRATES: 25 G   CHOLESTEROL: 80 MG   FAT: 5.9 G   FIBER: 2.9 G
PROTEIN: 28 G   SODIUM: 262 MG   CALCIUM: 36 MG

Choosing a Brisket

A slow-cooked brisket is a traditional part of many Jewish holiday meals. Although this cut of meat can be very fatty, when chosen carefully, even brisket can star in a light holiday menu. For the least fat, choose a flat half *brisket. This cut will have just over 5 grams of fat per 3-ounce cooked, trimmed serving. In contrast, a* point half *brisket has close to 12 grams of fat for the same size serving (untrimmed, this cut delivers about 24 grams of fat per serving!). Briskets that are labeled* whole *brisket include both the flat and point half sections, and will have an intermediate amount of fat.*

Asparagus Vinaigrette

YIELD: 8 SERVINGS

4 cups 1-inch pieces fresh asparagus
6 thin slices red onion, separated into rings
½ cup diced red bell pepper

DRESSING
3 tablespoons white wine vinegar
1½ to 2 tablespoons extra virgin olive oil
2 teaspoons sugar
½ teaspoon salt
¼ teaspoon dried thyme
⅛ teaspoon ground black pepper

1. Bring a large pot of water to a boil. Add the asparagus and boil for about 2 minutes, or just until the asparagus is crisp-tender. Drain the asparagus, then plunge into cold water (to stop the cooking process), and drain again.

2. Place the asparagus, onion rings, and bell pepper in a medium-sized bowl and toss to mix well. Combine the dressing ingredients in a small bowl, and stir to mix well. Pour the dressing over the salad and toss to mix well. Cover the salad and chill for several hours or overnight, stirring occasionally, before serving.

Nutritional Facts (per ½-cup serving)
CALORIES: 52 CARBOHYDRATES: 7 G CHOLESTEROL: 0 MG FAT: 2.7 G FIBER: 2 G
PROTEIN: 1.9 G SODIUM: 147 MG CALCIUM: 20 MG

Springtime Squash Salad

YIELD: 8 SERVINGS

2 cups thinly sliced yellow squash (about 5 medium)

2 cups thinly sliced zucchini squash (about 2 medium)

1 medium yellow onion, thinly sliced and separated into rings

DRESSING

¼ cup plus 1 tablespoon white wine vinegar

2 tablespoons extra virgin olive oil

2 tablespoons sugar

1 tablespoon finely chopped fresh dill or 1 teaspoon dried dill

½ teaspoon salt

¼ teaspoon ground black pepper

1. Place the squash and onion rings in a medium-sized bowl and toss to mix well. Combine the dressing ingredients in a small bowl, and stir to mix well. Pour the dressing over the salad and toss to mix well.

2. Cover the salad and chill for at least 8 hours or overnight, stirring occasionally, before serving.

Nutritional Facts (per ½-cup serving)
CALORIES: 56   CARBOHYDRATES: 6 G   CHOLESTEROL: 0 MG   FAT: 3.5 G   FIBER: 1 G
PROTEIN: 1 G   SODIUM: 148 MG   CALCIUM: 13 MG

Glazed Onions

YIELD: 8 SERVINGS

5 cups ½-inch wedges onions (about 5 medium)

½ cup plus 2 tablespoons dry sherry

2½ tablespoons reduced-fat margarine

2½ teaspoons light brown sugar

¼ teaspoon dried thyme
¼ teaspoon salt

1. Place all of the ingredients in a large nonstick skillet, and bring to a boil over medium-high heat. Reduce the heat to medium, cover, and cook, stirring occasionally, for about 8 minutes, or just until the onions are tender.
2. Remove the cover from the skillet and cook, stirring frequently, for another couple of minutes, or until most of the liquid has evaporated from the skillet. Serve hot.

Nutritional Facts (per ½-cup serving)
CALORIES: 59   CARBOHYDRATES: 8 G   CHOLESTEROL: 0 MG   FAT: 1.6 G   FIBER: 1.3 G
PROTEIN: 0.9 G   SODIUM: 107 MG   CALCIUM: 18 MG

Sweet and Savory Spinach

YIELD: 8 SERVINGS

½ cup chopped onion
½ cup chopped peeled Granny Smith apple
½ cup dark raisins
¼ cup orange juice
1 tablespoon plus 1 teaspoon extra virgin olive oil
1¼ pounds fresh prewashed spinach (about 10 cups)
¼ teaspoon salt
⅛ teaspoon ground black pepper
3 tablespoons toasted pine nuts (page 30)

1. Coat a large deep nonstick skillet with nonstick cooking spray, and place the onions, apples, raisins, and orange juice in the skillet. Place the skillet over medium heat, cover, and cook for about 3 minutes, stirring several times, until the onions and apples are tender. Add a little more orange juice if the skillet becomes too dry.
2. Add the olive oil to the skillet followed by the spinach, salt, pepper, and pine nuts. Toss over medium heat, for a couple of minutes, or just until the spinach is wilted. Serve hot.

Nutritional Facts (per ½-cup serving)
CALORIES: 78 CARBOHYDRATES: 10 G CHOLESTEROL: 0 MG FAT: 3.8 G FIBER: 2.4 G
PROTEIN: 2.8 G SODIUM: 105 MG CALCIUM: 61 MG

Spinach-Stuffed Tomatoes

YIELD: 8 SERVINGS

4 medium tomatoes (about 6 ounces each)
¾ cup finely chopped onion
1 teaspoon crushed garlic
1 teaspoon dried thyme
1 teaspoon dried oregano
10-ounces frozen chopped spinach,
   thawed and squeezed dry
1 cup matzo meal
2 to 3 tablespoons extra virgin olive oil
½ teaspoon salt
¼ teaspoon ground black pepper
3 tablespoons fat-free egg substitute
¼ cup plus 2 tablespoons vegetable or chicken broth
Olive oil nonstick cooking spray

1. Cut the tomatoes in half crosswise and scoop out and discard the seeds and juice. Coat a 9-by-13-inch baking dish with the cooking spray, and arrange the tomato halves, cut side up, in the dish.

2. Coat a large nonstick skillet with the cooking spray, and add the onions, garlic, thyme, oregano, and 1 tablespoon of water. Place the skillet over medium heat, cover, and cook, stirring several times, for about 3 minutes, or until the onions are tender.

3. Remove the skillet from the heat and stir in the spinach, matzo meal, olive oil, salt, and pepper, and toss to mix well. Combine the egg substitute and broth, and stir into the spinach mixture. The mixture should be moist, but not wet, and should hold together nicely. Add a little more broth if the mixture seems too dry.

4. Spoon one-eighth of the spinach mixture into each of the hollowed-out tomato halves, and spray the tops lightly with the cooking spray. Bake at 375°F for about 20 minutes, or until the stuffed tomatoes are heated through and lightly browned. Serve hot.

Nutritional Facts (per serving)
CALORIES: 98 CARBOHYDRATES: 14 G CHOLESTEROL: 0 MG FAT: 3.8 G FIBER: 2.1 G
PROTEIN: 3.7 G SODIUM: 189 MG CALCIUM: 51 MG

Almond-Crusted Fruit Tart

✿ *For variety, substitute hazelnuts for the almonds.*

YIELD: 10 SERVINGS

CRUST
Matzo cake meal (can use unbleached flour
   at other times of the year)
1½ cups sliced almonds
⅓ cup sugar
⅛ teaspoon salt
1 tablespoon fat-free egg substitute

GLAZE
4 cups diced fresh or frozen strawberries (about 1¼ pounds)
½ cup sugar
3 tablespoons frozen cranberry juice concentrate
1 teaspoon potato starch (can use cornstarch
   at other times of the year)

TOPPING
3 cups sliced fresh strawberries
1½ cups fresh raspberries, rinsed and patted dry
1½ cups fresh blackberries or blueberries, rinsed and patted dry

1. To make the crust, line a 10-inch pie pan with heavy-duty aluminum foil, pressing the foil firmly against the sides of the pan. Spray the foil with nonstick cooking spray, and lightly dust with the matzo cake meal. Set aside.

2. Place the almonds, sugar, and salt in the bowl of a food processor and process until the almonds are finely ground. Add the egg substitute and process for a few seconds, or just until the mixture is moist and crumbly and holds together when pinched.

3. Use the back of a spoon to spread the dough in an even layer over the bottom and sides of the foil-lined pan. Then use your fingers to finish pressing the crust into place (place your hand inside a small plastic bag or lay a piece of wax paper over the crust as you press to prevent sticking). Bake at 350°F for about 12 minutes, or until the crust feels firm and dry. Let the crust cool to room temperature, then remove from the pan, and carefully peel the foil from the crust. Return the crust to the pan, cover with plastic wrap, and store at room temperature for up to 24 hours before assembling the tart.

4. To make the glaze, place all of the glaze ingredients in a large nonstick skillet, and bring to a boil over medium-high heat. Cook, stirring frequently and mashing the berries with the back of a spoon, for 10 to 12 minutes, or until the mixture thickens and is reduced in volume to about 1½ cups. Dissolve the potato starch in a teaspoon of water and stir into the glaze. Cook and stir for another minute, or until the glaze thickens a bit more. Let the glaze cool to room temperature, then cover and refrigerate for up to 2 days before assembling the tart.

5. To assemble the tart, place the berries in a large bowl, add the glaze, and toss to mix well. Pile the filling into the crust. Cover and refrigerate 2 to 5 hours before serving.

Nutritional Facts (per serving)
CALORIES: 222 CARBOHYDRATES: 34 G CHOLESTEROL: 0 MG FAT: 8.5 G FIBER: 4.9 G
PROTEIN: 4.5 G SODIUM: 39 MG CALCIUM: 76 MG

Variation:

To save time, substitute 1½ cups ready-made strawberry glaze for the cooked glaze.

Crisp Hazelnut Cookies

✦ *For variety, substitute pecans or almonds for the hazelnuts.*

YIELD: 36 COOKIES

1¾ cups coarsely chopped hazelnuts
¾ cup sugar
2 large egg whites, brought to room temperature
Pinch salt
1 teaspoon vanilla extract

1. Combine 1½ cups of the hazelnuts and ¼ cup of the sugar in the bowl of a food processor and process until the nuts are finely ground. Set aside.
2. Place the egg whites in a large glass bowl and add the salt. Beat with an electric mixer until soft peaks form when the beaters are raised. Still beating, slowly add the remaining ½ cup of sugar, 1 tablespoonful at a time. Continue beating until all the sugar is mixed in and the mixture is thick and glossy. Beat in the vanilla extract.
3. Gently fold half of the ground hazelnut mixture into the beaten egg whites, and then fold in the remaining ground hazelnut mixture.
4. Line 2 large cookie sheets with aluminum foil (do not coat with cooking spray). Drop heaping teaspoons of the hazelnut mixture onto the sheets, spacing them 1½ inches apart. Sprinkle about ⅓ teaspoon of the chopped hazelnuts over each cookie, pressing them slightly onto the cookie to make them stick.
5. Bake at 350°F for 10 minutes. Switch the positions of the cookie sheets in the oven, and cook for an additional 6 minutes, or until the cookies are lightly browned and firm to the touch. Turn the oven off and let the cookies sit in the oven with the door slightly ajar for 30 minutes. Then remove the cookie sheets from the oven and allow the cookies to cool in the pan to room temperature. Peel the cookies from the foil and serve immediately or store in an airtight container.

Nutritional Facts (per cookie)
CALORIES: 52   CARBOHYDRATES: 5 G   CHOLESTEROL: 0 MG   FAT: 3.4 G   FIBER: 0.5 G
PROTEIN: 1 G   SODIUM: 7 MG   CALCIUM: 7 MG

Variation:

To make Chocolate-Hazelnut Crisps, reduce the nuts in the food processor mixture to ¾ cup, and add 4 ounces (about ⅔ cup) coarsely chopped semi-sweet chocolate or chocolate chips. Process the mixture until the nuts and chocolate are finely ground.

Nutritional Facts (per cookie)
CALORIES: 52   CARBOHYDRATES: 7 G   CHOLESTEROL: 0 MG   FAT: 2.9 G   FIBER: 0.5 G
PROTEIN: 0.8 G   SODIUM: 7 MG   CALCIUM: 5 MG

Easter

This section presents two delightful menus that will allow you to celebrate spring and still leave yourself time for that Easter egg hunt. Choose from a light, no-fuss Easter brunch or a simple but elegant Easter dinner.

The first menu proves that traditional brunch favorites can be both light and deliciously satisfying. The main course—a make-ahead Ham and Cheese Strata, made with lower-fat dairy and egg products and ultra-lean ham—has only a fraction of the fat and calories of a traditional version. A casserole of hearty cheese grits or crisp hash brown patties, a selection of store-bought bagels with light cream cheese spread and smoked salmon slices, and a plentiful platter of the season's freshest fruits round out the selections. But do save room for dessert. Indulge in a rich and creamy cherry-topped cheesecake, or linger over coffee with a slice of Cinnamon-Swirl Coffee Cake. Either confection adds that perfect finishing touch.

But perhaps you've decided to make an Easter dinner instead of a brunch. If so, our holiday feast is sure to delight family and friends alike. Simple, yet special enough for any occasion, this menu captures the essence of spring with its light and flavorful dishes. Dinner starts with a gloriously simple salad of gourmet greens tossed with a light raspberry vinaigrette dressing. The main course brings a marinated tenderloin of pork, fragrant with rosemary and garlic. Accompaniments like Easy Creamed Corn, Crunchy Carrot Salad, and fresh steamed asparagus add balance and color while continuing the spring theme. And the crowing touch? Present a lovely Chocolate-Raspberry Layer Cake or a heavenly White Chocolate Angel Trifle. Either choice will bring plenty of *oohs* and *ahhs* from guests. And both are amazingly simple to make.

Easter Brunch

SERVES 8 TO 10

Ham and Cheese Strata (page 192)

Creamy Cheese Grits (page 193)
or Hash Brown Potato Patties (page 194)

Assorted Bagels
with Light Cream Cheese Spread
and Sliced Smoked Salmon

Seasonal Fresh Fruit Platter

Light Cherry Cheesecake (page 195)
or Cinnamon-Swirl Coffee Cake (page 196)

ADVANCE PLANNING TIPS:

◆ *Prepare the Ham and Cheese Strata to the point of baking the day before and refrigerate for up to 24 hours. Remove from the refrigerator 30 to 60 minutes before baking.*

◆ *Make the Hash Brown Potato Patties mixture the day before and refrigerate until ready to shape and bake the patties.*

◆ *Light Cherry Cheesecake should be made the day before, so it has plenty of time to chill before serving. Cinnamon-Swirl Coffee Cake can also be made the day before and covered with a cake shield. It will become even moister when allowed to sit overnight.*

Ham and Cheese Strata

✿ *For variety, substitute diced lean smoked sausage or kielbasa for the ham.*

YIELD: 10 SERVINGS

8 cups ½-inch cubes crustless sourdough bread (about 9 slices)
1¾ cups diced lean ham, smoked sausage, or kielbasa
4-ounce can diced green chilies, drained
2 cups shredded reduced-fat Cheddar cheese
2 cups fat-free egg substitute
12-ounce can evaporated skim or low-fat milk
1 cup skim or low-fat milk
⅛ teaspoon ground black pepper
Butter-flavored nonstick cooking spray

1. Coat a 9-by-13-inch pan with the nonstick cooking spray, and spread half of the bread cubes over the bottom of the pan. Layer half of the ham, chilies, and cheese over the bread. Repeat the bread, ham, chilies, and cheese layers.

2. Combine the egg substitute, evaporated milk, skim or low-fat milk, and pepper in a medium-sized bowl, and whisk to mix well. Pour the egg mixture over the layers in the baking dish. Cover the dish with aluminum foil, and refrigerate for 2 to 24 hours.

3. When ready to bake, remove the dish from the refrigerator and let sit at room temperature for 30 to 60 minutes. Spray the top lightly with the cooking spray and bake at 350°F for about 50 minutes, or until the top is nicely browned and a sharp knife inserted in the center of the dish comes out clean.

4. Remove the dish from the oven and let sit for 15 minutes before cutting into squares and serving.

Nutritional Facts (per serving)
CALORIES: 209 CARBOHYDRATES: 18 G CHOLESTEROL: 20 MG FAT: 4.6 G FIBER: 0.6 G
PROTEIN: 22 G SODIUM: 669 MG CALCIUM: 362 MG

Variation:

To make **Ham and Swiss Strata,** substitute Swiss cheese for the Cheddar and 4-ounces canned drained sliced mushrooms for the chilies.

Nutritional Facts (per serving)
CALORIES: 200 CARBOHYDRATES: 18 G CHOLESTEROL: 16 MG FAT: 4.3 G FIBER: 0.6 G
PROTEIN: 22 G SODIUM: 663 MG CALCIUM: 363 MG

Creamy Cheese Grits

YIELD: 10 SERVINGS

1½ cups quick-cooking (5-minute) grits
3 cups skim or low-fat milk
3 cups water
⅛ teaspoon ground white pepper
2 cups shredded reduced-fat Cheddar cheese
½ cup fat-free egg substitute
Ground paprika
Butter-flavored nonstick cooking spray

1. Combine the grits, milk, water, and white pepper in a 4-quart nonstick pot, and place over medium-high heat. Cook, stirring frequently, for several minutes, or until the mixture comes to a boil. Reduce the heat to low, cover, and cook, stirring frequently, for about 5 minutes, or until the grits are tender and the mixture is thick. Add the cheese, and stir over low heat for another minute, or until the cheese is melted. (Note: If you prefer, you can serve the grits immediately after stirring in the cheese, or proceed with the recipe to prepare casserole-style cheese grits.)

2. Place the egg substitute in a small bowl and stir in ½ cup of the hot grits mixture, then stir the egg mixture into the grits.

3. Coat an 8-by-12-inch baking dish or a shallow 2½-quart casserole dish with the cooking spray, and spread the grits mixture evenly in the dish. Sprinkle the top lightly with the paprika, and spray the top lightly with the cooking spray.

4. Bake at 350°F for 30 minutes or until the casserole starts to bubble around the edges. Remove the dish from the oven and let sit for 10 minutes before serving.

Nutritional Facts (per ¾-cup serving)
CALORIES: 175 CARBOHYDRATES: 21 G CHOLESTEROL: 14 MG FAT: 3.6 G FIBER: 1.2 G
PROTEIN: 13 G SODIUM: 212 MG CALCIUM: 297 MG

Hash Brown Potato Patties

YIELD: 10 SERVINGS

1½ pounds (about 9 cups) frozen shredded hash brown potatoes, thawed or 1½ pounds
*   refrigerated shredded hash brown potatoes (about 5 cups lightly packed)*
¾ cup finely chopped onion
½ cup finely chopped green bell pepper
2 tablespoons dried seasoned bread crumbs
½ teaspoon salt
⅛ teaspoon ground black pepper
½ cup fat-free egg substitute
Butter-flavored nonstick cooking spray

1. Place all of the ingredients except for the cooking spray in a large bowl, and stir to mix well. (Note: The mixture can be made a day in advance and refrigerated until ready to use.) Coat 2 large nonstick baking sheets with the cooking spray. For each patty, spoon ¼ cup of the potato mixture onto the sheet and form into a 3-inch patty. Spray the tops of the patties with the cooking spray.

2. Bake at 425°F for 10 minutes, turn the pancakes with a spatula, spray again, and switch the positions of the pans in the oven. Bake for an additional 7 to 10 minutes, or until golden brown. If desired, spray the patties once again with a light coating of the cooking spray just before serving to give them a pan-fried appearance. Serve hot.

Nutritional Facts (per 2 patties)
CALORIES: 76 CARBOHYDRATES: 14 G CHOLESTEROL: 0 MG FAT: 0.9 G FIBER: 1.3 G
PROTEIN: 3 G SODIUM: 190 MG CALCIUM: 9 MG

Light Cherry Cheesecake

✧ *For variety, substitute blueberry, apple, or peach pie filling for the cherry.*

YIELD: 12 SERVINGS

2 tablespoons low-fat graham cracker crumbs*
15 ounces nonfat or part-skim ricotta cheese
1 cup sugar
2 teaspoons vanilla extract
12 ounces block-style reduced-fat (Neufchâtel) cream cheese,
    softened to room temperature
2 tablespoons lemon juice
3 tablespoons unbleached flour
3 tablespoons instant cheesecake or vanilla pudding mix
¾ cup fat-free egg substitute
20-ounce can light (reduced-sugar) cherry pie filling

1. Coat a 9-inch springform pan with nonstick cooking spray. Sprinkle the crumbs over the bottom of the pan, and tilt the pan to coat the bottom and 1 inch up the sides with the crumbs. Set the pan on a 12-inch square of heavy-duty aluminum foil and fold the foil up the sides of the pan (to protect against possible leakage). Set aside.

2. Place the ricotta cheese, sugar, and vanilla extract in the bowl of a food processor, and process until smooth. Add the cream cheese, lemon juice, flour, and pudding mix, and process until smooth. Add the egg substitute, and process to mix well.

3. Pour the batter into the prepared pan and bake at 325°F for about an hour, or until the edges are firm and the center is almost set. Turn the oven off and let the cake cool in the oven with the door ajar for 1 hour. Remove the cheesecake to a wire rack and let cool to room temperature.

4. Cover the cheesecake and chill for at least 6 hours. Spread the pie filling over the top of the cake and chill for at least 2 additional hours before slicing and serving.

Nutritional Facts (per serving)
CALORIES: 232   CARBOHYDRATES: 32 G   CHOLESTEROL: 22 MG   FAT: 6.7 G   FIBER: 0.7 G
PROTEIN: 10 G   SODIUM: 233 MG   CALCIUM: 198 MG

*If you prefer a thicker crust, substitute Graham Cracker Pie Crust (page 302) for the graham cracker crumbs. Pat the crust over the bottom and ¾-inch up the sides of the springform pan, bake for 5 minutes, and cool to room temperature before adding the cheese filling.

Cinnamon-Swirl Coffee Cake

YIELD: 16 SERVINGS

1 box (1 pound, 2.25 ounces) yellow cake mix
1 cup plus 2 tablespoons water
¼ cup plus 2 tablespoons unsweetened applesauce
½ cup fat-free egg substitute

CINNAMON FILLING

½ cup chopped walnuts or toasted pecans (page 30)

3 tablespoons light brown sugar

1 teaspoon ground cinnamon

GLAZE

⅔ cup powdered sugar

1 tablespoon skim or low-fat milk

¼ teaspoon vanilla extract

1. To make the filling, combine all of the filling ingredients in a small bowl and stir to mix well. Set aside.

2. Place the cake mix in a large bowl, and add the water, applesauce, and egg substitute. Beat with an electric mixer for 2 minutes.

3. Coat a 12-cup bundt pan with nonstick cooking spray, and spread one-third of the batter evenly in the pan. Sprinkle half of the cinnamon filling over the batter, repeat the batter and filling layers, then finish off with the remaining batter. Bake at 350°F for about 35 minutes, or just until the top springs back when lightly touched and a wooden toothpick inserted in the center of the cake comes out clean. Be careful not to overbake.

4. Allow the cake to cool in the pan for 40 minutes. Then invert onto a serving platter and cool to room temperature.

5. To make the glaze, combine all of the glaze ingredients in a microwave-safe bowl, and stir to mix well. Microwave at high power for about 25 seconds, or until hot and runny. Drizzle the hot glaze over the cake. Allow the cake to sit for at least 15 minutes before slicing and serving.

Nutritional Facts (per serving)

CALORIES: 188   CARBOHYDRATES: 35 G   CHOLESTEROL: 0 MG   FAT: 4.7 G   FIBER: 0.7 G
PROTEIN: 2.1 G   SODIUM: 220 MG   CALCIUM: 71 MG

Easter Dinner

SERVES 8 TO 10

Spring Greens with Raspberry Vinaigrette (page 199)

Rosemary Roasted Tenderloins (page 200)

Easy Creamed Corn (page 201)
or Cheddar Scalloped Potatoes (page 202)

Crunchy Carrot Salad (page 203)
or Creamy Ambrosia (page 204)

Asparagus with Honey-Mustard Sauce (page 205)
or Sugar Snap Peas with Dill (page 205)

Multigrain or Sourdough Dinner Rolls

White Chocolate Angel Trifle (page 206)
or Chocolate-Raspberry Layer Cake (page 207)

◆ *Make the dressing for the salad the day before. Purchase prewashed salad greens, and the salad can be put together in a matter of minutes.*

◆ *Place the pork tenderloin in the marinade the day before so that it will be ready to roast an hour or so before dinner.*

◆ *Cheddar Scalloped Potatoes can be prepared up to the point of baking the day before and refrigerated. Remove the dish from the refrigerator 30 to 60 minutes before baking.*

◆ *Purchase preshredded carrots for Crunchy Carrot Salad or shred the carrots the day before. Creamy Ambrosia can be made up to 12 hours in advance of your dinner.*

◆ *Rinse and trim either the asparagus spears or sugar snap peas the day before, pat dry, and store in a zip-type bag until ready to cook.*

◆ *If you are making White Chocolate Angel Trifle, prepare the pudding the day before. Then assemble the trifle up to 8 hours before serving. Make Chocolate-Raspberry Layer Cake the day before your dinner, as it becomes moister and more flavorful if chilled for 24 hours before serving.*

Spring Greens with Raspberry Vinaigrette

YIELD: 10 SERVINGS

8 ounces prewashed mixed baby salad greens (about 15 cups loosely packed)
¼ cup Raspberry Vinaigrette Salad Dressing (page 200)

1. Place the greens in a large salad bowl, and drizzle with the dressing.
2. Toss to mix well, and add a little more dressing if the mixture seems too dry. Serve immediately.

Nutritional Facts (per 1½-cup serving)
CALORIES: 41 CARBOHYDRATES: 3 G CHOLESTEROL: 0 MG FAT: 2.9 G FIBER: 1.5 G
PROTEIN: 1.4 G SODIUM: 36 MG CALCIUM: 30 MG

Raspberry Vinaigrette Salad Dressing

YIELD: ½ CUP

2 tablespoons seedless raspberry jam
¼ cup walnut oil
2 tablespoons raspberry vinegar
½ teaspoon salt
¼ teaspoon ground black pepper
¼ teaspoon dried thyme

1. Place all of the ingredients in a blender and blend until smooth.
2. Transfer the dressing to a covered container and refrigerate for at least 1 hour before serving.

Nutritional Facts (per tablespoon)
CALORIES: 74 CARBOHYDRATES: 3.5 G CHOLESTEROL: 0 MG FAT: 6.8 G FIBER: 0 G
PROTEIN: 0 G SODIUM: 143 MG CALCIUM: 1 MG

Rosemary Roasted Tenderloins

YIELD: 12 SERVINGS

3 pork tenderloins (1 pound each)

MARINADE
⅓ cup frozen apple juice concentrate, thawed
3 tablespoons Dijon mustard
2 tablespoons fresh rosemary, or 2 teaspoons dried rosemary

2 teaspoons crushed garlic

½ teaspoon coarsely ground black pepper

1. Rinse the tenderloins with cool water and pat dry with paper towels. Place the tenderloins in a shallow nonmetal dish.
2. Combine the marinade ingredients in a small bowl and stir to mix well. Pour the marinade over the meat, turning to coat all sides. Cover and refrigerate for several hours or overnight.
3. When ready to bake, coat an 11-by-13-inch roasting pan or the bottom of a broiler pan with nonstick cooking spray and place the tenderloins in the pan, spacing them at least 2 inches apart. Pour the marinade remaining in the dish over the tenderloins. Bake at 350°F for about 45 minutes, basting occasionally with the pan juices, or until a thermometer inserted in the thickest part of a tenderloin registers 160°F. Remove the pan from the oven, cover loosely with aluminum foil, and let sit for 5 minutes before slicing thinly at an angle. Serve hot.

Nutritional Facts (per 3-ounce serving)
CALORIES: 144   CARBOHYDRATES: 2 G   CHOLESTEROL: 79 MG   FAT: 4.2 G   FIBER: 0 G
PROTEIN: 35 G   SODIUM: 76 MG   CALCIUM: 7 MG

Easy Creamed Corn

YIELD: 10 SERVINGS

2 pounds frozen sweet white corn, thawed

1½ cups skim or low-fat milk

2 tablespoons reduced-fat margarine or light butter

¼ cup plus 2 tablespoons finely chopped onion

½ teaspoon salt

⅛ teaspoon ground white pepper

1. Place 3 cups of the corn and all of the milk in a blender or food processor and process until smooth. Set aside.
2. Combine the margarine or butter and the onions in a large nonstick skillet, and place over medium heat. Cover and cook, stirring occasionally, for about 3 minutes, or until the onions are tender. Add the pureed corn mixture, the remaining corn, and the salt and pepper to the pot.

3. Bring the mixture to a boil over medium-high heat, stirring frequently. Reduce the heat to medium-low and place a lid on the skillet, leaving it slightly ajar to allow steam to escape. Simmer, stirring occasionally, for about 5 minutes, or until the corn is tender. If the mixture seems too thin, remove the lid, and cook for another couple of minutes, stirring frequently, until some of the liquid evaporates. Serve hot.

Nutritional Facts (per ½ cup serving)
CALORIES: 106 CARBOHYDRATES: 21 G CHOLESTEROL: 0 MG FAT: 1.8 G FIBER: 2.3 G
PROTEIN: 4.3 G SODIUM: 160 MG CALCIUM: 58 MG

Cheddar Scalloped Potatoes

YIELD: 10 SERVINGS

2 pounds Yukon Gold potatoes (about 6 medium)
Butter-flavored nonstick cooking spray
2 tablespoons dried bread crumbs

SAUCE
¼ cup unbleached flour
3 tablespoons instant nonfat dry milk powder
½ teaspoon dry mustard
⅛ teaspoon ground white pepper
2½ cups skim or low-fat milk
1½ cups diced or shredded reduced-fat process Cheddar cheese (like Velveeta Light)

1. Scrub the potatoes, pat dry, and spray the skins lightly with the cooking spray. Pierce each potato in several places with a fork. Place the potatoes on a large baking sheet and bake at 400°F for about 40 minutes, or until tender. Allow the potatoes to cool, then slice ¼-inch thick.
2. To make the sauce, combine the flour, milk powder, mustard, and pepper in a 2-quart microwave-safe bowl. Add about ¼ cup of the milk, and whisk until the mixture is smooth and no lumps of flour remain. Slowly whisk in the remaining milk. Microwave the milk mixture at

high power for 4 minutes, whisking every 2 minutes. Then microwave for an additional 2 to 3 minutes, whisking every 45 to 60 seconds, or until the mixture is thickened and bubbly. Whisk in the cheese, and microwave for an additional minute, or just until the cheese is melted.

3. Coat a 9-by-13-inch baking dish with the cooking spray, and spread half of the potatoes over the bottom of the pan. Top with half of the sauce. Repeat the layers and sprinkle the bread crumbs over the top. Spray the top lightly with the cooking spray.

4. Bake at 350°F for about 30 minutes, or until the edges are bubbly and the top is lightly browned. Remove the dish from the oven and let sit for 10 minutes before serving.

Nutritional Facts (per ¾-cup serving)
CALORIES: 160 CARBOHYDRATES: 27 G CHOLESTEROL: 9 MG FAT: 2.1 G FIBER: 1.8 G
PROTEIN: 8 G SODIUM: 327 MG CALCIUM: 200 MG

Crunchy Carrot Salad

YIELD: 10 SERVINGS

3½ cups grated carrots
1½ cups diced peeled apple
⅔ cup dark raisins
⅓ cup chopped walnuts or toasted pecans (page 30)

DRESSING
½ cup nonfat or light mayonnaise
¼ cup nonfat or light sour cream
1 tablespoon sugar

1. Combine the carrots, apple, raisins, and walnuts or pecans in a medium bowl and toss to mix well.

2. To make the dressing, combine the mayonnaise, sour cream, and sugar in a small bowl, and stir to mix well. Add the dressing to the salad, and toss to mix well. Cover the salad, and refrigerate for 2 to 8 hours before serving.

Nutritional Facts (per ½-cup serving)
CALORIES: 99   CARBOHYDRATES: 18 G   CHOLESTEROL: 0 MG   FAT: 2.5 G   FIBER: 2.5 G
PROTEIN: 2 G   SODIUM: 106 MG   CALCIUM: 24 MG

Creamy Ambrosia

YIELD: 10 SERVINGS

2 cans (11 ounces each) mandarin orange sections in juice or light syrup, well drained
2 cans (8 ounces each) pineapple tidbits in juice, well drained
1 cup mini marshmallows
¼ cup plus 2 tablespoons sweetened shredded coconut
¼ cup chopped toasted pecans (page 30)
1 cup nonfat or light sour cream
1 tablespoon sugar

1. Combine the oranges, pineapple, marshmallows, coconut, and pecans in a medium-sized bowl and toss to mix well. Combine the sour cream and sugar in a small bowl and stir to mix well. Add the sour cream mixture to the fruit mixture and toss gently to mix.
2. Cover the salad and refrigerate for several hours or overnight before serving.

Nutritional Facts (per ½-cup serving)
CALORIES: 110   CARBOHYDRATES: 18 G   CHOLESTEROL: 0 MG   FAT: 3.5 G   FIBER: 1.6 G
PROTEIN: 2.2 G   SODIUM: 30 MG   CALCIUM: 38 MG

Asparagus with Honey-Mustard Sauce

2½ pounds fresh asparagus spears

SAUCE
½ cup plus 2 tablespoons nonfat or light mayonnaise
2 tablespoons Dijon or spicy brown mustard
2 tablespoons lemon juice
2 tablespoons honey

1. Rinse the asparagus with cool running water and snap off and discard the tough stem ends. Fill a 6-quart pot half full with water and bring to a boil over high heat. Add the asparagus and boil for about 2 minutes, or just until the asparagus are crisp-tender. Drain well and transfer to a serving platter.
2. While the asparagus are cooking, place all of the sauce ingredients in a 1-quart pot and stir to mix well. Cook over medium-low heat, stirring frequently, for a minute or two, or just until the sauce is heated through. Add a little water if the sauce seems too thick.
3. Drizzle the sauce over the asparagus and serve hot.

Nutritional Facts (per serving)
CALORIES: 52   CARBOHYDRATES: 10 G   CHOLESTEROL: 0 MG   FAT: 0.3 G   FIBER: 2 G
PROTEIN: 2.2 G   SODIUM: 180 MG   CALCIUM: 24 MG

Sugar Snap Peas with Dill

YIELD: 10 SERVINGS

6 cups fresh sugar snap peas (about 2¼ pounds), strings removed
1 tablespoon extra virgin olive oil or walnut oil
1 tablespoon finely chopped fresh dill, or 1 teaspoon dried dill
¼ teaspoon salt

1. Fill a 6-quart pot half full with water and bring to a boil over high heat. Add the sugar snap peas and boil for about 3 minutes, or just until the peas are tender.
2. Drain the peas well and return them to the pot. Add the oil, dill, and salt, and toss to mix well. Serve hot.

Nutritional Facts (per ½-cup serving)
CALORIES: 57 CARBOHYDRATES: 9 G CHOLESTEROL: 0 MG FAT: 1.4 G FIBER: 2.7 G
PROTEIN: 2.7 G SODIUM: 115 MG CALCIUM: 54 MG

Variation:

To make **Sesame Sugar Snap Peas,** substitute sesame oil for the olive or walnut oil and 2 teaspoons toasted sesame seeds for the dill.

Nutritional Facts (per ½-cup serving)
CALORIES: 60 CARBOHYDRATES: 9 G CHOLESTEROL: 0 MG FAT: 1.6 G FIBER: 2.8 G
PROTEIN: 2.8 G SODIUM: 115 MG CALCIUM: 55 MG

White Chocolate Angel Trifle

YIELD: 10 SERVINGS

10 (⅔-inch wedges) angel food cake (about 10 ounces)
¼ cup plus 1 tablespoon raspberry jam

PUDDING MIXTURE
3 cups skim or low-fat milk
2 packages (4 serving-size each) cook-and-serve or instant
   white chocolate pudding mix (sugar-free or regular)

FRUIT MIXTURE
1½ cups sliced fresh strawberries
1½ cups fresh or frozen raspberries, thawed
1 tablespoon sugar

TOPPING

2 cups nonfat or light whipped topping

½ cup nonfat or low-fat vanilla yogurt (sugar-free or regular)

3 tablespoons shaved dark chocolate

3 tablespoons sliced toasted almonds (page 30)

1. Use the milk to prepare the pudding according to package directions. Transfer to a covered container and refrigerate until well chilled.
2. To make the fruit mixture, combine the berries and sugar in a medium bowl, and toss to mix well.
3. To assemble the trifle, spread 1½ teaspoons of the jam over each of the cake slices, and arrange half of the cake slices over the bottom of a 3-quart glass bowl. Top the cake slices with half of the fruit mixture and then half of the pudding. Repeat the layers.
4. To make the topping, place the whipped topping in a medium-sized bowl, and gently fold in the yogurt. Swirl the mixture over the top of the trifle, cover, and chill for 5 to 8 hours. Just before serving, sprinkle with the chocolate and almonds.

Nutritional Facts (per serving)

CALORIES: 215 CARBOHYDRATES: 43 G CHOLESTEROL: 1 MG FAT: 2.5 G FIBER: 2.6 G
PROTEIN: 5.6 G SODIUM: 530 MG CALCIUM: 165 MG

Chocolate-Raspberry Layer Cake

YIELD: 16 SERVINGS

1 box (1 pound, 2.25 ounces) chocolate fudge cake mix

¼ teaspoon baking soda

¾ cup room temperature coffee

½ cup unsweetened applesauce

½ cup fat-free egg substitute

FILLINGS

4-serving size package instant chocolate pudding mix (sugar-free or regular)

1¾ cups skim or low-fat milk
¾ cup seedless raspberry jam

FROSTING
2½ cups nonfat or light whipped topping
½ cup nonfat or low-fat raspberry yogurt (sugar-free or regular)
2 tablespoons sliced toasted almonds (page 30)
2 tablespoons shaved dark chocolate

1. Place the cake mix and baking soda in a large bowl, and stir to mix well. Add the coffee, applesauce, and egg substitute, and beat with an electric mixer for 2 minutes.

2. Coat two 9-inch round cake pans with nonstick cooking spray, then lightly flour the bottom of each pan. Spread the batter evenly in the pans. Bake at 350°F for about 23 minutes, or just until the top springs back when lightly touched and a wooden toothpick inserted in the center of the cakes comes out clean. Be careful not to overbake. Remove the cakes from the oven, and cool in the pans on wire racks for 30 minutes. Remove the cakes from the pans and place on wire racks to cool completely.

3. To make the filling, combine the pudding mix and milk in a medium-sized bowl, and stir with a wire whisk for about 2 minutes, or until well mixed and thickened. Set aside.

4. Invert one cake layer onto a large cutting board. Using a bread knife, cut through the layer to separate it into two layers. Repeat this procedure with the second cake layer to make a total of four layers.

5. Place one cake layer, cut side up, on a serving plate, and spread it with half (about 1 cup) of the chocolate pudding, extending the filling all the way to the edges. Place another layer, cut side up, over the first layer. Stir the jam to soften it, and spread it over the cake layer. Place a third cake layer, cut side up, and spread with the remaining pudding. Place the top layer on the cake, right side up, and set aside.

6. To make the frosting, place the whipped topping in a large bowl, and gently fold in the yogurt. Spread the frosting over the sides and top of the cake, swirling with a knife. Cover the cake, and refrigerate for at least 12 hours (preferably for 24 hours) before slicing and serving. Sprinkle the almonds and chocolate over the top of the cake just before serving.

Nutritional Facts (per serving)
CALORIES: 227   CARBOHYDRATES: 46 G   CHOLESTEROL: 0 MG   FAT: 3.1 G   FIBER: 1.2 G
PROTEIN: 4.2 G   SODIUM: 395 MG   CALCIUM: 90 MG

PART FOUR

Celebrations and Parties

Each calendar year is studded with special days that invite us to share in celebrations ranging from a Halloween costume party to a Fourth of July fireworks display to the Saint Patrick's Day wearing of the green. For most of us, each of these days provides a welcome time of relaxation and festive events. Perhaps most important, each is a wonderful reason to get together with family and friends.

Over the years, the uniqueness of each holiday has come to be reflected by certain types of food and gatherings. The Fourth of July, for instance, almost always means a cookout or picnic, while Saint Patrick's Day wouldn't seem right without corned beef and a liberal sprinkling of green. With today's emphasis on healthy, low-fat eating, though, many people are now looking for new menu ideas that provide good nutrition without sacrificing good taste. The remainder of Part Four will fill the bill by presenting festive menus that will delight your guests with great-tasting, satisfying fare that is also high in nutrition.

New Year's Day

Resolving to eat more healthfully is probably *the* most common New Year's resolution. Fortunately, this hearty winter's meal, which presents two main-dish options, is just what the doctor ordered. The traditional New Year's Day meal of Hoppin' John—made with lean ham instead of fatty ham hocks—takes center stage as a high-nutrient, low-fat entrée. Rich in protein, fiber, vitamins, and minerals, beans are a perfect low-fat alternative to meat.

If Hoppin' John is not your pleasure, try an old-fashioned Pot Roast with Baby Carrots and New Potatoes. This down-home dish is sure to delight your family's meat-and-potato lovers while keeping fat and calories within reasonable limits. Side dishes like Country-Style Cabbage, Broccoli and Cauliflower Salad, Winter Fruit Salad, and Buttermilk Corn Muffins round out this simple yet satisfying meal. Last, but not least, is your choice of comforting Cranberry–Apple Crisp or luscious Chocolate Carrot Cake with cream cheese frosting. Either of these light and delicious desserts will bring a sweet conclusion to your meal.

New Year's Dinner

SERVES 6 TO 8

Hoppin' John (page 214) with Perfect Brown Rice (page 215)
or Pot Roast with Baby Carrots and New Potatoes (page 216)

Broccoli and Cauliflower Salad (page 217)
or Spinach Salad (page 218)

Country-Style Cabbage (page 219)

Winter Fruit Salad (page 219)
or Ambrosia Gelatin Salad (page 220)

Buttermilk Corn Muffins (page 221)

Cranberry-Apple Crisp (page 222)
or Chocolate Carrot Cake (page 223)

ADVANCE PLANNING TIPS:

◆ *Hoppin' John can be made the day before your dinner and reheated just before serving. Like most bean dishes, it is even better the next day.*

◆ *Wash and dry the broccoli and cauliflower florets for Broccoli and Cauliflower Salad the day before. Prepare the bacon crumbles and boiled eggs for the Spinach Salad the day before and refrigerate until ready to assemble the salads.*

◆ *Winter Fruit Salad can be made the day before your dinner if you add the bananas 30 to 60 minutes before serving. If you are making Ambrosia Gelatin Salad, do so the day before so that it has plenty of time to set.*

◆ *Mix the dry ingredients for Buttermilk Corn Muffins, cover, and set aside until ready to stir in the liquid ingredients and bake.*

◆ *Prepare Cranberry-Apple Crisp to the point of adding the topping a day in advance and refrigerate. Prepare the topping and refrigerate in a separate container. Remove from the refrigerator 30 to 60 minutes before ready to assemble and bake. Chocolate Carrot Cake can be made the day before and refrigerated until ready to serve.*

Hoppin' John

✦ *Serve over brown rice for a traditional Southern-style New Year's meal.*

YIELD: 10 SERVINGS

3 cups dried black-eyed peas
1 large, lean meaty ham bone or 2 cups diced lean ham
1½ cups chopped onion
2 teaspoons ham, chicken, or vegetable bouillon granules
2 bay leaves

1 teaspoon dried sage
¼ teaspoon ground black pepper
4 cups water

GARNISH
½ cup plus 2 tablespoons finely chopped seeded plum tomato
½ cup plus 2 tablespoons thinly sliced scallions

1. Rinse the peas well, and place in a 6-quart pot. Cover the peas with several inches of water, and discard any that float to the top. Soak the peas for at least 4 hours, or for as long as 12 hours. (If soaking for more than 4 hours, place the bowl or pot in the refrigerator.)
2. Discard the soaking water, and return the peas to the pot. Add the ham, onions, bouillon granules, bay leaves, sage, pepper, and water. Bring the mixture to a boil, then reduce the heat to low, cover, and simmer for about 1 hour, or until the beans are soft and the liquid is thick. Stir occasionally, and add more water if needed. (The liquid should barely cover the peas.)
3. Remove the ham bone to a cutting board, remove the meat from the bones, and cut into bite-sized pieces. Add the ham back to the pot. Remove the bay leaves. Serve hot, topping each serving with some of the tomatoes and scallions. Serve over brown rice if desired.

Nutritional Facts (per 1-cup serving)
CALORIES: 196 CARBOHYDRATES: 31 G CHOLESTEROL: 8 MG FAT: 1.7 G FIBER: 8 G
PROTEIN: 16 G SODIUM: 402 MG CALCIUM: 59 MG

Perfect Brown Rice

YIELD: 8 SERVINGS

2 cups long-grain brown rice
4½ cups water

1. Place the rice in a strainer, and rinse under running water. Place the rice and water in a 3-quart pot, and bring to a boil over high heat. Reduce the heat to low, stir the rice, and cover.

2. Allow the rice to simmer, covered, for 50 minutes, or until the rice is tender and the liquid has been absorbed. Do not stir the rice while it is cooking.

3. Remove the rice from the heat, and let sit, covered, for 5 minutes. Fluff the rice with a fork, and serve hot.

Nutritional Facts (per ¾-cup serving)
CALORIES: 172 CARBOHYDRATES: 35 G CHOLESTEROL: 0 MG FAT: 1.4 G FIBER: 2.8 G
PROTEIN: 4 G SODIUM: 8 MG CALCIUM: 15 MG

Pot Roast with Baby Carrots and New Potatoes

YIELD: 8 SERVINGS

2½- to 3-pound lean beef roast such as top round,
    eye round, bottom round, or round tip
½ teaspoon coarsely ground black pepper
10½-ounce can condensed French onion soup, undiluted
¾ cup water
½ cup medium-dry sherry
½ teaspoon dried thyme
½ teaspoon dried marjoram
1 pound baby carrots (about 3 cups)
1 pound new potatoes, halved if small or
    quartered if large (about 3 cups)

GRAVY
½ cup evaporated skim or low-fat milk
¼ cup unbleached flour

1. Trim the meat of visible fat, rinse with cool water, and pat it dry with paper towels. Sprinkle all sides of the roast with some of the pepper.

2. Coat a nonstick 6-quart pot with nonstick cooking spray, and preheat over medium-high heat. Place the meat in the pot, and cook for several minutes, or until all sides are nicely browned.

3. Add the undiluted soup, water, sherry, thyme, and marjoram to the pot, and let the mixture come to a boil. Reduce the heat to low, cover, and simmer for about 2¼ hours, turning the roast occasionally or until the roast is almost tender. Add the carrots and potatoes to the pot, and increase the heat to return the mixture to a boil. Reduce the heat to low, cover, and simmer for an additional 20 minutes, or until the meat and vegetables are tender.

4. Remove the roast to a cutting board, cover loosely with foil, and set aside. Using a slotted spoon, remove the vegetables to a bowl, and cover to keep warm.

5. To make the gravy, place the evaporated milk and flour in a jar with a tight-fitting lid, and shake until smooth. Set aside. Pour the pan juices into a 2-cup measure. If there is more than 1¾ cups of liquid, return it to the pot, and cook uncovered over medium-high heat for a few minutes to reduce the volume to 1¾ cups. Return the pan juices to the pot, and bring to a boil over high heat. Reduce the heat to medium-low, and slowly add the flour mixture while stirring constantly. Cook and stir for a minute or two, or until the gravy is thickened and bubbly.

6. Slice the roast thinly across the grain, and serve accompanied by the vegetables and gravy.

Nutritional Facts (per serving)
CALORIES: 301 CARBOHYDRATES: 25 G CHOLESTEROL: 75 MG FAT: 5.5 G FIBER: 2.5 G
PROTEIN: 34 G SODIUM: 391 MG CALCIUM: 48 MG

Broccoli and Cauliflower Salad

YIELD: 10 SERVINGS

3 cups small broccoli florets
3 cups small cauliflower florets
¾ cup shredded nonfat or reduced-fat Cheddar cheese
½ cup chopped red onion
½ cup dark raisins
¼ cup roasted salted sunflower seeds
3 slices extra-lean turkey bacon, cooked, drained, and crumbled

DRESSING

1 cup nonfat or light mayonnaise

2 tablespoons sugar

1 tablespoon apple cider vinegar

1. Combine the broccoli, cauliflower, cheese, onion, raisins, sunflower seeds, and bacon in a large bowl, and toss to mix well. Combine the dressing ingredients in a small bowl, and stir to mix well. Add the dressing to the salad, and toss to mix well.

2. Cover the salad and refrigerate for at least 2 hours before serving.

Nutritional Facts (per ¾-cup serving)
CALORIES: 100 CARBOHYDRATES: 16 G CHOLESTEROL: 7 MG FAT: 2 G FIBER: 2.3 G
PROTEIN: 5 G SODIUM: 319 MG CALCIUM: 84 MG

Spinach Salad

YIELD: 8 SERVINGS

8 ounces prewashed fresh spinach leaves (about 12 cups loosely packed)

2 cups sliced fresh mushrooms

1 medium carrot, shredded with a potato peeler

4 hard-boiled eggs, chopped

4 slices extra-lean turkey bacon, cooked, drained, and crumbled

½ cup shredded nonfat or reduced-fat Cheddar cheese

1 cup bottled nonfat or light ranch or buttermilk-herb salad dressing

1. Combine the spinach, mushrooms, and carrot in a large bowl and toss to mix well.

2. Place about 1½ cups of the mixture on each of 8 salad plates, and top each salad with some of the eggs, bacon, and cheese. Serve immediately accompanied by the dressing.

Nutritional Facts (per serving)
CALORIES: 124 CARBOHYDRATES: 15 G CHOLESTEROL: 116 MG FAT: 3.1 G FIBER: 1.9 G
PROTEIN: 8 G SODIUM: 542 MG CALCIUM: 92 MG

Country-Style Cabbage

1 medium-large head cabbage (about 2 pounds)
Butter-flavored nonstick cooking spray or 1 tablespoon canola oil
1 medium yellow onion, thinly sliced
1½ teaspoons ham bouillon granules
1 teaspoon dry mustard
½ cup water

1. Cut the cabbage into quarters, and trim away the core. Cut the cabbage quarters into ½ inch slices, and set aside.

2. Coat a 6-quart nonstick pot with the cooking spray or canola oil and place over medium heat. Add the onions, cover, and cook, stirring occasionally, for about 3 minutes or until the onions start to soften (do not let them brown).

3. Add the cabbage, bouillon granules, mustard, and water to the skillet, cover, and cook for 5 minutes, stirring occasionally. Reduce the heat to medium-low and cook, stirring occasionally, for an additional 7 to 10 minutes, or until the cabbage is wilted and tender. Add a little more water during cooking if the skillet becomes too dry, keeping only enough liquid in the skillet to prevent scorching. Serve hot.

Nutritional Facts (per ¾-cup serving)
CALORIES: 31 CARBOHYDRATES: 7 G CHOLESTEROL: 0 MG FAT: 0.4 G FIBER: 2.5 G
PROTEIN: 1.4 G SODIUM: 138 MG CALCIUM: 50 MG

Winter Fruit Salad

YIELD: 8 SERVINGS

6 medium navel oranges
2 tablespoons honey
1½ cups seedless red grapes

2 medium Empire, Red Delicious, or Gala apples, unpeeled and diced

¼ cup plus 2 tablespoons sliced toasted almonds or pecans (page 30)

2 medium-small bananas, peeled and sliced

1. Peel the oranges, cutting down to the flesh. Cut the orange segments away from the membranes, and place the orange segments and the juices that have accumulated in a large bowl. Mix the honey into 2 tablespoons of the juice from the bowl of oranges, then add the honey-juice mixture to the oranges and toss to mix well.

2. Add the grapes, apples, and almonds or pecans to the oranges, and toss to mix well. Cover the mixture and refrigerate for at least 1 hour. Add the bananas to the salad 30 to 60 minutes before serving.

Nutritional Facts (per 1-cup serving)
CALORIES: 155 CARBOHYDRATES: 33 G CHOLESTEROL: 0 MG FAT: 3 G FIBER: 4.7 G
PROTEIN: 2.6 G SODIUM: 2 MG CALCIUM: 58 MG

Ambrosia Gelatin Salad

YIELD: 9 SERVINGS

8-ounce can crushed pineapple in juice, undrained

11-ounce can mandarin oranges in juice or light syrup, undrained

1 package (4-serving size) sugar-free or regular orange gelatin mix

8 ounces nonfat or low-fat coconut cream or piña colada yogurt

½ cup mini marshmallows

¼ cup chopped toasted pecans (page 30)

1½ cups nonfat or light whipped topping

1. Drain the fruits, reserving ½ cup plus 2 tablespoons of the combined juices. Set aside.

2. Place the gelatin mix in a large bowl. Place the juice in a small pot, and bring to a boil over high heat. Pour the boiling juice over the gelatin mix, and stir with a wire whisk for 3 minutes, or until the gelatin mix is completely dissolved. Set aside for 20 minutes, or until the mixture has cooled to room temperature.

3. When the gelatin mixture has reached room temperature, add the yogurt, and whisk until smooth. Place the gelatin mixture in the refrigerator for 15 minutes. Stir the mixture; it should be the consistency of pudding. If it is too thin, return it to the refrigerator for a few minutes.

4. When the gelatin mixture has reached the proper consistency, stir it with a wire whisk until smooth. Fold in first the drained pineapple, oranges, marshmallows, and pecans, and then the whipped topping.

5. Spread the mixture evenly into an 8-by-8-inch (2-quart) square dish, and chill for at least 6 hours, or until firm, before cutting into squares and serving. Alternatively, spread the mixture into a 6-cup mold, chill for at least 6 hours, and unmold onto a large serving plate just before serving.

Nutritional Facts (per serving)
CALORIES: 102   CARBOHYDRATES: 18 G   CHOLESTEROL: 0 MG   FAT: 2.7 G   FIBER: 0.7 G
PROTEIN: 2.3 G   SODIUM: 51 MG   CALCIUM: 46 MG

Buttermilk Corn Muffins

✴ *For the softest, lightest texture, be sure to use only finely ground cornmeal in this recipe.*

YIELD: 12 MUFFINS

1¾ cups finely ground cornmeal
2 tablespoons sugar
2 teaspoons baking powder
¼ teaspoon baking soda
⅛ teaspoon salt
2 cups nonfat or low-fat buttermilk
¼ cup plus 2 tablespoons fat-free egg substitute
   or 2 large eggs, lightly beaten
2 tablespoons canola oil

1. Place the cornmeal, sugar, baking powder, baking soda, and salt in a large bowl, and stir to mix well.

2. Place the buttermilk, egg substitute or eggs, and oil in a small bowl, and stir to mix well. Add the buttermilk mixture to the cornmeal mixture, and stir to mix well.

3. Coat muffin cups with nonstick cooking spray, and fill three-quarters full with the batter. Bake at 375°F for about 16 minutes, or just until a wooden toothpick inserted in the center of a muffin comes out clean. Be careful not to overbake.

4. Remove the muffin tin from the oven, and allow it to sit for 5 minutes before removing the muffins. Serve warm.

Nutritional Facts (per muffin)
CALORIES: 132 CARBOHYDRATES: 22 G CHOLESTEROL: 1 MG FAT: 2.9 G FIBER: 1.7 G
PROTEIN: 4 G SODIUM: 215 MG CALCIUM: 96 MG

Variation:

To make **Buttermilk Cornbread,** coat a large ovenproof skillet with nonstick cooking spray and spread the batter evenly in the skillet. Bake at 400°F for about 25 minutes, or until a wooden toothpick inserted in the center of the bread comes out clean. Be careful not to overbake. Let sit for 5 minutes before cutting into wedges and serving.

Cranberry-Apple Crisp

YIELD: 8 SERVINGS

2 cans (20-ounces each) light (reduced-sugar) apple pie filling
¼ cup dried sweetened cranberries
1 quart low-fat vanilla ice cream (optional)

TOPPING
½ cup old-fashioned (5-minute) rolled oats
3 tablespoons whole wheat pastry flour or unbleached flour
¼ cup plus 2 tablespoons light brown sugar
½ teaspoon ground cinnamon
2 tablespoons margarine or butter, cut into pieces

2 teaspoons frozen apple juice concentrate, thawed
⅓ to ½ cup chopped walnuts or pecans

1. Place the pie filling and the cranberries in a large bowl, and stir to mix well. Coat a 9-inch deep-dish pie pan with nonstick cooking spray, and spread the mixture evenly in the dish.
2. To make the topping, place the oats, flour, brown sugar, and cinnamon in a medium-sized bowl, and stir to mix well. Using a pastry cutter or two knives, cut in the margarine or butter until the mixture is crumbly. Add the juice concentrate, and stir lightly to mix. Add a little more juice concentrate if the mixture seems too dry. Add the nuts, and toss lightly to mix.
3. Spread the oat mixture over the fruit mixture, bake at 375°F for 30 to 35 minutes, or until the fruit mixture is bubbly around the edges and the topping is golden brown. Cover the dish loosely with foil during the last few minutes of baking if the topping starts to brown too quickly. Remove the dish from the oven, and let sit for at least 20 minutes before serving warm. Top each serving with a scoop of vanilla ice cream if desired.

Nutritional Facts (per serving)
CALORIES: 241 CARBOHYDRATES: 42 G CHOLESTEROL: 0 MG FAT: 6.1 G FIBER: 3.1 G
PROTEIN: 2.5 G SODIUM: 94 MG CALCIUM: 16 MG

Chocolate Carrot Cake

YIELD: 18 SERVINGS

1½ cups unbleached flour
½ cup cocoa powder (preferably Dutch processed cocoa powder)
1½ cups sugar
1¼ teaspoons baking soda
1 teaspoon ground cinnamon
¼ teaspoon salt
½ cup orange juice
½ cup plus 1 tablespoon fat-free egg substitute
   or 3 large eggs, lightly beaten
⅓ cup canola oil

1½ teaspoons vanilla extract

3 cups (not packed) grated carrots (about 6 medium)

½ cup dark raisins

½ cup chopped walnuts or toasted pecans (page 30) (optional)

FROSTING

8-ounce block nonfat or reduced-fat cream cheese,
*   softened to room temperature*

¼ cup sugar

1 package (4-serving size) instant white chocolate
*   pudding mix (sugar-free or regular)*

½ cup skim or low-fat milk

1½ cups nonfat or light whipped topping

1. Place the flour, cocoa powder, sugar, baking soda, cinnamon, and salt in a large bowl, and stir to mix well. Add the orange juice, egg substitute or eggs, oil, vanilla extract, and carrots, and stir to mix well. Fold in the raisins, and if desired, the nuts.

2. Coat a 9-by-13-inch pan with nonstick cooking spray, and spread the batter evenly in the pan. Bake at 300°F for about 40 minutes, or until the top springs back when lightly touched and a wooden toothpick inserted in the center of the cake comes out clean or coated with a few fudgy crumbs. Remove the cake from the oven, and cool to room temperature.

3. To make the frosting, place the cream cheese and sugar in a medium-sized bowl, and beat with an electric mixer until smooth. Add the pudding mix and milk, and beat to mix well. (If you are using reduced-fat cream cheese instead of nonfat, increase the milk to ⅔ cup.) Gently fold in the whipped topping.

4. Spread the frosting over the cake, cover, and refrigerate for at least 3 hours before cutting into squares and serving.

Nutritional Fact (per serving)
CALORIES: 218 CARBOHYDRATES: 41 G CHOLESTEROL: 1 MG FAT: 4.5 G FIBER: 1.7 G
PROTEIN: 4.7 G SODIUM: 285 MG CALCIUM: 60 MG

Valentine's Day

If great food is the key to your loved one's heart, this simple but elegant Valentine's Day dinner is sure to win his or her affections. Get things started with a beautiful salad of mixed baby greens topped with fresh raspberries and a sprinkling of feta cheese and walnuts. For the main course, choose from robust Penne with Shrimp and Sun-Dried Tomatoes or sweet and savory Apricot-Glazed Tenderloins with Broccoli-Rice Pilaf. Paired with Parsleyed Baby Carrots, either entrée will fill you up without weighing you down. For dessert, this menu offers two delightful options—Chocolate-Raspberry Sundaes made with light ice cream or a light and luscious cherry mousse garnished with shaved chocolate and glazed almonds. So set the mood with lovely dishes, linens, flowers, and candlelight, and settle in for a romantic evening for two.

Valentine's Day Dinner

SERVES 2

Mixed Baby Salad Greens with Fresh Raspberries (page 227)

Penne with Shrimp and Sun-Dried Tomatoes (page 228)
or Apricot-Glazed Tenderloins (page 229)
with Broccoli-Rice Pilaf (page 230)

Parsleyed Baby Carrots (page 230)

Multigrain or Sourdough Dinner Rolls

Chocolate-Raspberry Sundaes (page 231)
or Light Cherry Mousse (page 232)

Mixed Baby Salad Greens with Fresh Raspberries

YIELD: 2 SERVINGS

4 cups prewashed mixed baby salad greens

½ cup fresh raspberries

2 tablespoons crumbled nonfat or reduced-fat feta cheese

1½ tablespoons chopped walnuts

3 tablespoons bottled light raspberry vinaigrette salad dressing

1. Place half of the greens on each of 2 serving plates. Top the greens on each plate with half of the raspberries, feta cheese, and walnuts.

2. Drizzle some of the dressing over each salad and serve immediately.

Nutritional Facts (per serving)
CALORIES: 109 CARBOHYDRATES: 10 G CHOLESTEROL: 1 MG FAT: 6.8 G FIBER: 4.8 G
PROTEIN: 4.5 G SODIUM: 253 MG CALCIUM: 100 MG

Penne with Shrimp and Sun-Dried Tomatoes

YIELD: 2 SERVINGS

4 ounces penne pasta

1½ teaspoons extra virgin olive oil

8 ounces shelled and deveined raw shrimp

¼ cup chopped sun-dried tomatoes

3 tablespoons sliced black olives

½ cup chicken or vegetable broth

¾ teaspoon crushed garlic

½ teaspoon dried Italian seasoning

⅛ teaspoon coarsely ground black pepper

½ cup coarsely chopped canned artichoke hearts, drained

2 tablespoons finely chopped fresh parsley

2 to 3 tablespoons crumbled nonfat or reduced-fat feta cheese

1. Cook the pasta al dente according to package directions. Drain well, return to the pot, and toss with the olive oil. Cover to keep warm.
2. While the pasta is cooking, place the shrimp, sun-dried tomatoes, olives, broth, garlic, Italian seasoning, and pepper in a large nonstick skillet. Cover and cook over medium heat for 4 minutes, or until the shrimp turn pink and the tomatoes have plumped. Add the artichoke hearts and cook for another 30 seconds to heat through.
3. Reduce the heat to low and add the pasta to the skillet mixture. Tossing gently, cook for a minute or two, or until the mixture is heated through.
4. Serve hot, topping each serving with a sprinkling of parsley and feta cheese.

Nutritional Facts (per 2-cup serving)
CALORIES: 416   CARBOHYDRATES: 52 G   CHOLESTEROL: 173 MG   FAT: 7.4 G   FIBER: 5.1 G
PROTEIN: 34 G   SODIUM: 650 MG   CALCIUM: 134 MG

Apricot-Glazed Tenderloins

✿ *For variety, substitute orange marmalade or raspberry jam for the apricot preserves.*

YIELD: 2 SERVINGS

8 ounces turkey or pork tenderloins,
   sliced crosswise into 4 equal pieces
⅛ teaspoon garlic powder
⅛ teaspoon salt
⅛ teaspoon coarsely ground black pepper
¼ teaspoon dried rosemary or thyme
1½ teaspoons extra virgin olive oil
1 tablespoon thinly sliced scallions

SAUCE
2 tablespoons apricot jam or fruit spread
¼ cup chicken broth
1½ teaspoons balsamic vinegar
¾ teaspoon Dijon mustard

1. To make the sauce, place the sauce ingredients in a small bowl and stir to mix well. Set aside.
2. Rinse the tenderloins with cool water and pat dry with paper towels. With the cut side up, use the palm of your hand to flatten each piece to slightly less than ½ inch thick. Sprinkle both sides of the tenderloins with some of the garlic powder, salt, pepper, and rosemary or thyme and set aside.
3. Coat a large nonstick skillet with the olive oil and preheat over medium-high heat. Add the tenderloins and cook for about 2 to 3 minutes on each side or until nicely browned and no longer pink inside. Remove the tenderloins from the skillet and set aside to keep warm.
4. Pour the sauce into the skillet and cook, stirring constantly, for a couple of minutes, or until the sauce is reduced by about half and is syrupy.
5. To serve, place half of the tenderloins on each of 2 serving plates, drizzle with the sauce, and top with a sprinkling of the scallions. Serve hot accompanied by Broccoli-Rice Pilaf (page 230).

Nutritional Facts (per serving)
CALORIES: 210   CARBOHYDRATES: 14 G   CHOLESTEROL: 70 MG   FAT: 4.3 G   FIBER: 0.3 G
PROTEIN: 28 G   SODIUM: 321 MG   CALCIUM: 21 MG

Broccoli-Rice Pilaf

✷ *For variety, substitute whole wheat couscous, bulgur wheat, or orzo for the rice.*

YIELD: 2 SERVINGS

1 cup small fresh broccoli florets
1½ cups cooked brown rice (or half brown rice and half wild rice)
2 teaspoons reduced-fat margarine or light butter
⅛ teaspoon salt

1. Place the broccoli and 2 tablespoons of water in a small nonstick skillet and place over medium heat. Cover and cook, stirring several times, for about 3 minutes or until the broccoli is crisp-tender. Add a little more water if needed but only enough to prevent scorching.
2. Add the rice, margarine or butter, and salt to the broccoli and cook, stirring frequently, for a minute or two, or until the margarine or butter is melted and the mixture is heated through. Serve hot.

Nutritional Facts (per 1¼-cup serving)
CALORIES: 187   CARBOHYDRATES: 35 G   CHOLESTEROL: 0 MG   FAT: 3.1 G   FIBER: 3.7 G
PROTEIN: 4.8 G   SODIUM: 195 MG   CALCIUM: 31 MG

Parsleyed Baby Carrots

YIELD: 2 SERVINGS

1½ cups baby carrots
¼ cup water

Pinch salt

2 teaspoons reduced-fat margarine or light butter

1½ teaspoons finely chopped fresh parsley

1. Place the carrots, water, and salt in a small nonstick skillet and bring to a boil over medium-high heat. Reduce the heat to medium, cover, and cook for 5 minutes, or just until tender. Add a little more water during cooking if the skillet becomes too dry, but only enough to prevent scorching.

2. Add the margarine or butter to the skillet, and raise the heat to medium-high. Cook, stirring frequently, for another minute or two, or until most of the liquid evaporates. Toss in the parsley, and serve hot.

Nutritional Facts (per ⅔ cup serving)
CALORIES: 47 CARBOHYDRATES: 7 G CHOLESTEROL: 0 MG FAT: 2.1 G FIBER: 1.6 G
PROTEIN: 0.7 G SODIUM: 133 MG CALCIUM: 21 MG

Chocolate-Raspberry Sundaes

YIELD: 2 SERVINGS

1½ cups low-fat vanilla, chocolate, or cappuccino ice cream

¾ cup fresh raspberries

2 tablespoons chocolate syrup

1½ tablespoons Glazed Almonds (page 322) or chopped walnuts

1. Place a ¾-cup scoop of the ice cream in each of two 10-ounce balloon wineglasses. Top the ice cream in each glass with half of the raspberries.

2. Drizzle 1 tablespoon of chocolate syrup over each dessert and top with a sprinkling of the almonds or walnuts. Serve immediately.

Nutritional Facts (per serving)
CALORIES: 251 CARBOHYDRATES: 46 G CHOLESTEROL: 7 MG FAT: 6.6 G FIBER: 5.5 G
PROTEIN: 6.2 G SODIUM: 89 MG CALCIUM: 170 MG

Light Cherry Mousse

YIELD: 2 SERVINGS

1⅓ cups coarsely chopped fresh or frozen sweet pitted cherries
2 tablespoons sugar
2 tablespoons orange juice
⅓ cup nonfat or light sour cream
1 cup nonfat or light whipped topping
1 tablespoon shaved dark chocolate
1 tablespoon Glazed Almonds (page 322)

1. Place the cherries, sugar, and orange juice in a small nonstick skillet, and stir to mix well. Place over medium heat, cover, and cook, stirring occasionally, for 3 minutes, or until the cherries have softened and released their juices.

2. Increase the heat to medium-high, and cook uncovered, stirring frequently, for about 8 minutes more, or until the mixture is very thick and is reduced to about ⅓ cup. Transfer to a covered container and refrigerate for several hours or until well chilled.

3. When ready to assemble the desserts, fold the cherry mixture into the sour cream, then gently fold the whipped topping into the cherry–sour cream mixture. Divide the dessert between two 8-ounce balloon wineglasses. Cover and refrigerate for 1 to 3 hours before serving. Top each dessert with a sprinkling of the chocolate and almonds just before serving.

Nutritional Facts (per serving)
CALORIES: 259 CARBOHYDRATES: 52 G CHOLESTEROL: 0 MG FAT: 2 G FIBER: 3.2 G
PROTEIN: 4 G SODIUM: 54 MG CALCIUM: 72 MG

Saint Patrick's Day

Green is the theme of this lighthearted Irish holiday. In keeping with tradition, this hearty home-style dinner features green aplenty.

Get things started with a fresh Spinach and Mushroom Salad tossed with crumbled turkey bacon and a light Apple Cider Vinaigrette Dressing. Corned Beef and Cabbage, a Saint Patrick's Day tradition, is a featured entrée. By choosing the leanest brisket available, you can enjoy this hearty dish and still keep fat and calories under control. If corned beef is not your pleasure, try a steaming bowl of Chunky Split Pea Soup. Rich in fiber and protein, this tasty dish perfectly complements this holiday's green color scheme. On the side, dishes like Dilled Baby Carrots, Shamrock Fruit Salad, and a loaf of bakery-fresh caraway-rye bread round out this down-home meal. What's for dessert? Try a low-fat fudge brownie topped with a scoop of minty green ice cream or opt for a light and tender Pistachio-Almond Pound Cake.

Saint Patrick's Day Dinner

SERVES 6 TO 8

Spinach and Mushroom Salad (page 235)
with Apple Cider Vinaigrette Dressing (page 236)

Corned Beef and Cabbage (page 236)
or Chunky Split Pea Soup (page 238)

Dilled Baby Carrots (page 239)
or Sautéed Squash and Onions (page 239)

Caraway-Rye Bread

Shamrock Fruit Salad (page 240)
Saint Paddy's Day Fruit Platter (page 241)

Fudge Brownies à la Mode (page 241)
or Pistachio-Almond Pound Cake (page 242)

ADVANCE PLANNING TIPS:

◆ *Prepare the dressing and cook the bacon for Spinach and Mushroom Salad a day in advance, and refrigerate until needed.*

◆ *Cook the corned beef the day before, cover, and refrigerate overnight. Skim any fat that rises to the surface, then reheat the brisket, and proceed with the recipe as directed. Chunky Split Pea Soup can also be made the day before. Like most soups, it is even better the next day.*

◆ *Prepare Shamrock Fruit Salad the day before so that it has plenty of time to set.*

◆ *Bake the brownies for Fudge Brownies à la Mode the day before. If you are making Pistachio-Almond Pound Cake, you can do so the day before and cover with a cake shield. It will become even moister when allowed to sit overnight.*

Spinach and Mushroom Salad

Yield: 8 servings

8 ounces prewashed fresh spinach leaves (about 12 cups loosely packed)
2 cups sliced fresh mushrooms
4 thin slices red onion, separated into rings
4 slices turkey bacon, cooked, drained, and crumbled
¼ cup Apple Cider Vinaigrette Salad Dressing (page 236)

1. Combine the spinach, mushrooms, onion rings, and bacon in a large salad bowl, and drizzle with the dressing.
2. Toss to mix well, and add a little more dressing if the mixture seems too dry. Serve immediately.

Nutritional Facts (per 1½-cup serving)
CALORIES: 57 CARBOHYDRATES: 3 G CHOLESTEROL: 10 MG FAT: 3.8 G FIBER: 1.5 G
PROTEIN: 2.9 G SODIUM: 172 MG CALCIUM: 30 MG

Apple Cider Vinaigrette Salad Dressing

YIELD: ½ CUP

¼ cup extra virgin olive oil
2 tablespoons apple cider vinegar
1 tablespoon frozen apple juice concentrate, thawed
1 tablespoon honey
1½ teaspoons Dijon mustard
½ teaspoon salt
¼ teaspoon ground black pepper

1. Combine all of the ingredients in a small bowl and whisk to mix well.
2. Use immediately or cover and refrigerate until ready to serve. Let the chilled dressing sit at room temperature for a few minutes, if necessary, to liquefy the olive oil.

Nutritional Facts (per tablespoon)
CALORIES: 72 CARBOHYDRATES: 3 G CHOLESTEROL: 0 MG FAT: 6.8 G FIBER: 0 G
PROTEIN: 0 G SODIUM: 153 MG CALCIUM: 1 MG

Corned Beef and Cabbage

YIELD: 8 SERVINGS

2½- to 3-pound flat half corned beef brisket, trimmed of visible fat
1 teaspoon black peppercorns*
2 bay leaves*
1 medium-large head cabbage, cut into 8 wedges

1. Place the brisket in a 6-quart pot or Dutch oven and add the juices from the package. Add water to the pot to cover the meat by a couple of inches, then add the peppercorns and bay leaves. Bring the pot to a boil over high heat, and reduce the heat to low. Skim off and discard any foam that rises to the surface. Cover and simmer for 2½ to 3 hours, or until the meat is very tender. Add a little more water during cooking, if needed, to keep the brisket covered with water.
2. Remove the meat to a serving platter, reserving the liquid, cover loosely with foil, and let sit for 10 minutes.
3. Add the cabbage to the brisket cooking liquid and raise the heat slightly to return the mixture to a boil. Reduce the heat to low, cover, and cook for about 10 minutes, or until the cabbage is tender. Remove and discard the bay leaves.
4. To serve, slice the corned beef thinly across the grain and serve hot, accompanied by the cabbage.

Nutritional Facts (per serving)
CALORIES: 187   CARBOHYDRATES: 5 G   CHOLESTEROL: 80 MG   FAT: 5.5 G   FIBER: 2.3 G
PROTEIN: 28 G   SODIUM: 982 MG   CALCIUM: 51 MG

Note: If your brisket comes with a spice packet, omit the peppercorns and bay leaves from the recipe and use the spice packet instead.

Choosing a Corned Beef Brisket

Corned Beef and Cabbage is a Saint Patrick's Day tradition. And although brisket can be very fatty, when chosen carefully, even this dish can star in a light holiday menu. For the least fat, choose corned beef made from a flat half *brisket. After trimming away the visible fat, this cut will have just over 5 grams of fat per 3-ounce cooked serving. In contrast, a* point half *brisket has close to 12 grams of fat for the same size serving (untrimmed, this cut delivers about 24 grams of fat per serving!). Briskets that are labeled* whole brisket *include both the flat and point half sections, and will have an intermediate amount of fat.*

Many grocery stores also sell precooked corned beef briskets around the Saint Patrick's Day holiday. These products are real time-savers because all you do is heat and eat. Be sure to read labels, though, as the fat content of these products can vary from less than 5 to over 15 grams of fat per serving.

Chunky Split Pea Soup

YIELD: 8 SERVINGS

2½ cups dried split green peas

8 cups water

1 large meaty ham bone or 2 cups diced ham or smoked
    sausage (at least 97-percent lean)

1 large Spanish onion, chopped

2 cups diced potatoes

1½ cups diced carrots

1 cup sliced celery (include the leaves)

2 teaspoons ham or chicken bouillon granules

1½ teaspoons crushed garlic

2 bay leaves

1 teaspoon dried sage

½ teaspoon dried thyme

¼ teaspoon ground black pepper

1. Place all of the ingredients in a 6-quart pot and bring to a boil over high heat. Reduce the heat to low, cover, and simmer, stirring occasionally, for about 1 hour, or until the peas are soft and the liquid is thick.

2. Remove and discard the bay leaves. Remove the ham bone to a cutting board, trim the meat from the bones, and cut into bite-sized pieces. Add the ham back to the soup, and serve hot.

Nutritional Facts (per 1½-cup serving)
CALORIES: 317   CARBOHYDRATES: 53 G   CHOLESTEROL: 9 MG   FAT: 2.7 G   FIBER: 11 G
PROTEIN: 23 G   SODIUM: 544 MG   CALCIUM: 46 MG

Dilled Baby Carrots

Yield: 8 servings

6 cups baby carrots (about 1½ pounds)

¾ cup water

⅛ teaspoon salt

3 tablespoons reduced-fat margarine or light butter

1 tablespoon finely chopped fresh dill, or 1 teaspoon dried dill

1. Place the carrots, water, and salt in a large nonstick skillet and bring to a boil over medium-high heat. Reduce the heat to medium, cover, and cook for 5 to 7 minutes, or just until the carrots are tender. Add a little more water during cooking if the skillet becomes too dry, but only enough to prevent scorching.

2. Add the margarine or butter to the skillet, and raise the heat to medium-high. Cook, stirring frequently, for another minute or two, or until most of the liquid evaporates. Toss in the dill, and serve hot.

Nutritional Facts (per ⅔-cup serving)
Calories: 49 Carbohydrates: 7 g Cholesterol: 0 mg Fat: 2.3 g Fiber: 1.7 g
Protein: 0.7 g Sodium: 104 mg Calcium: 22 mg

Sautéed Squash and Onions

Yield: 8 servings

2 tablespoons reduced-fat margarine or light butter

3½ cups sliced zucchini squash (about 1 pound)

3½ cups sliced yellow squash (about 1 pound)

1 medium yellow onion, sliced ¼ inch thick and separated into rings

¾ teaspoon dried savory, dill, or parsley

½ teaspoon salt

¼ teaspoon ground black pepper

1. Place the margarine or butter in a large, deep nonstick skillet, and place over medium-high heat. Add the remaining ingredients to the skillet, cover, and cook, stirring a couple of times, for 3 minutes.

2. Reduce the heat to medium and cook, stirring occasionally, for an additional 5 minutes, or just until the squash is crisp-tender. Serve hot.

Nutritional Facts (per ¾-cup serving)
CALORIES: 36 CARBOHYDRATES: 5.5 G CHOLESTEROL: 0 MG FAT: 1.5 G FIBER: 2.1 G
PROTEIN: 1.3 G SODIUM: 172 MG CALCIUM: 23 MG

Shamrock Fruit Salad

YIELD: 9 SERVINGS

2 cans (8 ounces each) crushed pineapple in juice, undrained
½ cup boiling water
4-serving size sugar-free or regular lime gelatin mix
8-ounce block nonfat or reduced-fat (Neufchâtel) cream cheese,
    softened to room temperature
11-ounce can mandarin oranges, drained
⅓ cup chopped toasted pecans (page 30) (optional)
1½ cups nonfat or light whipped topping

1. Drain the pineapple, pouring the juices into a 1-cup measure. If necessary, add water to bring the volume up to ½ cup. Set aside.

2. Pour the boiling water into a blender and add the gelatin mix. Cover the blender, and carefully blend at low speed with the lid slightly ajar (to allow steam to escape) for about 30 seconds or until the gelatin mix is completely dissolved. Add the pineapple juice and blend again. Allow the mixture to sit in the blender for about 20 minutes, or until it reaches room temperature. Add the cream cheese and blend until smooth.

3. Pour the cream cheese mixture into a large bowl and chill for 40 minutes. Stir the mixture; it should be the consistency of pudding. If it is too thin, return it to the refrigerator for a few minutes, or until it reaches the proper consistency.

4. When the gelatin reaches the proper consistency, stir with a wire whisk until smooth. Gently fold in first the drained pineapple, mandarin oranges, and pecans and then the whipped topping. Pour the mixture into an 8-inch square pan and chill for at least 6 hours, or until firm. Cut into squares to serve.

Nutritional Facts (per ¾-cup serving)
CALORIES: 86 CARBOHYDRATES: 16 G CHOLESTEROL: 2 MG FAT: 0.5 G FIBER: 0.9 G
PROTEIN: 4.9 G SODIUM: 153 MG CALCIUM: 86 MG

Saint Paddy's Day Fruit Platter

YIELD: 8 SERVINGS

5 kiwi fruits, peeled and sliced
½ honeydew melon, peeled, seeded, and cut into small wedges
1 pound seedless green grapes

1. Arrange the kiwi slices around the outer edges of a 12-inch platter. Arrange the melon wedges, slightly overlapping in a circle within the larger circle created by the kiwi slices.
2. Arrange the grapes in the center of the platter, and serve.

Nutritional Facts (per serving)
CALORIES: 102 CARBOHYDRATES: 25 G CHOLESTEROL: 0 MG FAT: 0.6 G FIBER: 2.4 G
PROTEIN: 1.6 G SODIUM: 23 MG CALCIUM: 25 MG

Fudge Brownies à la Mode

YIELD: 8 SERVINGS

1 box (9-by-13-inch pan size) low-fat fudge brownie mix
½ cup chopped walnuts (optional)
2 cups low-fat green ice cream such as mint chocolate chip or pistachio
½ cup chocolate syrup

1. Prepare the brownies according to package directions, adding the walnuts to the batter if desired. Let the brownies cool to room temperature, then cut into 15 pieces, each 2½ by 3 inches. (Note that you will need only 8 of the brownies for this recipe.)
2. Place a brownie on a serving plate, and top with a ½-cup scoop of the ice cream. Drizzle 1 tablespoon of chocolate syrup over the top. Serve immediately.

Nutritional Facts (per serving)
CALORIES: 328   CARBOHYDRATES: 64 G   CHOLESTEROL: 5 MG   FAT: 5.2 G   FIBER: 2.7 G
PROTEIN: 5.9 G   SODIUM: 204 MG   CALCIUM: 103

Pistachio-Almond Pound Cake

YIELD: 16 SERVINGS

1 box (1 pound, 2.25 ounces) French vanilla or yellow cake mix
1 package (4-serving size) instant pistachio pudding mix
¾ cup nonfat or light sour cream
¾ cup fat-free egg substitute
¾ cup water
¼ teaspoon almond extract
3 to 4 drops green food coloring

GLAZE
⅔ cup powdered sugar
1 tablespoon nonfat or light sour cream
¼ teaspoon vanilla extract
2 tablespoons sliced almonds

1. Place the cake mix and pudding mix in a large bowl, and stir to mix well. Add the sour cream, egg substitute, water, almond extract, and food coloring and beat with an electric mixer for 2 minutes.
2. Coat a 12-cup bundt pan with nonstick cooking spray, and spread the batter evenly in the pan. Bake at 350°F for about 35 to 40 minutes, or just until the top springs back when lightly

touched and a wooden toothpick inserted in the center of the cake comes out clean. Be careful not to overbake.

3. Allow the cake to cool in the pan for 40 minutes. Then invert onto a serving platter and cool to room temperature.

4. To make the glaze, combine the powdered sugar, sour cream, and vanilla extract in a small microwave-safe bowl, and stir to mix well. Add a little more sour cream, if needed, to form a thick glaze. Microwave the glaze uncovered at high power for about 35 seconds, or until hot and runny. Drizzle the hot glaze over the cake and sprinkle with the almonds. Allow the cake to sit for at least 15 minutes before slicing and serving.

Nutritional Facts (per serving)
CALORIES: 195   CARBOHYDRATES: 39 G   CHOLESTEROL: 0 MG   FAT: 2.8 G   FIBER: 0.5 G
PROTEIN: 2.8 G   SODIUM: 319 MG   CALCIUM: 195 MG

Memorial Day

A balmy afternoon in May is the perfect time to fire up the grill and invite family and friends to enjoy this Mediterranean-inspired menu. Start your meal with a beautiful salad of mixed gourmet greens tossed in a light balsamic vinaigrette, or create a colorful salad of fresh asparagus, tomatoes, and onions garnished with feta cheese and walnuts. The main course brings two options: a grilled tenderloin of pork marinated with herbs, orange juice, and balsamic vinegar, or a Mediterranean version of that cook-out favorite, the burger. Dishes like Broccoli Twice-Baked Potatoes, Grilled Portobello Mushrooms, and a platter of seasonal fresh fruit round out the meal. For dessert, indulge guests in rich and creamy Cherry Tiramisu or cool off with dazzling Very Raspberry Pafaits. Both of these elegant desserts are a snap to make.

Memorial Day Cookout

SERVES 6 TO 8

Mixed Baby Salad Greens with Balsamic Vinaigrette (page 246)
or Springtime Asparagus Salad (page 247)

Grilled Tuscan Tenderloins (page 248)
or Burgers Mediterranean-Style (page 250)

Broccoli Twice-Baked Potatoes (page 251)
or Potato Salad Dijon (page 252)

Grilled Portobello Mushrooms (page 253)

Seasonal Fresh Fruit Platter

Cherry Tiramisu (page 254)
or Very Raspberry Parfaits (page 255)

ADVANCE PLANNING TIPS:

◆ *Make the dressing for Mixed Baby Salad Greens with Balsamic Vinaigrette the day before. Purchase prewashed salad greens, and the salad can be put together in a matter of minutes. If you are making Springtime Asparagus Salad, cook the asparagus the day before. Cover and refrigerate until you are ready to assemble the salad.*

◆ *Place the pork tenderloin in the marinade the day before so that it will be ready to grill when you are. If you are making the burgers instead, prepare the burger mixture the day before, cover, and refrigerate until ready to shape the patties. Make the sauce a day in advance, and refrigerate until ready to serve.*

◆ *Assemble Broccoli Twice-Baked Potatoes to the point of baking the day before. Cover and refrigerate. Remove from the refrigerator 30 to 60 minutes before you are ready to pop them in the oven. Potato Salad Dijon can be prepared the day before and refrigerated until ready to serve.*

◆ *Make Cherry Tiramisu the day before and refrigerate until ready to serve. If you are making Very Raspberry Parfaits, place the raspberries in the refrigerator to thaw a day in advance, so they are ready when you are.*

Mixed Baby Salad Greens with Balsamic Vinaigrette

YIELD: 8 SERVINGS

6 ounces mixed baby salad greens (about 12 cups loosely packed)
3½ tablespoons Balsamic Vinaigrette Salad Dressing (page 247)
¾ cup low-fat sourdough croutons (optional)

1. Place the greens in a large salad bowl and drizzle with the dressing.

2. Toss to mix well, and add a little more dressing if the mixture seems too dry. Toss in the croutons if desired, and serve immediately.

Nutritional Facts (per 1½-cup serving)
CALORIES: 42 CARBOHYDRATES: 3 G CHOLESTEROL: 0 MG FAT: 3.2 G FIBER: 1.4 G
PROTEIN: 1.4 G SODIUM: 71 MG CALCIUM: 31 MG

Balsamic Vinaigrette Salad Dressing

YIELD: ½ CUP

¼ cup extra virgin olive oil
2 tablespoons balsamic vinegar
2 tablespoons frozen white grape juice concentrate, thawed
½ teaspoon salt
¼ teaspoon ground black pepper
¼ teaspoon dried thyme
¼ teaspoon dry mustard

1. Combine all of the ingredients in a small jar with a tight-fitting lid, and shake to mix well.
2. Refrigerate for at least 1 hour, or until well chilled before serving. (Let the chilled dressing sit at room temperature for a few minutes to liquefy the olive oil.)

Nutritional Facts (per tablespoon)
CALORIES: 69 CARBOHYDRATES: 2 G CHOLESTEROL: 0 MG FAT: 6.7 G FIBER: 0 G
PROTEIN: 0 G SODIUM: 147 MG CALCIUM: 2 MG

Springtime Asparagus Salad

YIELD: 8 SERVINGS

1½ pounds fresh asparagus
¾ cup nonfat or light red wine vinaigrette salad dressing

3 medium plum tomatoes, thinly sliced

6 thin slices of red onion, separated into rings

¼ cup plus 2 tablespoons crumbled nonfat or reduced-fat feta cheese

3 tablespoon chopped walnuts or toasted pecans (page 30)

1. Rinse the asparagus with cool water and snap off the tough stem ends. Bring a large pot of water to a boil over high heat, add the asparagus spears, and cook for 2 to 3 minutes, or just until the spears are crisp-tender. Drain the spears, then plunge them into a bowl of ice water to stop the cooking process. Drain again and arrange the spears in a single layer on a large serving platter.

2. Drizzle the asparagus with half of the salad dressing. Arrange the tomato slices over the asparagus spears, and top with the onion rings. Drizzle the remaining dressing over the onion layer. Cover the salad and refrigerate for 1 to 3 hours. Sprinkle the feta cheese and the nuts over the salad and serve immediately.

Nutritional Facts (per serving)

CALORIES: 72 CARBOHYDRATES: 11 G CHOLESTEROL: 0 MG FAT: 2 G FIBER: 3.3 G
PROTEIN: 3.8 G SODIUM: 301 MG CALCIUM: 35 MG

Grilled Tuscan Tenderloins

YIELD: 8 SERVINGS

2 to 2½ pounds pork tenderloin

MARINADE

⅓ cup frozen orange or apple juice concentrate, thawed

2 tablespoons balsamic vinegar

2 tablespoons Dijon mustard

2 tablespoons extra virgin olive oil

2 tablespoons honey

2 teaspoons crushed garlic

1 teaspoon dried rosemary

½ teaspoon dried thyme

½ teaspoon coarsely ground black pepper

½ teaspoon salt

1. Combine all of the marinade ingredients in a small bowl, and whisk until smooth. Remove ¼ cup of the marinade, place in a small bowl, and refrigerate until ready to cook the tenderloins.

2. Rinse the tenderloins, pat dry with paper towels, and place in a shallow nonmetal container. Pour the remaining marinade over the tenderloins and lift the meat to allow the marinade to flow underneath. Cover and refrigerate for 6 to 24 hours, turning occasionally.

3. Lightly grease the grill rack with a paper towel saturated with nonstick cooking spray or dipped in a little canola oil. Place the tenderloins on the grill rack and cook, covered, over medium coals for about 25 minutes, turning occasionally, until a thermometer inserted in the thickest part of the meat reads 155° to 160° F. Baste occasionally with the reserved marinade during the last 10 minutes of cooking. If the meat starts to cook too quickly, move it slightly off center, away from the coals. Or if you have a gas grill, reduce the heat under one of the burners to low, and move the tenderloins to the low-heat side of the grill.

4. Remove the tenderloins from the grill, cover loosely with foil, and let sit for 5 minutes before slicing thinly at an angle. Serve immediately.

Nutritional Facts (per 3-ounce serving)
CALORIES: 166 CARBOHYDRATES: 3 G CHOLESTEROL: 67 MG FAT: 5 G FIBER: 0 G
PROTEIN: 24 G SODIUM: 121 MG CALCIUM: 8 MG

Variations:

To make **Grilled Tuscan Chicken,** substitute boneless skinless chicken breasts for the pork tenderloin. Cook covered, as for the pork, turning and basting occasionally, for about 12 minutes, or until the juices run clear and the meat is no longer pink inside.

For bone-in breasts, legs, and thighs, cook for about 25 minutes. If the chicken starts to cook too quickly, move the pieces slightly off center, away from the coals. Or if you have a gas grill, reduce the heat under one of the burners to low, and move the chicken to the low-heat side of the grill.

Nutritional Facts (per 3-ounce serving)
CALORIES: 167 CARBOHYDRATES: 3 G CHOLESTEROL: 72 MG FAT: 3.9 G FIBER: 0 G
PROTEIN: 26 G SODIUM: 134 MG CALCIUM: 15 MG

To make **Grilled Tuscan Tuna,** substitute tuna steaks for the pork tenderloin. Cook covered, as for the pork, but only for about 5 minutes on each side, basting occasionally, until the meat is easily flaked with a fork.

Nutritional Facts (per 3-ounce serving)
CALORIES: 143 CARBOHYDRATES: 3 G CHOLESTEROL: 51 MG FAT: 2 G FIBER: 0 G
PROTEIN: 26 G SODIUM: 112 MG CALCIUM: 20 MG

To make **Grilled Tuscan Shrimp,** substitute large peeled and deveined raw shrimp for the pork tenderloin, marinating them for only 30 minutes. Thread the shrimp onto eight 12-inch skewers as follows: Bend each shrimp almost in half, so that the large end nearly touches the smaller tail end. Insert the skewer just above the tail so that it passes through the shrimp twice. (If you are using wooden skewers, soak them in water for 20 minutes before using, to prevent burning.) Grill the skewers over medium coals for about 6 minutes, turning occasionally, or until the shrimp turn pink and are cooked through.

Nutritional Facts (per 3-ounce serving)
CALORIES: 146 CARBOHYDRATES: 3 G CHOLESTEROL: 172 MG FAT: 3 G FIBER: 0 G
PROTEIN: 23 G SODIUM: 241 MG CALCIUM: 62 MG

Burgers Mediterranean-Style

YIELD: 8 SERVINGS

1¾ pounds 95 percent lean ground beef
10-ounces frozen chopped spinach, thawed and squeezed dry
1 cup very finely chopped fresh mushrooms
¾ cup very finely chopped onion
1½ teaspoons crushed garlic
1 teaspoon beef bouillon granules
1 teaspoon dried oregano
½ teaspoon coarsely ground black pepper

SAUCE

½ cup nonfat or light mayonnaise

½ cup chopped bottled roasted red peppers

½ teaspoon crushed garlic

TOPPINGS

8 whole multigrain or sourdough burger buns

8 slices tomato

8 slices red onion

8 leaves romaine lettuce

1. To make the sauce, combine all of the sauce ingredients in a blender or food processor and process until smooth. Cover and chill until ready to cook the burgers.
2. Combine the ground beef, spinach, mushrooms, onion, garlic, bouillon granules, oregano, and pepper in a large bowl and mix thoroughly. Shape the mixture into eight 4-inch patties.
3. Lightly grease the grill rack with a paper towel saturated with nonstick cooking spray or dipped in a little canola oil. Place the patties on the rack, and cook over medium coals for about 6 minutes on each side, or until the burgers are no longer pink inside, and the internal temperature of the patties reaches 160°F. (To retain moisture, avoid pressing down on the patties as they cook.)
4. Place each burger in a bun and top with some of the sauce, a tomato slice, an onion slice, and a lettuce leaf. Serve hot.

Nutritional Facts (per serving)
CALORIES: 278 CARBOHYDRATES: 32 G CHOLESTEROL: 53 MG FAT: 6.3 G FIBER: 6.3 G
PROTEIN: 28 G SODIUM: 560 MG CALCIUM: 94 MG

Broccoli Twice-Baked Potatoes

YIELD: 10 SERVINGS

10 medium Yukon Gold baking potatoes (about 6 ounces each)
Butter-flavored nonstick cooking spray

½ cup plus 2 tablespoons skim or low-fat milk

½ cup plus 2 tablespoons nonfat or light sour cream

¼ teaspoon salt

⅛ teaspoon ground white pepper

1¼ cups shredded reduced-fat Cheddar cheese or ½ cup
*   plus 2 tablespoons grated Parmesan cheese*

10 ounces frozen chopped broccoli, thawed and squeezed dry

Ground paprika

1. Scrub the potatoes, pat dry, and spray the skins lightly with the cooking spray. Pierce each potato in several places with a fork. Place the potatoes on a large baking sheet and bake at 400°F for about 40 minutes, or until easily pierced. Allow the potatoes to cool until they can be handled easily.

2. Cut a slice ½ inch deep from the top of each potato, and carefully scoop out the pulp, leaving a ¼-inch-thick shell. Place the scooped-out potatoes and the milk, sour cream, salt, and white pepper in a large bowl, and mash with a potato masher or beat with an electric mixer until smooth. Add the cheese and broccoli, and stir to mix well.

3. Spoon the filling back into the potato skins. Arrange the potatoes on a large baking sheet, spray the tops and sides lightly with the cooking spray, and sprinkle some paprika over the top of each. Bake at 350°F for 25 to 30 minutes, or until the filling is heated through and the tops are lightly browned. Serve hot.

Nutritional Facts (per serving)
CALORIES: 206 CARBOHYDRATES: 37 G CHOLESTEROL: 8 MG FAT: 2.3 G FIBER: 3.9 G
PROTEIN: 9.6 G SODIUM: 185 MG CALCIUM: 191 MG

Potato Salad Dijon

YIELD: 8 SERVINGS

6 cups ¾-inch chunks unpeeled Yukon Gold potatoes (about 2 pounds)

¼ teaspoon salt

1 cup frozen green peas, thawed

⅓ cup coarsely chopped black olives

⅓ cup chopped red onion

DRESSING

¾ cup nonfat or light mayonnaise

1 tablespoon plus 1½ teaspoons Dijon mustard

2 teaspoons honey

⅛ teaspoon ground white pepper

1. Place the potatoes and salt in a 3-quart pot, cover with water, and bring to a boil over high heat. Reduce the heat to medium-low, cover, and cook for about 10 minutes, or until tender. Drain the potatoes, rinse with cool water, and drain again.
2. Place the potatoes in a large bowl. Add the peas, olives, and onion, and toss to mix well.
3. Place all of the dressing ingredients in a small bowl, and stir to mix. Pour the dressing over the potato mixture, and toss to mix well. Add a little more mayonnaise if the mixture seems too dry.
4. Cover the salad, and chill for at least 2 hours before serving.

Nutritional Facts (per ¾-cup serving)
CALORIES: 146 CARBOHYDRATES: 30 G CHOLESTEROL: 0 MG FAT: 1 G FIBER: 3.3 G
PROTEIN: 3.4 G SODIUM: 330 MG CALCIUM: 24 MG

Grilled Portobello Mushrooms

YIELD: 8 SERVINGS

8 large Portobello mushrooms, sliced ½ inch thick (about 1¼ pounds)

Olive oil nonstick cooking spray

½ teaspoon dried marjoram or thyme

¼ teaspoon salt

⅛ teaspoon ground black pepper

1. Spread the mushrooms in a single layer on a large baking sheet, spray both sides with the cooking spray, and sprinkle with the marjoram or thyme, salt, and pepper.

2. Transfer the mushroom slices to the grill, and cook, covered, over medium coals for about 2 minutes on each side or until browned and tender. Serve immediately.

Nutritional Facts (per serving)
CALORIES: 19 CARBOHYDRATES: 3 G CHOLESTEROL: 0 MG FAT: 0.4 G FIBER: 0.9 G
PROTEIN: 2 G SODIUM: 75 MG CALCIUM: 4 MG

Cherry Tiramisu

YIELD 9 SERVINGS

8-ounce block reduced-fat (Neufchâtel) cream cheese, softened to room temperature
1¼ cups skim or low-fat milk
1 package (4-serving size) instant cheesecake or vanilla pudding mix
18 ladyfinger cookies (about 4½ ounces) or 10 slices (½ inch thick)
   fat-free vanilla loaf cake or low-fat pound cake
6 to 8 tablespoons coffee liqueur
1¼ cups light (reduced-sugar) cherry pie filling
2 cups nonfat or light whipped topping
1½ teaspoons Dutch processed cocoa powder

1. Place the cream cheese in a medium-sized bowl, and beat with an electric mixer until smooth. Still beating, gradually add the milk, and beat until smooth. Add the pudding mix, and beat for another minute, or until well mixed and thickened. Set aside.
2. Split the ladyfingers open (most ladyfingers come presplit) and arrange half of them, split side up, in a single layer over the bottom of an 8-inch square (2-quart) dish. Alternatively, arrange half of the cake slices over the bottom of the dish. Drizzle half of the liqueur over the ladyfingers or cake slices, then spread with half of the pudding mixture. Repeat the lady-finger, liqueur, and pudding layers. Finish off with a layer of cherry pie filling and then the whipped topping. Sift the cocoa powder over the top.
3. Cover the dish and refrigerate for at least 8 hours or overnight before cutting into squares and serving.

Very Raspberry Parfaits

YIELD: 8 SERVINGS

2 packages (10 ounces each) frozen sweetened raspberries, thawed
8 (½-inch) slices angel food cake (about 6 ounces)
6 cups low-fat vanilla or chocolate swirl ice cream
¼ cup Glazed Almonds (page 322) or shaved dark chocolate

1. Place 1 tablespoon of the raspberries in the bottom of each of eight 10-ounce balloon wine-glasses.
2. Crumble a half-slice of cake over the raspberries in each glass. Top the cake with ⅓ cup of the ice cream and 2 tablespoons of the raspberries.
3. Repeat the cake, ice cream, and raspberry layers. Top each serving with some of the almonds or chocolate. Serve immediately.

Nutritional Facts (per serving)
CALORIES: 283 CARBOHYDRATES: 55 G CHOLESTEROL: 7 MG FAT: 4.4 G FIBER: 4.6 G
PROTEIN: 6.6 G SODIUM: 238 MG CALCIUM: 193 MG

The Fourth of July

This midsummer holiday is a great excuse to fire up the grill and invite friends and family to share in the bounty. Celebrate your independence from heavy eating with this light and refreshing menu. Munch on some cool, fresh melon while you wait for dinner—cantaloupes, honeydew melons, and watermelon are all plentiful this time of year.

The main course brings a slimmed-down version of that all-American favorite, the burger. Made from the leanest ground beef available and kept flavorful and juicy with plenty of chopped onions and mushrooms, these burgers are a sure-fire hit.

Keep cool with a variety of chilled make-ahead side dishes such as Picnic Potato Salad, Fresh Tomato-Basil Salad, and Three Bean Salad, all of which are substantially lighter than traditional versions. For the crowning touch, serve Summertime Short-cakes. Bursting with colorful berries, this dish is almost as American as apple pie. Don't feel like cooking? Try Patriotic Parfaits instead. This elegant dessert is a snap to assemble and appropriately displays the colors of Old Glory.

Fourth of July Cookout

S E R V E S 6 T O 8

All-American Burgers (page 258)

Picnic Potato Salad (page 259)
or Primavera Pasta Salad (page 260)

Fresh Tomato-Basil Salad (page 261)

Creamy Coleslaw (page 262)
or Three-Bean Salad (page 263)

Summertime Shortcakes (page 264)
or Patriotic Parfaits (page 265)

ADVANCE PLANNING TIPS

◆ *Prepare the burger mixture the day before. Cover and refrigerate until ready to shape the patties.*

◆ *Both Picnic Potato Salad and Primavera Pasta Salad can be made the day before and refrigerated until ready to serve.*

◆ *Both Creamy Coleslaw and Three Bean Salad can be made the day before and refrigerated until ready to serve.*

◆ *The biscuits for Summertime Shortcakes can be made the day before and stored in a covered container until ready to assemble the desserts. The topping can also be made the day before and refrigerated until needed.*

All-American Burgers

Yield: 8 servings

1¾ pounds 95 percent lean ground beef
1⅓ cups very finely chopped fresh mushrooms
1 cup very finely chopped onion
1 tablespoon plus 1 teaspoon Worcestershire sauce
1 tablespoon plus 1 teaspoon spicy mustard
1 teaspoon beef bouillon granules
¼ teaspoon ground black pepper

TOPPINGS
8 slices (¾ ounce each) reduced-fat Cheddar cheese (optional)
8 whole wheat or multigrain burger buns
½ cup ketchup, mustard, or nonfat or reduced-fat mayonnaise

8 slices tomato

8 slices onion

8 leaves lettuce

1. Combine the ground beef, mushrooms, onion, Worcestershire sauce, mustard, bouillon granules, and pepper in a large bowl and mix thoroughly. Shape the mixture into eight 4-inch patties.

2. Lightly grease the grill rack with a paper towel saturated with nonstick cooking spray or dipped in a little canola oil. Place the patties on the rack and cook over medium coals for about 6 minutes on each side, or until the burgers are no longer pink inside, and the internal temperature reaches 160°F. (To retain moisture, avoid pressing down on the patties as they cook.) If desired, lay a slice of cheese over each burger, cover the grill, and cook for another minute or just until the cheese is melted.

3. Place each burger in a bun and top with your choice of condiments, the tomato and onion slices, and a lettuce leaf. Serve hot.

Nutritional Facts (per serving)
CALORIES: 280 CARBOHYDRATES: 33 G CHOLESTEROL: 53 MG FAT: 6.3 G FIBER: 5.6 G PROTEIN: 27 G SODIUM: 624 MG CALCIUM: 63 MG

Picnic Potato Salad

YIELD: 8 SERVINGS

6 cups ¾-inch chunks unpeeled Yukon Gold potatoes
   (about 2 pounds)

¼ teaspoon salt

½ cup finely chopped celery

½ cup coarsely chopped sweet or dill pickles

¼ cup finely chopped onion

¼ cup grated carrot

2 hard-boiled eggs, chopped

Ground paprika

DRESSING

¾ cup nonfat or light mayonnaise
1 tablespoon yellow mustard
⅛ teaspoon salt
⅛ teaspoon ground black pepper

1. Place the potatoes and salt in a 3-quart pot, barely cover with water, and bring to a boil over high heat. Reduce the heat to medium-low, cover, and cook for about 10 minutes, or until tender. Drain the potatoes, rinse with cool water, and drain again.

2. Place the potatoes in a large bowl. Add the celery, pickles, onion, carrot, and eggs, and toss to mix well.

3. Place all of the dressing ingredients in a small bowl, and stir to mix. Pour the dressing over the potato mixture, and toss to mix well. Add a little more mayonnaise if the mixture seems too dry.

4. Cover the salad and chill for at least 2 hours. Sprinkle the paprika over the top just before serving.

Nutritional Facts (per ¾-cup serving)
CALORIES: 151 CARBOHYDRATES: 29 G CHOLESTEROL: 52 MG FAT: 1.4 G FIBER: 2.6 G
PROTEIN: 3.9 G SODIUM: 298 MG CALCIUM: 20 MG

Primavera Pasta Salad

YIELD: 8 SERVINGS

8 ounces tricolor rotini pasta (about 3 cups)
2 cups fresh broccoli florets
1 cup frozen whole-kernel corn, thawed
½ cup diced red bell pepper
½ cup sliced black olives
¼ cup sliced scallions
½ cup plus 2 tablespoons bottled nonfat or light red
wine vinaigrette or Italian salad dressing

1. Cook the pasta al dente according to package directions. One minute before the pasta is done, add the broccoli to the pot, and cook for another minute, or until the broccoli turns bright green and is crisp-tender. Rinse the pasta and broccoli with cool water, drain well, and return to the pot.

2. Add the corn, bell pepper, olives, and scallions to the pasta mixture, and toss to mix well. Add the salad dressing and toss again. Transfer the salad to a covered container and refrigerate for at least 2 hours before serving. Toss in a little more dressing just before serving if the salad seems too dry.

Nutritional Facts (per ⅞-cup serving)
CALORIES: 164 CARBOHYDRATES: 33 G CHOLESTEROL: 0 MG FAT: 1.5 G FIBER: 2.2 G
PROTEIN: 5 G SODIUM: 237 MG CALCIUM: 18 MG

Fresh Tomato-Basil Salad

YIELD: 8 SERVINGS

3 medium-large tomatoes, cut into wedges
  (about 3 cups)
1 medium sweet onion, cut into thin wedges
  (about 1 cup)
1 medium green bell pepper, cut into
  thin strips (about 1 cup)
¼ cup finely chopped fresh basil

DRESSING
3 tablespoons red or white wine vinegar
1 tablespoon extra virgin olive oil
1 tablespoon sugar
½ teaspoon salt
⅛ teaspoon ground black pepper

1. Combine the tomatoes, onions, bell pepper, and basil in a large bowl, and toss to mix well. Set aside.
2. Place all of the dressing ingredients in a small bowl, and stir to mix well.
3. Pour the dressing over the salad, and toss to mix well. Transfer the salad to a shallow container, cover, and refrigerate for 2 to 5 hours, stirring occasionally, before serving.

Nutritional Facts (per ½-cup serving)
CALORIES: 45 CARBOHYDRATES: 7 G CHOLESTEROL: 0 MG FAT: 2 G FIBER: 1.3 G
PROTEIN: 1 G SODIUM: 152 MG CALCIUM: 10 MG

Creamy Coleslaw

YIELD: 8 SERVINGS

6 cups finely shredded cabbage (about 1 small head)
½ cup grated carrot
¼ cup finely chopped green bell pepper

DRESSING
½ cup plus 2 tablespoons nonfat or light mayonnaise
½ cup nonfat or light sour cream
1½ to 2 tablespoons sugar
⅛ teaspoon ground black pepper

1. Place the cabbage, carrots, and bell pepper in a large bowl and toss to mix well. Combine all of the dressing ingredients in a small bowl, and stir to mix well. Add the dressing to the coleslaw mixture, and toss to mix well.
2. Cover the salad and chill for at least 8 hours or overnight before serving. Stir well before serving.

Nutritional Facts (per ⅔-cup serving)
CALORIES: 54 CARBOHYDRATES: 11 G CHOLESTEROL: 0 MG FAT: 0.2 G FIBER: 1.5 G
PROTEIN: 2 G SODIUM: 154 MG CALCIUM: 45 MG

Three-Bean Salad

2 cans (15 ounces each) green beans, drained

15-ounce can red kidney beans, rinsed and drained

15-ounce can garbanzo (chickpea) beans, rinsed and drained

½ cup finely chopped onion

3 slices extra-lean turkey bacon, cooked, drained, and crumbled

DRESSING

¼ cup plus 2 tablespoons tomato juice

¼ cup red wine vinegar

2 tablespoons sugar

1 to 2 tablespoons extra virgin olive oil

1 teaspoon crushed garlic

¼ teaspoon dried oregano

¼ teaspoon ground black pepper

1. Place the green beans, kidney beans, garbanzo beans, and onions in a large bowl and toss to mix well. Set aside.
2. Place all of the dressing ingredients in a small bowl and stir to mix well. Pour the dressing over the salad, and toss to mix well. Transfer the salad to a shallow container, cover, and refrigerate for several hours or overnight, stirring occasionally. Just before serving, sprinkle with the bacon.

Nutritional Facts (per ¾-cup serving)
CALORIES: 159 CARBOHYDRATES: 26 G CHOLESTEROL: 0 MG FAT: 2.9 G FIBER: 8 G
PROTEIN: 8 G SODIUM: 262 MG CALCIUM: 35 MG

Summertime Shortcakes

1⅔ cups unbleached flour
¼ cup plus 2 tablespoons sugar
1½ teaspoons baking powder
¼ teaspoon baking soda
⅛ teaspoon salt
¾ cup nonfat or low-fat buttermilk
2 tablespoons canola oil

BERRY MIXTURE
2½ cups sliced fresh strawberries
1¼ cups fresh raspberries
1¼ cups fresh blueberries or blackberries
½ cup sugar
3 tablespoons orange juice

TOPPING
1½ cups nonfat or light whipped topping
⅓ cup nonfat or low-fat vanilla yogurt
⅓ cup Glazed Almonds (page 322) or sliced toasted almonds (page 30) (optional)

1. To make the berry mixture, place the berries, sugar, and orange juice in a medium-sized bowl, and toss to mix well. Cover and chill for 1 to 3 hours.
2. To make the topping, place the whipped topping in a small bowl, and fold in the yogurt. Cover and chill until ready to serve.
3. To make the biscuits, place the flour, sugar, baking powder, baking soda, and salt in a medium-sized bowl, and stir to mix well. Combine the buttermilk and oil in a small bowl and stir to mix well. Add the buttermilk mixture to the flour mixture and stir just until moistened. Add a little more buttermilk if the batter seems too thick.
4. Coat a medium-sized baking sheet with nonstick cooking spray and drop heaping tablespoons of the batter onto the sheet to make 8 biscuits. Bake at 400°F for about 12 minutes, or

until the biscuits are just beginning to brown. Be careful not to overbake. Remove the biscuits from the oven and let sit for at least 15 minutes before assembling the desserts.

5. To assemble the desserts, split each biscuit open and place each biscuit bottom on an individual dessert plate. Top the biscuit half with ¼ cup of the berry mixture, the top half of the biscuit, and 2 more tablespoons of the berry mixture. Crown with a dollop of the topping, and a sprinkling of the almonds if desired. Serve immediately.

Nutritional Facts (per serving)
CALORIES: 257 CARBOHYDRATES: 51 G CHOLESTEROL: 1 MG FAT: 4.4 G FIBER: 3.6 G
PROTEIN: 4.4 G SODIUM: 172 MG CALCIUM: 107 MG

Patriotic Parfaits

YIELD: 8 SERVINGS

2 cups sliced fresh strawberries
1 cup fresh raspberries
1 cup fresh blueberries
¼ cup sugar
3 tablespoons orange juice
8 (½-inch) slices angel food cake (about 7 ounces)
6 cups low-fat vanilla ice cream

1. Place the berries, sugar, and orange juice in a medium-sized bowl and toss to mix well. Cover and chill for 1 to 3 hours.

2. To assemble the parfaits, place 1 tablespoon of the berry mixture in the bottom of each of eight 10-ounce balloon wineglasses or parfait glasses. Crumble a half-slice of cake over the berries in each glass. Top the cake with ⅓ cup of the ice cream and 2½ tablespoons of the berry mixture.

3. Repeat the cake, ice cream, and berry layers. Serve immediately.

Nutritional Facts (per serving)
CALORIES: 270 CARBOHYDRATES: 55 G CHOLESTEROL: 7 MG FAT: 3.5 G FIBER: 4.4 G
PROTEIN: 6.5 G SODIUM: 262 MG CALCIUM: 196 MG

Labor Day

As summer turns to fall, and thoughts of the school year begin, celebrate one of the last great cookout days of the year with this delightful menu. The main course brings tasty grilled chicken marinated with pineapple juice and Asian seasonings. A cool and refreshing salad, and side dishes like fresh Grilled Corn on the Cob, Citrus-Sauced Broccoli, and a platter of seasonal fresh fruit add balance and a pleasing contrast of colors and textures. For dessert, treat guests to a divine Frozen Peanut Butter Pie or spectacular Caramel Fudge Cake. Either of these confections will bring a sweet ending to a memorable holiday meal.

Labor Day Cookout

SERVES 6 TO 8

Cantonese Grilled Chicken (page 268)

Layered Garden Salad (page 270)
or Crunchy Cabbage Salad (page 271)

Grilled Corn on the Cob (page 271)

Fresh Grilled Asparagus (page 272)
or Citrus-Sauced Broccoli (page 273)

Seasonal Fresh Fruit Platter

Multigrain Dinner Rolls

Frozen Peanut Butter Pie (page 274)
or Caramel Fudge Cake (page 275)

Cantonese Grilled Chicken

YIELD: 8 SERVINGS

8 boneless skinless chicken breast halves (2 to 2½ pounds) or 4 pounds bone-in skinless chicken breast halves, thighs, and drumsticks

MARINADE
½ cup pineapple or orange juice
¼ cup reduced-sodium soy sauce
¼ cup hoisin sauce*
3 tablespoons honey
1 tablespoon roasted (dark) sesame oil
2½ teaspoons crushed garlic
1 tablespoon freshly grated ginger root or 1 teaspoon ground ginger

1. Combine all of the marinade ingredients in a small bowl, and stir to mix well. Remove ⅓ cup of the marinade, place in a small bowl, and refrigerate until ready to cook the chicken.

2. Rinse the chicken, pat dry with paper towels, and place in a shallow nonmetal container. Pour the remaining marinade over the chicken and lift the chicken to allow the marinade to flow underneath. Cover, and refrigerate for 6 to 24 hours, turning occasionally.

3. Lightly grease the grill rack with a paper towel saturated with nonstick cooking spray or dipped in a little canola oil. Place the chicken on the grill rack and cook, covered, over medium coals for about 12 minutes, turning occasionally, or until the juices run clear and the meat is no longer pink inside. Baste occasionally with the reserved marinade during the last 5 minutes of cooking. For bone-in breasts, drumsticks, and thighs, cook for about 25 minutes. If the meat starts to cook too quickly, move it slightly off center, away from the coals. Or if you have a gas grill, reduce the heat under one of the burners to low, and move the chicken to the low-heat side of the grill. Serve immediately.

Nutritional Facts (per 3-ounce serving)
CALORIES: 165 CARBOHYDRATES: 4 G CHOLESTEROL: 72 MG FAT: 3.9 G FIBER: 0 G
PROTEIN: 26 G SODIUM: 196 MG CALCIUM: 14 MG

Hoisin sauce is available in the Asian foods section of most grocery stores.

Variations:

To make **Cantonese Grilled Pork Tenderloin,** substitute pork tenderloin for the chicken. Grill the tenderloins, covered, over medium coals for about 25 minutes, turning occasionally, until a thermometer inserted in the thickest part of the meat reads 155° to 160° F. Baste occasionally with the marinade during the last 10 minutes of cooking. If the meat starts to cook too quickly, move it slightly off center, away from the coals. Or if you have a gas grill, reduce the heat under one of the burners to low, and move the tenderloins to the low-heat side of the grill. Remove the tenderloins from the grill, cover loosely with foil, and let sit for 5 minutes before slicing thinly at an angle and serving.

Nutritional Facts (per 3-ounce serving)
CALORIES: 172 CARBOHYDRATES: 4 G CHOLESTEROL: 67 MG FAT: 4.9 G FIBER: 0 G
PROTEIN: 24 G SODIUM: 180 MG CALCIUM: 7 MG

To make **Cantonese Grilled Shrimp,** substitute large shelled and deveined raw shrimp for the chicken, marinating them for only 30 minutes. Thread the shrimp onto eight 12-inch skewers as follows: Bend each shrimp almost in half, so that the large end nearly touches the smaller tail end. Insert the skewer just above the tail so that it passes through the shrimp twice. (If you are using wooden skewers, soak them in water for 20 minutes before using, to prevent burning.) Grill the skewers over medium coals for about 6 minutes, turning occasionally, or until the shrimp turn pink and are cooked through.

Nutritional Facts (per 3-ounce serving)
CALORIES: 145 CARBOHYDRATES: 4 G CHOLESTEROL: 172 MG FAT: 2.8 G FIBER: 0 G
PROTEIN: 23 G SODIUM: 301 MG CALCIUM: 61 MG

Layered Garden Salad

YIELD: 8 SERVINGS

10 cups coarsely shredded romaine lettuce (about 1 medium head)
2 cups sliced fresh mushrooms
1 cup frozen green peas, thawed
1 medium-large carrot, shredded with a potato peeler
2 hard-boiled eggs, sliced
4 thin slices red onion, separated into rings
1 cup shredded nonfat or reduced-fat Cheddar cheese
1¼ cups nonfat or light mayonnaise
5 slices turkey bacon, cooked, drained, and crumbled

1. Place the lettuce in a 4-quart glass bowl and layer the mushrooms, peas, carrots, eggs, onion rings, and ¾ cup of the cheese over the top.
2. Spread the mayonnaise in an even layer over the top of the salad, extending it all the way to the edges.
3. Cover the bowl with plastic wrap and chill for 2 to 24 hours. Just before serving, sprinkle the bacon and the remaining ¼ cup of cheese over the top of the salad, toss to mix well, and serve immediately.

Nutritional Facts (per 1½-cup serving)
CALORIES: 112 CARBOHYDRATES: 14 G CHOLESTEROL: 0 MG FAT: 1.9 G FIBER: 2.9 G
PROTEIN: 9.4 G SODIUM: 498 MG CALCIUM: 136 MG

Crunchy Cabbage Salad

YIELD: 8 SERVINGS

5 cups coarsely shredded cabbage

1-pound can pineapple tidbits in juice, well drained

8-ounce can water chestnuts, drained and chopped

½ cup shredded nonfat or reduced-fat Cheddar cheese

⅓ cup chopped toasted pecans (page 30)

¾ cup nonfat or light mayonnaise

1. Place all of the ingredients except for the mayonnaise in a large bowl and toss to mix well. Add the mayonnaise and toss again. Add a little more mayonnaise if the salad seems too dry.
2. Cover the salad and refrigerate for 2 to 12 hours before serving.

Nutritional Facts (per ¾-cup serving)
CALORIES: 100 CARBOHYDRATES: 13 G CHOLESTEROL: 0 MG FAT: 3.9 G FIBER: 3.7 G
PROTEIN: 3.6 G SODIUM: 242 MG CALCIUM: 76 MG

Grilled Corn on the Cob

YIELD: 8 SERVINGS

8 ears fresh corn with the husks on

1. Carefully peel away the outer layers of husk from each ear of corn, leaving only the silk and a single layer of husk covering the corn kernels. Trim away the long silk ends protruding from the tips of the ears.
2. Grill the corn over medium coals for 8 to 10 minutes, turning the ears every couple of minutes, until the kernels are tender and the husks are lightly charred and beginning to peel away from the ears of corn.

3. Remove the husks and silk from the ears, and serve hot, sprinkling each ear lightly with salt, pepper, and butter-flavored nonstick cooking spray or reduced-fat margarine or light butter if desired.

Nutritional Facts (per serving)
CALORIES: 83 CARBOHYDRATES: 19 G CHOLESTEROL: 0 MG FAT: 1 G FIBER: 2.5 G
PROTEIN: 2.6 G SODIUM: 13 MG CALCIUM: 2 MG

Fresh Grilled Asparagus

YIELD: 8 SERVINGS

2 pounds fresh asparagus spears
Olive oil or butter-flavored nonstick cooking spray
¼ teaspoon salt
⅛ teaspoon ground black pepper

1. Rinse the asparagus with cool water, snap off the tough stem ends, and pat dry with paper towels. Spread the asparagus in a single layer on a large baking sheet, spray all sides with the cooking spray, and sprinkle with the salt and pepper.
2. Transfer the asparagus to a grill, and cook, covered, over medium coals for about 2 minutes on each side, or just until crisp-tender. Serve hot.

Nutritional Facts (per serving)
CALORIES: 31 CARBOHYDRATES: 4 G CHOLESTEROL: 0 MG FAT: 0.4 G FIBER: 2.1 G
PROTEIN: 2.1 G SODIUM: 73 MG CALCIUM: 21 MG

Citrus-Sauced Broccoli

✿ *For variety, substitute fresh asparagus spears for the broccoli.*

YIELD: 8 SERVINGS

2 pounds fresh broccoli spears

SAUCE
3 tablespoons reduced-fat margarine or light butter
1 tablespoon lemon juice
1 tablespoon frozen orange juice concentrate
1½ teaspoons honey
¼ teaspoon dried parsley, tarragon, or thyme
⅛ teaspoon salt
⅛ teaspoon ground black pepper

1. Fill a 6-quart pot half full with water and bring to a boil over high heat. Add the broccoli and boil for about 3 minutes, or just until the broccoli is crisp-tender. Drain well and transfer to a serving platter.
2. While the broccoli is cooking, place all of the sauce ingredients in a 1-quart pot and bring to a boil over medium heat. Cook, stirring frequently, for a minute or two, or until the sauce is reduced by about one-fourth. Drizzle the sauce over the broccoli, and serve hot.

Nutritional Facts (per serving)
CALORIES: 55   CARBOHYDRATES: 6 G   CHOLESTEROL: 0 MG   FAT: 1.9 G   FIBER: 2.2 G
PROTEIN: 2.5 G   SODIUM: 74 MG   CALCIUM: 54 MG

Frozen Peanut Butter Pie

CRUST

3 large egg whites, brought to room temperature

¼ teaspoon cream of tartar

Pinch salt

¾ cup sugar

½ teaspoon vanilla extract

1 tablespoon cocoa powder

FILLING

1 cup skim or low-fat milk

1 package (4-serving size) instant white chocolate pudding mix

½ cup smooth peanut butter

8-ounce container nonfat or light whipped topping, thawed

2 tablespoons shaved dark chocolate

1. To make the crust, line a 9-inch pie pan with aluminum foil, pressing the foil firmly over the bottom and sides of the pan (do not spray with cooking spray). Set aside.
2. Place the egg whites, cream of tartar, and salt in a medium-sized bowl and beat with an electric mixer until soft peaks form when the beaters are removed. Gradually add the sugar, a tablespoon at a time, while beating continuously, until all of the sugar has been incorporated, the mixture is glossy, and stiff peaks form when the beaters are removed. Beat in the vanilla extract. Sift the cocoa over the top, then gently fold the cocoa into the whipped egg white mixture.
3. Use the back of a spoon to spread the egg white mixture evenly over the bottom and sides of the prepared pan. Build the sides up so that they are about ¾-inch higher than the rim of the pan.
4. Bake at 250°F for 1½ hours, or until the crust is dry and firm to the touch. Turn the oven off, and allow the crust to cool in the oven for 30 minutes with the door slightly ajar. Cool the crust to room temperature, carefully peel away the foil, and return the crust to the pan. (Note: The crust can be made up to 3 days in advance and stored in an airtight container until ready to use.)
5. To make the filling, place the milk and pudding mix in a large bowl, and beat with an electric mixer for 1 minute or until well mixed and thickened. Add the peanut butter and beat until

smooth, and then gently fold in the whipped topping. Spread the filling in the crust and sprinkle the shaved chocolate over the top. Cover the pie and freeze for at least 6 hours. Remove the pie from the freezer and let sit for about 15 minutes, or until slightly softened, before cutting into wedges and serving.

Nutritional Facts (per serving)
CALORIES: 281   CARBOHYDRATES: 44 G   CHOLESTEROL: 0 MG   FAT: 8.7 G   FIBER: 1.2 G
PROTEIN: 6.6 G   SODIUM: 307 MG   CALCIUM: 46 MG

Variation:

To make **Cool Ice Cream Pie,** substitute 6 cups of slightly softened low-fat ice cream such as cappuccino, cookies and cream, rocky road, peanut butter cup, or mint chocolate chip for the peanut butter filling. Be careful not to crush the crust as you fill it with the ice cream. Sprinkle the top with 2 tablespoons of shaved dark chocolate or 3 to 4 tablespoons of Glazed Almonds (page 322).

Nutritional Facts (per serving)
CALORIES: 266   CARBOHYDRATES: 53 G   CHOLESTEROL: 15 MG   FAT: 3.5 G   FIBER: 1.8 G
PROTEIN: 6 G   SODIUM: 128 MG   CALCIUM: 152 MG

Caramel Fudge Cake

YIELD: 16 SERVINGS

1 box (1 pound, 2.25 ounces) chocolate fudge cake mix
¼ teaspoon baking soda
¾ cup room temperature coffee
½ cup unsweetened applesauce
½ cup fat-free egg substitute

FILLING
4-serving size package instant butterscotch or chocolate pudding mix
*   (sugar-free or regular)*
1½ cups skim or low-fat milk
¾ cup ready-made caramel topping

FROSTING

2½ cups nonfat or light whipped topping
¼ cup ready-made caramel topping
2 tablespoons chopped toasted pecans or sliced toasted almonds (page 30)
2 tablespoons shaved dark chocolate

1. Place the cake mix and baking soda in a large bowl, and stir to mix well. Add the coffee, applesauce, and egg substitute, and beat with an electric mixer for about 2 minutes, or until well mixed.

2. Coat two 9-inch round cake pans with nonstick cooking spray, then lightly flour the bottom of each pan. Spread the batter evenly in the pans. Bake at 350°F for about 23 minutes, or just until the top springs back when lightly touched and a wooden toothpick inserted in the center of the cakes comes out clean. Be careful not to overbake. Remove the cakes from the oven, cool in the pans, on wire racks, for 30 minutes. Remove the cakes from the pans and place on wire racks to cool completely.

3. To make the filling, place the pudding mix and milk in a medium-sized bowl, and stir with a wire whisk for about 2 minutes, or until well mixed and thickened. Set aside.

4. Invert one cake layer onto a large cutting board. Using a bread knife, cut through the layer to separate it into two layers. Repeat this procedure with the second cake layer to make a total of 4 layers.

5. Place one cake layer, cut side up on a serving plate, and spread it with ¼ cup of the caramel topping followed by ½ cup of the pudding, extending the fillings all the way to the edges. Place another layer, cut side up over the first layer, and spread it with caramel topping and pudding. Place the third layer, cut side up, over the second layer, and spread with the remaining caramel topping and pudding. Place the top layer on the cake, right side up, and set aside.

6. To make the icing, combine the whipped topping and the caramel topping in a medium-sized bowl, and gently fold the two ingredients together. Spread the frosting over the sides and top of the cake, swirling with a knife. Sprinkle the pecans or almonds and shaved chocolate over the top. Cover the cake and refrigerate for at least 12 hours (preferably for 24 hours) before slicing and serving.

Nutritional Facts (per serving)
CALORIES: 237   CARBOHYDRATES: 48 G   CHOLESTEROL: 0 MG   FAT: 3.1 G   FIBER: 1 G
PROTEIN: 4.2 G   SODIUM: 421 MG   CALCIUM: 92 MG

Halloween

When the ghosts and goblins have finished making their rounds, lure them in from the chill of an October evening and warm them up with this hot and hearty buffet. As your guests arrive, greet them with steaming mugs of Hot Apple Cider, kept warm and fragrant in a Crock-Pot heated casserole or coffeemaker.

This meal's main course, Fiesta Chili, is made with lean ground beef and perked up with stewed tomatoes, green chilies, and whole kernel corn. Country Cornbread is the perfect accompaniment to a steaming bowl of chili, and a duo of make-ahead salads adds festive color and a contrast of textures. Homemade Caramel Apples or spicy Pumpkin Gingerbread add the finishing touch to this fuss-free menu.

Halloween Buffet

SERVES 8 TO 10

Hot Apple Cider (page 83)

Fiesta Chili (page 279)

Country Cornbread (page 280)

*Apple Crunch Coleslaw (page 281)
or Orange-Avocado Salad (page 282)*

Golden Glow Gelatin Salad (page 282)

*Caramel Apples (page 283)
Pumpkin Gingerbread (page 284)*

ADVANCE PLANNING TIPS:

◆ *Fiesta Chili can be made the day before the party, reheated, and kept warm in a Crock-Pot heated casserole dish or a chafing dish.*

◆ *Mix the dry ingredients for Country Cornbread, cover, and set aside until ready to stir in the liquid ingredients and bake.*

◆ *Purchase preshredded cabbage for making Apple Crunch Coleslaw, or prewashed romaine or spinach for Orange-Avocado Salad, and either dish can be assembled in a matter of minutes.*

◆ *Make Golden Glow Gelatin Salad the day before so it has plenty of time to set. Refrigerate until ready to unmold or serve.*

◆ *Make Caramel Apples the day before, and refrigerate until ready to serve. If you are making Pumpkin Gingerbread, you can do so the day before, and cover until ready to cut into squares and serve.*

Fiesta Chili

YIELD: 10 SERVINGS

2 pounds 95 percent lean ground beef
2 cans (14½ ounces each) stewed tomatoes, crushed
16-ounce can tomato sauce
1½ cups chopped onion
3 to 4 tablespoons chili powder
1 teaspoon ground cumin
2 cans (15 ounces each) red kidney or black beans, drained
2 cups frozen whole kernel corn

4-ounce can chopped green chilies

1½ cup shredded nonfat or reduced-fat Cheddar or Monterey Jack cheese (optional)

1. Coat a 6-quart pot with nonstick cooking spray, and preheat over medium heat. Add the ground beef, and cook, stirring to crumble, until the meat is no longer pink. Drain off and discard any excess fat.

2. Add the undrained tomatoes, tomato sauce, onions, chili powder, and cumin to the pot, and bring the mixture to a boil. Reduce the heat to low, cover, and simmer for 20 minutes. Add the beans, corn, and chilies, and simmer for 10 minutes more, or until the flavors are well blended. Serve hot, topping each serving with some of the cheese if desired.

Nutritional Facts (per 1¼-cup serving)
CALORIES: 261   CARBOHYDRATES: 30 G   CHOLESTEROL: 49 MG   FAT: 4.8 G   FIBER: 9.3 G
PROTEIN: 25 G   SODIUM: 488 MG   CALCIUM: 41

Country Cornbread

✲ *For the softest, lightest texture, be sure to use only finely ground cornmeal in this recipe.*

YIELD: 12 SERVINGS

2 cups finely ground cornmeal

2 tablespoons sugar

1 tablespoon plus 1 teaspoon baking powder

⅛ teaspoon salt

1¾ cups skim or low-fat milk

8-ounce can cream-style corn

¼ cup plus 2 tablespoons fat-free egg substitute or 2 large eggs, beaten

2 tablespoons canola oil

1. Place the cornmeal, sugar, baking powder, and salt in a large bowl, and stir to mix well. Add the milk, corn, egg substitute or eggs, and canola oil, and stir with a wire whisk until smooth.

2. Coat a large ovenproof skillet with nonstick cooking spray, and spread the batter evenly in the pan. Bake at 400°F for about 30 minutes, or just until a wooden toothpick inserted in the center of the bread comes out clean. Be careful not to overbake. Let sit for 5 minutes before cutting into wedges and serving.

Nutritional Facts (per serving)
CALORIES: 142 CARBOHYDRATES: 25 G CHOLESTEROL: 0 MG FAT: 2.8 G FIBER: 1.9 G
PROTEIN: 4.3 G SODIUM: 251 MG CALCIUM: 138 MG

Variations:

For a change of pace, after whisking in the liquid ingredients, fold one or more of the following ingredients into the batter:

◆ ¾ cup shredded reduced-fat Cheddar cheese

◆ 2 to 3 tablespoons finely chopped pickled jalapeño peppers

◆ 4-ounce can chopped (drained) green chilies

◆ ¼ cup cooked crumbled turkey bacon

Apple Crunch Coleslaw

YIELD: 10 SERVINGS

6 cups coarsely shredded cabbage
1 medium-small carrot, peeled and shredded with a potato peeler
1 cup diced unpeeled red apple, such as Gala or Empire
½ cup dark raisins
¼ cup plus 2 tablespoons roasted salted sunflower or pumpkin seeds
¾ cup plus 2 tablespoons nonfat or light mayonnaise

1. Combine the cabbage, carrot, apple, raisins, and sunflower or pumpkin seeds in a large bowl and toss to mix well. Add the mayonnaise, and toss again.
2. Cover the salad and refrigerate for at least 2 hours before serving.

Orange-Avocado Salad

YIELD: 10 SERVINGS

12 cups torn romaine lettuce or fresh spinach leaves
1½ cups fresh (well drained) orange sections or canned drained mandarin oranges
1½ small avocados, peeled and cut into small wedges (about 1½ cups)
5 slices red onion, separated into rings
¼ cup Citrus Vinaigrette Salad Dressing (page 173)

1. Combine the romaine or spinach, oranges, avocado wedges, and onion rings in a large bowl.
2. Pour the dressing over the salad, and toss to mix well. Add a little more dressing if the salad seems too dry. Serve immediately.

Nutritional Facts (per 1½-cup serving)
CALORIES: 93 CARBOHYDRATES: 9 G CHOLESTEROL: 0 MG FAT: 6.3 G FIBER: 3.3 G
PROTEIN: 2 G SODIUM: 66 MG CALCIUM: 42 MG

Golden Glow Gelatin Salad

YIELD: 10 SERVINGS

2 cans (8 ounces each) crushed pineapple in juice
2 packages (4-serving size each) orange gelatin mix (sugar-free or regular)
1½ cups orange juice
1½ cups grated carrots
⅓ cup finely chopped celery

½ cup chopped toasted pecans (page 30) (optional)
1 pound seedless green grapes

1. Drain the pineapple juice into a 2-cup measure and add enough water to bring the volume up to 2 cups. Place the juice mixture in a small pot and bring to a boil over high heat.
2. Place the gelatin mix in a large bowl, and add the boiling juice mixture. Stir for about 2 minutes, or until the gelatin mix is completely dissolved. Add the orange juice and stir to mix well.
3. Place the mixture in the refrigerator and chill for about 1 hour, or until the gelatin is the consistency of raw egg whites. Fold in the drained pineapple, carrots, celery, and if desired, the pecans.
4. Pour the mixture into a 2-quart ring mold lightly coated with nonstick cooking spray. Cover, and refrigerate for at least 6 hours, or until firm. Unmold* the gelatin onto a serving plate. Arrange some of the grapes in the center of the ring, and the rest around the outer edges. Slice and serve chilled. Alternatively, spread the gelatin mixture into an 8-inch (2-quart) square dish, chill until firm, and cut into squares to serve.

Nutritional Facts (per serving)
CALORIES: 90   CARBOHYDRATES: 21 G   CHOLESTEROL: 0 MG   FAT: 0.4 G   FIBER: 1.5 G
PROTEIN: 2.1 G   SODIUM: 54 MG   CALCIUM: 21 MG

*To unmold the ring, loosen the edges of the gelatin with a knife. Place a serving platter upside down over the mold, and invert the mold onto the platter. It should slide out easily. If it does not, dip the mold in warm (not hot) water for 5 to 10 seconds before unmolding.

Caramel Apples

YIELD: 10 SERVINGS

10 medium red apples, such as Empire, Red Delicious, or Gala
10 wooden popsicle sticks
10 paper cupcake liners
Butter-flavored nonstick cooking spray
1¼ pounds caramels

3 tablespoons water

¾ cup chopped walnuts (optional)

1. Rinse the apples and dry thoroughly. Insert one of the wooden sticks into the stem end of each apple. Flatten the cupcake liners and place on a large baking sheet. Spray each liner lightly with the cooking spray.

2. Place the caramels and water in a 1-quart microwave-safe bowl. Microwave at high power for 1 minute. Stir the mixture, then microwave for an additional 30 to 60 seconds, or until the caramels are melted and the mixture is smooth.

3. Quickly dip the apples into the warm caramel mixture, and turn to coat the entire surface of the apple. (If the mixture is too thick, stir in a little water, a half-teaspoon at a time, until the desired consistency is reached.) Scrape off the excess caramel, and, if desired, dip the bottom of the apples in the nuts. Set each apple in one of the prepared cupcake liners. Rewarm the mixture as necessary by placing back in the microwave for about 15 seconds.

4. Place the apples in the refrigerator for at least 30 minutes before serving.

Nutritional Facts (per serving)

CALORIES: 260 CARBOHYDRATES: 56 G CHOLESTEROL: 3 MG FAT: 3.9 G FIBER: 5.2 G PROTEIN: 2.3 G SODIUM: 120 MG CALCIUM: 67 MG

Pumpkin Gingerbread

YIELD: 18 SERVINGS

1½ cups unbleached flour

1 cup whole wheat pastry flour

1 cup sugar

1¼ teaspoons baking soda

¼ teaspoon salt

3 to 4 teaspoons ground ginger

1½ teaspoons ground cinnamon

1 teaspoon ground allspice

¾ cup cooked mashed or canned pumpkin

¾ cup molasses

¾ cup plus 2 tablespoons orange or apple juice

½ cup canola oil

¼ cup plus 2 tablespoons fat-free egg substitute or 2 large eggs, lightly beaten

Nonfat or light whipped topping (optional)

1. Place the flours, sugar, baking soda, salt, and spices in a large bowl, and stir to mix well. Combine the pumpkin, molasses, orange or apple juice, oil, and egg substitute or eggs in a medium-sized bowl, and whisk to mix well. Add the pumpkin mixture to the flour mixture, and stir with a wire whisk to mix well. Set the batter aside for 10 minutes.

2. Coat a 9-by-13-inch pan with nonstick cooking spray, whisk the batter for 15 seconds, and spread the batter evenly in the pan. Bake at 350°F for about 30 minutes, or just until the top springs back when lightly touched and a wooden toothpick inserted in the center of the cake comes out clean.

3. Let the cake cool to room temperature before cutting into squares and serving. Top each serving with a dollop of whipped topping if desired.

Nutritional Facts (per serving)

CALORIES: 202 CARBOHYDRATES: 35 G CHOLESTEROL: 0 MG FAT: 5.9 G FIBER: 1.4 G PROTEIN: 2.6 G SODIUM: 136 MG CALCIUM: 35 MG

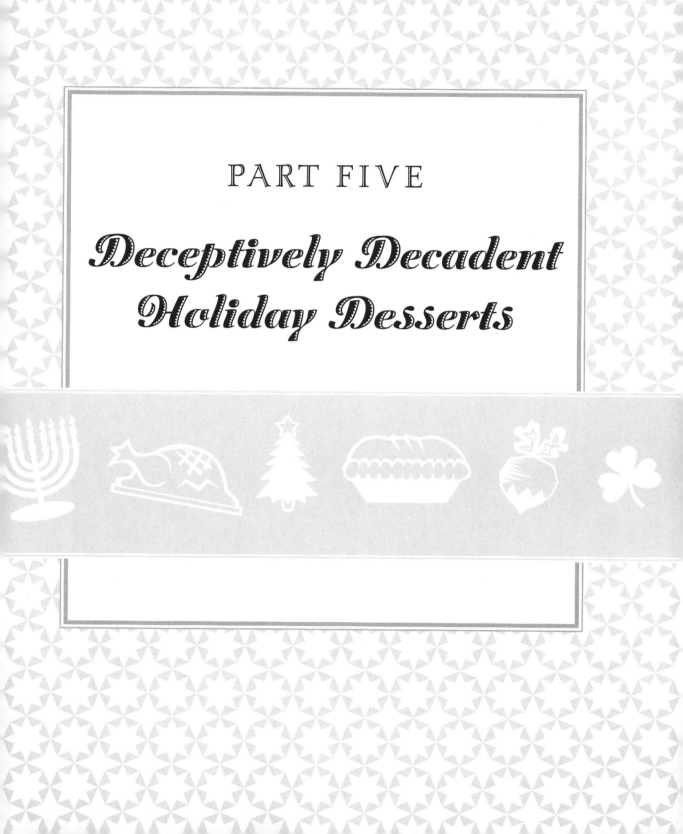

PART FIVE

Deceptively Decadent Holiday Desserts

THE HOLIDAYS BRING AN ABUNDANCE of deliciously decadent desserts and baked goods. These sweet treats are the stars of holiday parties, and are often given as gifts, as well. The recipes in this section—as well as in the holiday and party menus found in Parts Three and Four—will allow you to serve great-tasting treats that are also lighter than traditional holiday fare.

You will be delighted to discover that most of the recipes in this section are also very simple to prepare and can be made well in advance, allowing you to enjoy your party. So even if you're short on time, these simple, easy-to-follow recipes will help make your next special-occasion gathering an event to remember.

Chocolate-Raspberry Bundt Cake

1 box (1 pound, 2.25 ounces) chocolate fudge cake mix
1 teaspoon instant coffee granules
1¼ cups water
½ cup applesauce
½ cup fat-free egg substitute
½ cup seedless raspberry jam
2 tablespoons sliced almonds or chopped walnuts

1. Place the cake mix and coffee granules in a large bowl, and add the water, applesauce, and egg substitute. Beat with an electric mixer for 2 minutes. Spread the batter evenly in a 12-cup bundt pan, and bake at 350°F for about 40 minutes, or just until the top springs back when lightly touched and a wooden toothpick inserted in the center of the cake comes out clean or coated with a few fudgy crumbs. Be careful not to overbake.

2. Allow the cake to cool in the pan for 40 minutes. Then invert onto a serving platter and cool to room temperature.

3. To make the glaze, place the jam in a small pot. Place the pot over medium heat, and cook, stirring frequently, for a minute or two, or until the jam is hot and runny. Alternatively, place the jam in a 2-cup glass measure, and microwave at high power for about 1½ minutes, stirring every 30 seconds, until the jam is hot and runny. Slowly drizzle the hot jam over the top of the cake, and let the cake sit for at least 15 minutes to allow the jam to cool. Sprinkle with the almonds or walnuts just before slicing and serving. Serve with a scoop of vanilla ice cream if desired.

Nutritional Facts (per serving)
CALORIES: 166   CARBOHYDRATES: 34 G   CHOLESTEROL: 0 MG   FAT: 2.3 G   FIBER: 0.9 G
PROTEIN: 2.5 G   SODIUM: 257 MG   CALCIUM: 37 MG

Chocolate-Ripple Coffee Cake

YIELD: 16 SERVINGS

1 box (1 pound, 2.25 ounces) yellow cake mix

1 cup water

½ cup fat-free egg substitute

¼ cup plus 2 tablespoons unsweetened applesauce

COCOA FILLING

3 tablespoons Dutch processed cocoa powder

3 tablespoons chocolate syrup

½ cup finely chopped walnuts

GLAZE

⅔ cup powdered sugar

1 tablespoon Dutch processed cocoa powder

1 tablespoon skim or low-fat milk

¼ teaspoon vanilla extract

1. Place the cake mix in a large bowl, and add the water, egg substitute, and applesauce. Beat with an electric mixer for 2 minutes.

2. To make the cocoa filling, place ¾ cup of the batter in a small bowl, add the cocoa powder and chocolate syrup, and beat to mix well. Fold in the walnuts.

3. Coat a 12-cup bundt pan with nonstick cooking spray, and spread three-fourths of the yellow batter evenly in the pan. Pour all of the cocoa batter over the yellow batter, and finish off with the remaining yellow batter. Bake at 350°F for about 35 to 40 minutes, or just until the top springs back when lightly touched and a wooden toothpick inserted in the center of the cake comes out clean. Be careful not to overbake.

4. Allow the cake to cool in the pan for 40 minutes. Then invert onto a serving platter and cool to room temperature.

5. To make the glaze, combine all of the glaze ingredients in a microwave-safe bowl, and stir to mix well. Add a little more milk, if necessary, to form a thick glaze. Microwave at high power

for about 35 seconds, or until hot and runny. Drizzle the hot glaze over the cake. Allow the cake to sit for at least 15 minutes before slicing and serving.

Nutritional Facts (per serving)
CALORIES: 203   CARBOHYDRATES: 37 G   CHOLESTEROL: 0 MG   FAT: 5.1 G   FIBER: 1.8 G
PROTEIN: 3.2 G   SODIUM: 222 MG   CALCIUM: 75 MG

Lemon Poppy Seed Cake

YIELD: 16 SERVINGS

1 box (1 pound, 2.25 ounces) lemon cake mix
¾ cup nonfat or low-fat lemon yogurt
¾ cup water
½ cup fat-free egg substitute
2 tablespoons poppy seeds

GLAZE
¾ cup powdered sugar
1 tablespoon plus 1 teaspoon nonfat or low-fat lemon yogurt

1. Place the cake mix in a large bowl, and add the yogurt, water, and egg substitute. Beat with an electric mixer for 2 minutes. Mix in the poppy seeds.
2. Coat a 12-cup bundt pan with nonstick cooking spray, and spread the batter evenly in the pan. Bake at 350°F for about 35 minutes, or just until the top springs back when lightly touched and a wooden toothpick inserted in the center of the cake comes out clean. Be careful not to overbake.
3. Allow the cake to cool in the pan for 40 minutes. Then invert onto a serving platter and cool to room temperature.
4. To make the glaze, combine the powdered sugar and yogurt in a small microwave-safe bowl, and stir to mix well. Add a little more yogurt, if necessary, to form a thick glaze. Microwave uncovered at high power for about 35 seconds, or until hot and runny. Drizzle the hot glaze over the cake. Allow the cake to sit for at least 15 minutes before slicing and serving.

German Chocolate Torte

YIELD: 16 SERVINGS

1 box (1 pound, 2.25 ounces) German chocolate cake mix
¼ teaspoon baking soda
¾ cup water
½ cup unsweetened applesauce
½ cup fat-free egg substitute

FILLING
2 packages (4-serving size each) instant butterscotch
    pudding mix (sugar-free or regular)
3 cups skim or low-fat milk
¼ cup plus 2 tablespoons chopped toasted pecans (page 30)
¼ cup plus 2 tablespoons shredded sweetened coconut

FROSTING
2½ cups nonfat or light whipped topping
2 tablespoons chopped toasted pecans (page 30)
2 tablespoons shredded sweetened coconut

1. Place the cake mix and baking soda in a large bowl, and stir to mix well. Add the water, applesauce, and egg substitute, and beat with an electric mixer for 2 minutes.
2. Coat two 9-inch round cake pans with nonstick cooking spray, then lightly flour the bottom of each pan. Spread the batter evenly in the pans. Bake at 350°F for about 23 minutes, or just until the top springs back when lightly touched and a wooden toothpick inserted in the center of the cakes comes out clean. Be careful not to overbake. Remove the cakes from the oven,

and cool in the pans on wire racks for 30 minutes. Remove the cakes from the pans and place on wire racks to cool completely.

3. To make the filling, place the pudding mix and milk in a medium-sized bowl, and stir with a wire whisk for about 2 minutes, or until well mixed and thickened. Remove ½ cup of the pudding and set aside to use in the frosting. Stir the pecans and coconut into the remaining pudding and set aside.

4. Invert one cake layer onto a large cutting board. Using a bread knife, cut through the layer to separate it into two layers. Repeat this procedure with the second cake layer to make a total of four layers.

5. Place one cake layer, cut side up, on a serving plate, and spread it with one-third (about 1 cup) of the pecan-coconut filling, extending the filling all the way to the edges. Place another layer, cut side up, over the first layer, and spread it with filling in the same manner. Repeat this procedure with a third layer. Place the top layer on the cake, right side up, and set aside.

6. To make the frosting, place the whipped topping in a large bowl, and gently fold in the reserved ½ cup of pudding. Spread the frosting over the sides and top of the cake, swirling with a knife. Sprinkle the pecans and coconut over the top. Cover the cake, and refrigerate for at least 12 hours (preferably for 24 hours) before slicing and serving.

Nutritional Facts (per serving)
CALORIES: 219 CARBOHYDRATES: 38 G CHOLESTEROL: 1 MG FAT: 6 G FIBER: 1 G
PROTEIN: 4.4 G SODIUM: 362 MG CALCIUM: 93 MG

Apple-Spice Layer Cake

YIELD: 16 SERVINGS

1 box (1 pound, 2.25 ounces) spice cake mix
¼ teaspoon baking soda
¾ cup water
½ cup unsweetened applesauce
½ cup fat-free egg substitute
½ cup finely chopped walnuts (optional)

FILLING

1 package (4-serving size) instant cheesecake or
   vanilla pudding mix (sugar-free or regular)
1¼ cups skim or low-fat milk
20-ounce can apple pie filling

FROSTING

2½ cups nonfat or light whipped topping
2 tablespoons chopped walnuts

1. Place the cake mix and baking soda in a large bowl, and stir to mix well. Add the water, applesauce, and egg substitute, and beat with an electric mixer for 2 minutes. Fold in the walnuts if desired.

2. Coat two 9-inch round cake pans with nonstick cooking spray, then lightly flour the bottom of each pan. Spread the batter evenly in the pans. Bake at 350°F for about 23 minutes, or just until the top springs back when lightly touched and a wooden toothpick inserted in the center of the cakes comes out clean. Be careful not to overbake. Remove the cakes from the oven, cool in the pans, on wire racks, for 30 minutes. Remove the cakes from the pans and place on wire racks to cool completely.

3. To make the filling, place the pudding mix and milk in a medium-sized bowl, and stir with a wire whisk for about 2 minutes, or until well mixed and thickened. Set aside. Place the pie filling in a food processor and process, pulsing for several seconds at a time until the apples are finely chopped.

4. Invert one cake layer onto a large cutting board. Using a bread knife, cut through the layer to separate it into two layers. Repeat this procedure with the second cake layer to make a total of four layers.

5. Place one cake layer, cut side up, on a serving plate, and spread it with half of the apple pie filling, extending the filling all the way to the edges. Place another layer, cut side up, over the first layer, and spread it with ¾ cup of the pudding. Place the third layer, cut side up, over the second layer, and spread it with the remaining apple pie filling. Place the top layer on the cake, right side up, and set aside.

6. To make the icing, add the whipped topping to the remaining ½ cup of the pudding, and gently fold the two ingredients together. Spread the frosting over the sides and top of the cake,

swirling with a knife. Cover the cake, and refrigerate for at least 12 hours (preferably for 24 hours) before slicing and serving. Sprinkle the walnuts over the top just before serving.

Nutritional Facts (per serving)
CALORIES: 207 CARBOHYDRATES: 41 G CHOLESTEROL: 0 MG FAT: 3.3 G FIBER: 0.9 G
PROTEIN: 2.7 G SODIUM: 300 MG CALCIUM: 98 MG

Black Forest Fudge Cake

YIELD: 18 SERVINGS

1¼ cups unbleached flour

¾ cup oat flour*

½ cup Dutch processed cocoa powder

1½ cups sugar

1½ teaspoons baking soda

½ teaspoon salt

12 ounces (about 2½ cups) frozen pitted sweet cherries, thawed

½ cup room temperature coffee

¼ cup fat-free egg substitute

⅓ cup canola oil

2 teaspoons vanilla extract

½ cup chopped walnuts (optional)

FROSTING
1¼ cups nonfat or low-fat vanilla or white chocolate yogurt (sugar-free or regular)

1 (4-serving size) package instant white or dark chocolate pudding mix

2 cups nonfat or light whipped topping

3 tablespoons shaved dark chocolate or chopped walnuts

1. Place the flours, cocoa powder, sugar, baking soda, and salt in a large bowl, and stir with a wire whisk to mix well. Set aside.

2. Place the cherries, including the juice that has accumulated during thawing, and the coffee in a blender, and process until smooth. Add the cherry mixture, egg substitute, oil, and vanilla extract to the flour mixture, and whisk to mix well. Fold in the walnuts if desired.

3. Coat a 9-by-13-inch pan with nonstick cooking spray, and spread the batter evenly in the pan. Bake at 325°F for about 35 minutes, or until the top springs back when lightly touched and a wooden toothpick inserted in the center of the cake comes out clean or coated with a few fudgy crumbs. Be careful not to overbake. Remove the cake from the oven, and cool to room temperature.

4. To make the frosting, place the yogurt and pudding mix in a large bowl, and whisk to mix well. Gently fold in the whipped topping.

5. Spread the frosting over the cake, cover, and refrigerate for at least 3 hours before cutting into squares and serving. Sprinkle the chocolate or walnuts over the top just before serving.

Nutritional Facts (per serving)
CALORIES: 206 CARBOHYDRATES: 38 G CHOLESTEROL: 0 MG FAT: 4.7 G FIBER: 2 G
PROTEIN: 3.4 G SODIUM: 264 MG CALCIUM: 42 MG

*To make oat flour, process about 1 cup quick-cooking rolled oats in a food processor or blender until very finely ground. Ready-made oat flour is also available in most health foods stores and some grocery stores.

Cinnamon-Mocha Fudge Cake

YIELD: 18 SERVINGS

1¼ cups unbleached flour
¾ cup oat flour*
½ cup Dutch processed cocoa powder
1½ cups sugar
1½ teaspoons baking soda
¾ teaspoon ground cinnamon
¾ teaspoon instant coffee granules
½ teaspoon salt
1¼ cups unsweetened applesauce

½ cup water

¼ cup fat-free egg substitute

¼ cup vegetable oil

2 teaspoons vanilla extract

GLAZE

1½ cups powdered sugar

1 tablespoon Dutch processed cocoa powder

⅛ teaspoon ground cinnamon

⅛ teaspoon instant coffee granules

2 tablespoons skim or low-fat milk

½ teaspoon vanilla extract

½ cup chopped walnuts

1. Place the flours, cocoa powder, sugar, baking soda, cinnamon, coffee granules, and salt in a large bowl, and stir with a wire whisk to mix well. Add the applesauce, water, egg substitute, oil, and vanilla extract, and whisk to mix well.

2. Coat a 9-by-13-inch pan with nonstick cooking spray, and spread the batter evenly in the pan. Bake at 325°F for about 35 minutes, or just until the top springs back when lightly touched and a wooden toothpick inserted in the center of the cake comes out clean or coated with a few fudgy crumbs. Be careful not to overbake. Remove the cake from the oven, and cool to room temperature.

3. To make the glaze, place all of the glaze ingredients in a microwave-safe bowl and stir to mix well. Add a little more milk, if necessary, to form a thick glaze. Microwave uncovered at high power for about 45 to 60 seconds, or until the glaze is hot and runny. Drizzle the glaze back and forth over the cake in an S pattern, and allow the glaze to harden for at least 15 minutes before cutting into squares and serving.

Nutritional Facts (per serving)
CALORIES: 188 CARBOHYDRATES: 38 G CHOLESTEROL: 0 MG FAT: 5.8 G FIBER: 2 G
PROTEIN: 2.9 G SODIUM: 178 MG CALCIUM: 13 MG

To make oat flour, process about 1 cup quick-cooking rolled oats in a food processor or blender until very finely ground. Ready-made oat flour is also available in most health foods stores and some grocery stores.

Berries and Cream Cake

YIELD: 10 SERVINGS

1 angel food cake (1 pound)
4 cups low-fat vanilla ice cream, slightly softened
3 cups fresh strawberry slices, or 1½ cups each sliced strawberries and fresh raspberries
1½ cups fresh blueberries or blackberries
8 ounces nonfat or light whipped topping (optional)

1. With a serrated knife, cut out the center of the cake, leaving a shell that is ⅝ inch thick on the sides and ¾ inch thick on the bottom. (Reserve the cut out portion of the cake for another use.) Fill the hollowed-out cake with enough ice cream to bring the ice cream even with the top of the cake. Wrap the cake with plastic wrap and freeze for at least 12 hours.

2. Up to 2 hours before assembling the dessert, combine the berries in a large bowl. Cover and chill until ready to serve.

3. When ready to serve, place the cake in the center of a 12-inch round platter. Frost the top and sides of the cake with the whipped topping if desired. Arrange 2 cups of the fruit mixture over the top of the cake; then arrange the remaining fruit around the base. Let the cake sit for 5 minutes before slicing and serving, accompanying each piece of cake with some of the mixed fruit.

Nutritional Facts (per serving)
CALORIES: 173 CARBOHYDRATES: 36 G CHOLESTEROL: 4 MG FAT: 2.1 G FIBER: 2.9 G
PROTEIN: 4.4 G SODIUM: 233 MG CALCIUM: 124

Pumpkin Cake Roll

YIELD: 12 SERVINGS

¾ cup unbleached flour
1 cup sugar
1⅛ teaspoons baking powder

⅛ teaspoon salt

1 tablespoon pumpkin pie spice

3 large eggs

⅔ cup mashed cooked or canned pumpkin

1 teaspoon lemon juice

¼ cup powdered sugar

FILLING

8-ounce block reduced-fat (Neufchâtel) cream cheese,
*   softened to room temperature*

½ teaspoon vanilla extract

¾ cup powdered sugar

1. Line a 10-by-15-inch rimmed baking sheet or jellyroll pan with waxed paper by laying an 11-by-16-inch piece of waxed paper in the pan and folding up the sides to cover the bottom and sides of the pan. Set aside.

2. Place the flour, sugar, baking powder, salt, and pumpkin pie spice in a medium-sized bowl, and stir to mix well.

3. Place the eggs in a small bowl and beat lightly with a wire whisk. Whisk in the pumpkin and then the lemon juice. Add the pumpkin mixture to the flour mixture, and whisk until smooth.

4. Spread the batter evenly in the prepared pan, and bake at 375°F for about 10 to 12 minutes or just until the top springs back when lightly touched.

5. While the cake is baking, sift the ¼ cup of powdered sugar over a clean kitchen towel. Remove the cake from the oven and immediately invert it onto the towel. Carefully peel off the waxed paper. Starting at the short end, roll the cake and towel up together. Place on a wire rack to cool to room temperature.

6. To make the filling, place the cream cheese and vanilla extract in a medium-sized bowl and beat with an electric mixer until smooth. Add the powdered sugar and beat to mix well. Gently unroll the cooled cake and spread the filling over the cake to within ½-inch of the edges. Roll the cake up and transfer to a serving platter. Cover and refrigerate for at least 12 hours (preferably for 24 hours) before cutting into slices and serving.

Nutritional Facts (per serving)
CALORIES: 201   CARBOHYDRATES: 34 G   CHOLESTEROL: 67 MG   FAT: 5.7 G   FIBER: 0.5 G
PROTEIN: 4.3 G   SODIUM: 138 MG   CALCIUM: 24 MG

Crunchy Nutty Pie Crust

YIELD: 8 SERVINGS

Unbleached flour
1¼ cups sliced almonds
¼ cup sugar
⅛ teaspoon salt
2 teaspoons fat-free egg substitute

1. Line a 9-inch pie pan with heavy-duty aluminum foil, pressing the foil firmly against the sides of the pan. Spray the foil with nonstick cooking spray, and lightly dust with the flour. Set aside.
2. Place the almonds, sugar, and salt in the bowl of a food processor and process until the almonds are finely ground. Add the egg substitute and process for a few seconds, or just until the mixture is moist and crumbly and holds together when pinched.
3. Use the back of a spoon to spread the dough in an even layer over the bottom and sides of the foil-lined pan. Then use your fingers to finish pressing the crust into place (place your hand inside a small plastic bag or lay a piece of waxed paper over the crust as you press to prevent sticking).
4. Bake at 350°F for about 12 minutes, or until the crust feels firm and dry. Let the crust cool to room temperature, then remove from the pan, and carefully peel the foil from the crust. Return the crust to the pan, cover with plastic wrap, and store at room temperature for up to 24 hours before filling.

Nutritional Facts (per serving)
CALORIES: 120   CARBOHYDRATES: 9 G   CHOLESTEROL: 0 MG   FAT: 8.3 G   FIBER: 1.7 G
PROTEIN: 3.7 G   SODIUM: 44 MG   CALCIUM: 36 MG

Pat-In Pie Crust

YIELD: 8 SERVINGS

½ cup plus 2 tablespoons quick-cooking (1-minute) oats
½ cup plus 2 tablespoons unbleached flour

⅛ teaspoon salt

2 to 3 tablespoons canola oil

2 tablespoons skim or low-fat milk

1. Place the oats, flour, and salt in a medium bowl, and stir to mix well. Add the oil and milk, and stir until the mixture is moist and crumbly and holds together when pinched. Add a little more milk if needed.
2. Coat a 9-inch deep-dish pie pan with nonstick cooking spray. Press the dough in a thin layer over the sides and bottom of the pan, forming an even crust.
3. For a prebaked crust, prick the crust with a fork at 1-inch intervals, and bake at 400°F for about 12 minutes, or until lightly browned. Allow the crust to cool to room temperature before filling. When a prebaked crust is not desired, simply fill and bake the crust as directed in the recipe.

Nutritional Facts (per serving)
CALORIES: 86 CARBOHYDRATES: 11 G CHOLESTEROL: 0 MG FAT: 3.8 G FIBER: 0.9 G
PROTEIN: 2.1 G SODIUM: 38 MG CALCIUM: 8 MG

Graham Cracker Pie Crust

YIELD: 8 SERVINGS

1 cup reduced-fat graham cracker crumbs*

¼ cup toasted wheat germ

2 tablespoons sugar

3 tablespoons melted margarine or butter

1 tablespoon honey

1½ teaspoons fat-free egg substitute

1. Place the graham cracker crumbs, wheat germ, and sugar in the bowl of a food processor and process for a few seconds to mix well. Add the margarine or butter, honey, and egg substitute, and process, pulsing the food processor for several seconds at a time, until the mixture is

moist and crumbly and holds together when pinched. Add a little more egg substitute if the mixture seems too dry.

2. Coat a 9-inch pie pan with nonstick cooking spray, and use the back of a spoon to spread the mixture in an even layer over the bottom and sides of the pan. Then use your fingers to finish pressing the crust into place (place your hand inside a small plastic bag or lay a piece of waxed paper over the crust as you press to prevent sticking).

3. Bake at 350°F for 6 minutes, or until the edges feel dry. Let the crust cool to room temperature before filling.

Nutritional Facts (per serving)
CALORIES: 119   CARBOHYDRATES: 19 G   CHOLESTEROL: 0 MG   FAT: 4.5 G   FIBER: 0.7 G
PROTEIN: 2.1 G   SODIUM: 137 MG   CALCIUM: 2 MG

To make the graham cracker crumbs, break about 8 graham cracker sheets into small pieces, place in the bowl of a food processor, and process into fine crumbs. Or purchase ready-made graham cracker crumbs.

Simply Strawberry Pie

YIELD: 8 SERVINGS

1 prebaked Crunchy Nutty Pie Crust (page 301) or Graham Cracker Pie Crust (page 302)

FILLING
5 cups fresh strawberry halves
1½ cups ready-made strawberry glaze
1 cup nonfat or light whipped topping (optional)

1. Place the strawberries and glaze in a large bowl and toss to mix well. Spread the mixture evenly in the crust.

2. Cover the pie and refrigerate for 2 to 5 hours before cutting into wedges and serving. Top each slice with some of the whipped topping if desired.

Nutritional Facts (per serving)
CALORIES: 208 CARBOHYDRATES: 30 G CHOLESTEROL: 0 MG FAT: 8.6 G FIBER: 3.9 G
PROTEIN: 4.3 G SODIUM: 89 MG CALCIUM: 49 MG

Variation:

To make **Mixed Berry Pie,** reduce the strawberry halves to 3 cups and add 1 cup fresh raspberries plus 1 cup fresh blueberries or blackberries.

Nutritional Facts (per serving)
CALORIES: 214 CARBOHYDRATES: 31 G CHOLESTEROL: 0 MG FAT: 8.6 G FIBER: 5 G
PROTEIN: 4.3 G SODIUM: 89 MG CALCIUM: 53 MG

Light Key Lime Pie

YIELD: 8 SERVINGS

1 prebaked Graham Cracker Pie Crust (page 302) or ready-made 9-inch graham cracker
   pie crust

FILLING
14-ounce can nonfat or low-fat sweetened condensed milk
¼ cup plus 2 tablespoons fat-free egg substitute
½ cup key lime juice

TOPPING
1½ cups nonfat or light whipped topping
⅓ cup nonfat or low-fat vanilla yogurt
3 tablespoons toasted shredded sweetened coconut (optional)*

1. Place the sweetened condensed milk and egg substitute in a medium-sized bowl, and whisk to mix well. Slowly whisk in the lime juice, stirring just until combined.
2. Spread the filling evenly in the crust, and bake at 325°F for 20 minutes. Cool the pie to room temperature, then cover and chill for at least 3 hours.

3. To make the topping, place the whipped topping in a medium-sized bowl, and fold in the yogurt. Spread the topping over the pie, swirling with a knife. Sprinkle the coconut over the top if desired. Cover the pie and chill for an additional hour before cutting into wedges and serving.

Nutritional Facts (per serving)
CALORIES: 295 CARBOHYDRATES: 55 G CHOLESTEROL: 3 MG FAT: 4.8 G FIBER: 0.9 G
PROTEIN: 8.2 G SODIUM: 129 MG CALCIUM: 169 MG

*To toast the coconut, spread the coconut on a small baking sheet and bake at 350°F for about 4 minutes, stirring several times, or until lightly browned.

Creamy Lemon Pie

YIELD: 8 SERVINGS

1 prebaked Graham Cracker Pie Crust (page 302) or ready-made 9-inch graham cracker pie crust

FILLING
1 package (6-serving size) cook-and-serve lemon pudding and pie filling mix
½ cup sugar
2 tablespoons fat-free egg substitute or 2 egg yolks
¼ cup water
2 cups skim or low-fat milk
2 tablespoons frozen orange juice concentrate, thawed

TOPPING
2 cups nonfat or light whipped topping
⅓ cup nonfat or low-fat lemon yogurt

1. To make the filling, place the pudding mix, sugar, egg substitute or egg yolks, and water in a 2-quart microwave-safe bowl and stir with a wire whisk until smooth. Whisk in the milk.

Microwave at high power for 4 minutes, whisking every 2 minutes. Microwave for an additional 2 to 3 minutes, stirring every 45 to 60 seconds, or until the mixture is thick and bubbly. (The mixture may look curdled at first, but will become smooth as you keep cooking and whisking.) Remove the pudding from the microwave, whisk in the orange juice concentrate, and let sit at room temperature for 5 minutes, whisking every 2 minutes. Spread the pudding evenly into the pie crust.

2. Let the pie cool at room temperature for 30 minutes, then cover the pie and refrigerate for 3 hours.

3. To make the topping, place the whipped topping in a medium-sized bowl, and fold in the yogurt. Spread the topping over the filling, swirling with a knife. Refrigerate for an additional hour, or until the filling is well chilled and set, before cutting into wedges and serving.

Nutritional Facts (per serving)
CALORIES: 243 CARBOHYDRATES: 45 G CHOLESTEROL: 6 MG FAT: 4.8 G FIBER: 0.7 G
PROTEIN: 5 G SODIUM: 200 MG CALCIUM: 97 MG

Colossal Chocolate Cream Pie

YIELD: 8 SERVINGS

1 prebaked Graham Cracker Pie Crust (page 302) or
  ready-made 9-inch graham cracker pie crust

FILLING
2 packages (4-serving size each) sugar-free or regular
  cook-and-serve chocolate pudding mix
3½ cups skim or low-fat milk

TOPPING
1½ cups nonfat or light whipped topping
⅓ cup nonfat or low-fat vanilla yogurt
2 tablespoons sliced toasted almonds (page 30)
2 tablespoons shaved dark chocolate

1. To make the filling, place the pudding mix in a 2-quart microwave-safe bowl and slowly whisk in the milk. Microwave at high power for 4 minutes, whisking every 2 minutes. Microwave for an additional 4 minutes, whisking every minute, or until the mixture is thick and bubbly. Let the pudding sit at room temperature for 5 minutes, whisking every 2 minutes, and then spread the pudding evenly into the pie crust. Cover the pie and refrigerate for 3 hours.
2. To make the topping, place the whipped topping in a medium-sized bowl, and fold in the yogurt. Spread the topping over the filling, swirling with a knife. Refrigerate for an additional hour, or until the filling is well chilled and set, before cutting into wedges and serving. Sprinkle the almonds and chocolate over the top of the pie just before serving.

Nutritional Facts (per serving)
CALORIES: 225 CARBOHYDRATES: 35 G CHOLESTEROL: 2 MG FAT: 6.2 G FIBER: 0.9 G
PROTEIN: 6.6 G SODIUM: 424 MG CALCIUM: 154 MG

Cranberry-Pear Pie

YIELD: 8 SERVINGS

1 unbaked Pat-In Pie Crust (page 301) or 1 frozen 9-inch deep-dish pie crust, thawed

FILLING
6 cups peeled sliced pears
¼ cup dried sweetened cranberries or dried pitted sweet cherries
3 tablespoons sugar
1 tablespoon plus 1 teaspoon cornstarch
½ teaspoon ground cinnamon
¼ teaspoon ground nutmeg

TOPPING
⅓ cup honey crunch wheat germ or finely chopped pecans or walnuts
⅓ cup light brown sugar
¼ cup whole wheat pastry flour or unbleached flour
1 tablespoon reduced-fat margarine or light butter, softened to room temperature

1. To make the filling, place the pears and cranberries or cherries in a large bowl, and set aside. Combine the sugar, cornstarch, cinnamon, and nutmeg in small bowl, and stir to mix well. Sprinkle the sugar mixture over the pears, and toss to mix well.

2. Spread the filling evenly in the crust. Cover the pie loosely with a piece of aluminum foil, and bake at 400°F for 25 minutes, or until the pears begin to soften and release their juices.

3. While the pie is baking, prepare the topping by placing the wheat germ or nuts, brown sugar, and flour in a small bowl. Stir to mix well. Add the margarine or butter, and stir until the mixture is moist and crumbly. Add a little more margarine or butter if the mixture seems too dry.

4. Remove the pie from the oven, and sprinkle the topping over the pie. Reduce the oven temperature to 375°F, and bake, uncovered, for an additional 25 to 30 minutes, or until the topping is nicely browned and the filling is bubbly around the edges. Cover loosely with aluminum foil during the last few minutes of baking if the topping starts to brown too quickly.

5. Allow the pie to cool at room temperature for at least 1 hour before cutting into wedges and serving. Serve warm or at room temperature.

Nutritional Facts (per serving)
CALORIES: 267   CARBOHYDRATES: 53 G   CHOLESTEROL: 0 MG   FAT: 5.5 G   FIBER: 5.2 G   PROTEIN: 4.4 G   SODIUM: 55 MG   CALCIUM: 33 MG

Biscuit-Topped Cherry Cobbler

✲ *For variety, substitute blueberry, peach, or apple pie filling for the cherry pie filling.*

YIELD: 10 SERVINGS

2 cans (20 ounces each) light (reduced-sugar) cherry pie filling
4 cups low-fat vanilla ice cream (optional)

BISCUIT TOPPING
1¼ cups unbleached flour
⅓ cup plus 2 teaspoons sugar

1¼ teaspoon baking powder

⅛ teaspoon salt

3 tablespoons margarine or butter

¾ cup nonfat or low-fat buttermilk

1. Coat a 2½-quart casserole dish with nonstick cooking spray, and spread the cherry pie filling evenly in the dish. Cover the pan with aluminum foil and bake at 375°F for 45 minutes, or until hot and bubbly.
2. To make the biscuit topping, place the flour, ⅓ cup sugar, baking powder, and salt in a medium-sized bowl, and stir to mix well. Add the margarine or butter and buttermilk and stir just until moistened.
3. Drop heaping tablespoonfuls of the batter over the hot filling to make 8 biscuits. Sprinkle the remaining 2 teaspoons of sugar over the biscuits.
4. Bake uncovered at 375°F for about 18 minutes, or until the biscuits are just beginning to brown. Cool at room temperature for at least 20 minutes before serving warm. Top each serving with a scoop of vanilla ice cream if desired.

Nutritional Facts (per serving)

CALORIES: 244 CARBOHYDRATES: 44 G CHOLESTEROL: 0 MG FAT: 4.5 G FIBER: 2 G
PROTEIN: 2.7 G SODIUM: 188 MG CALCIUM: 70 MG

Peppermint Brownies

YIELD: 24 SERVINGS

1 package (9-by-13-inch pan size) low-fat brownie mix

¾ cup (about 4 ounces) coarsely chopped chocolate-covered peppermint wafers (like Peppermint Patties)

1. Prepare the brownie mix according to package directions. Fold in the chopped peppermint wafers.
2. Coat the bottom only of a 9-by-13-inch pan with nonstick cooking spray, and spread the mixture evenly in the pan. Bake at 325°F for about 27 minutes, or until the edges are firm and

the center is almost set. A wooden toothpick inserted 2 inches from the edges of the pan should come out coated with fudgy crumbs. Be careful not to overbake.

3. Remove the pan from the oven, and let cool to room temperature before cutting into squares and serving. For the easiest cutting, use a plastic knife.

Nutritional Facts (per brownie)
CALORIES: 118 CARBOHYDRATES: 24 G CHOLESTEROL: 0 MG FAT: 2.3 G FIBER: 0.8 G
PROTEIN: 1.5 G SODIUM: 92 MG CALCIUM: 4 MG

Variation:

Peanut Butter Brownies

Substitute diced peanut butter cup candies (like Reese's Peanut Butter Cups) for the peppermint candies.

Nutritional Facts (per brownie)
CALORIES: 124 CARBOHYDRATES: 23 G CHOLESTEROL: 0 MG FAT: 3.4 G FIBER: 0.9 G
PROTEIN: 2 G SODIUM: 106 MG CALCIUM: 4 MG

Variation:

Coconut Brownies

Substitute diced chocolate-covered coconut candy bars (like Mounds bars) for the peppermint candies.

Nutritional Facts (per brownie)
CALORIES: 121 CARBOHYDRATES: 23 G CHOLESTEROL: 0 MG FAT: 3.1 G FIBER: 1 G
PROTEIN: 1.7 G SODIUM: 98 MG CALCIUM: 1 MG

Glazed Mocha Brownies

YIELD: 24 BROWNIES

1 package (9-by-13-inch pan size) low-fat brownie mix
¾ teaspoon instant coffee granules

½ teaspoon ground cinnamon

½ cup chopped walnuts or pecans (optional)

GLAZE

1 cup powdered sugar

¼ teaspoon instant coffee granules

⅛ teaspoon ground cinnamon

1 tablespoon plus 1 teaspoon skim or low-fat milk

½ teaspoon vanilla extract

1. Combine the brownie mix, coffee granules, and cinnamon in a large bowl, and stir to mix well. Then prepare the brownie mix according to package directions. Fold in the nuts if desired.

2. Coat the bottom only of a 9-by-13-inch pan with nonstick cooking spray, and spread the mixture evenly in the pan. Bake at 325°F for about 27 minutes, or until the edges are firm and the center is almost set. A wooden toothpick inserted 2 inches from the edges of the pan should come out coated with fudgy crumbs. Be careful not to overbake. Remove the pan from the oven, and let cool to room temperature.

3. To make the glaze, combine all of the glaze ingredients in a microwave-safe bowl, and stir to mix well. Add a little more milk, if necessary, to form a thick glaze. Microwave at high power for about 45 seconds, or until hot and runny. Drizzle the hot glaze back and forth over the brownies in an S pattern. Allow the brownies to sit for at least 15 minutes before cutting into squares and serving. For the easiest cutting, use a plastic knife.

Nutritional Facts (per brownie)

CALORIES: 118   CARBOHYDRATES: 25 G   CHOLESTEROL: 0 MG   FAT: 1.9 G   FIBER: 0.8 G
PROTEIN: 1.5 G   SODIUM: 91 MG   CALCIUM: 1 MG

Golden Oatmeal Cookies

YIELD: 45 COOKIES

¼ cup plus 2 tablespoons margarine or butter,
   softened to room temperature

¾ cup light brown sugar

¼ cup pure maple syrup

3 tablespoons orange juice

1½ teaspoons vanilla extract

1½ cups quick-cooking (1-minute) oats

1 cup whole wheat pastry flour

¾ teaspoon baking soda

½ teaspoon ground cinnamon (optional)

¾ cup golden or dark raisins, pitted dried cherries, dried
   sweetened cranberries, or chopped dried apricots

¾ cup chopped almonds, walnuts, or pecans

1. Place the margarine or butter, sugar, and maple syrup in a large bowl, and beat with an electric mixer until smooth. Add the orange juice and vanilla extract, and beat to mix well.

2. Place the oats, flour, baking soda, and if desired, the cinnamon in a medium-sized bowl, and stir to mix well. Add the flour mixture to the margarine or butter mixture, and beat to mix well. Stir in the fruit and nuts.

3. Coat a large baking sheet with nonstick cooking spray, and drop level tablespoonfuls of the dough onto the sheets, spacing them at least 1½ inches apart. Flatten each cookie slightly with the tip of a spoon. Bake one sheet at a time at 325°F, for about 10 to 12 minutes, or until the cookies are lightly browned.

4. Remove the cookies from the oven, and cool the cookies on the pan for 3 minutes. Then transfer the cookies to wire racks to cool completely. Serve immediately, or transfer to an airtight container until ready to serve.

Nutritional Facts (per cookie)
CALORIES: 65 CARBOHYDRATES: 10 G CHOLESTEROL: 0 MG FAT: 2.6 G FIBER: 0.7 G
PROTEIN: 1.1 G SODIUM: 38 MG CALCIUM: 8 MG

Variation:

To make **Mocha-Oatmeal Cookies,** beat ½ teaspoon instant coffee granules into the margarine mixture and substitute cocoa powder for ⅓ cup of the whole wheat flour. Substitute semisweet chocolate chips for half of the raisins if desired.

Nutritional Facts (per cookie)
CALORIES: 69 CARBOHYDRATES: 10 G CHOLESTEROL: 0 MG FAT: 2.8 G FIBER: 1.1 G
PROTEIN: 1.3 G SODIUM: 39 MG CALCIUM: 14 MG

Fudge-Walnut Drops

YIELD: 40 COOKIES

½ cup dark raisins

⅓ cup brandy

3 cups powdered sugar

⅔ cup Dutch processed cocoa powder

2 tablespoons unbleached flour

1 teaspoon instant coffee granules

¼ teaspoon salt

⅛ teaspoon baking soda

½ cup fat-free egg substitute

1 teaspoon vanilla extract

2 cups chopped walnuts

1. Combine the raisins and brandy in a small bowl, cover, and allow the raisins to soak for at least 12 hours. (You can soak the raisins in the brandy in the refrigerator for up to 1 week.)
2. Combine the powdered sugar, cocoa powder, flour, coffee granules, salt, and baking soda in a medium bowl, and stir to mix well. (Note: When measuring the sugar and cocoa, lightly spoon them into measuring cups; then level the top with the flat edge of a knife.)
3. Add the egg substitute and vanilla extract to the cocoa mixture, and stir to mix well. The mixture will seem dry at first, but will form a thick brownie-like batter as you keep stirring. Drain the raisins, without pressing, and add them to the batter. Stir in the walnuts.

4. Coat a large baking sheet with aluminum foil; then spray the foil with nonstick cooking spray. Drop level tablespoonfuls of the batter onto the sheet, spacing them 1½ inches apart. Flatten each cookie with the tip of a spoon to ½ inch thickness. Bake one sheet at a time at 350°F for 12 to 14 minutes, or until the tops are firm to the touch and the centers are almost set. Cool the cookies on the pan for 2 minutes; then transfer to a wire rack to cool completely. Serve immediately, or transfer to an airtight container until ready to serve.

Nutritional Facts (per cookie)
CALORIES: 82 CARBOHYDRATES: 11 G CHOLESTEROL: 0 MG FAT: 4 G FIBER: 0.9 G
PROTEIN: 1.6 G SODIUM: 26 MG CALCIUM: 11 MG

Raspberry-Walnut Bars

✤ *For variety, substitute apricot jam for the raspberry jam and pecans for the walnuts.*

YIELD: 16 SERVINGS

¾ cup unbleached flour
¾ cup quick-cooking (1-minute) oats
¼ cup plus 2 tablespoons light brown sugar
½ teaspoon baking powder
3 tablespoons chilled margarine or butter, cut into pieces
2 tablespoons pure maple syrup
1 tablespoon fat-free egg substitute
1 teaspoon vanilla extract
⅓ cup chopped walnuts
½ cup raspberry jam

1. Place the flour, oats, brown sugar, and baking powder in the bowl of a food processor, and process for a few seconds to mix well. Add the margarine or butter, maple syrup, egg substitute, and vanilla extract, and process, pulsing the food processor for several seconds at a time, until the mixture is moist and crumbly and holds together when pinched.

2. Remove ½ cup of the crumbs, and mix with the walnuts. Set aside.

3. Coat an 8-inch square pan with nonstick cooking spray, and pat the remaining crumb mixture firmly into the bottom of the pan, forming an even layer. Spread the jam in an even layer over the crust, extending the filling to within ⅛ inch of each edge. Sprinkle the crumb-walnut mixture over the jam.

4. Bake at 325°F for about 30 minutes, or until the jam starts to bubble around the edges and the top is lightly browned. Cool to room temperature, cut into squares, and serve.

Nutritional Facts (per cookie)
CALORIES: 149   CARBOHYDRATES: 27 G   CHOLESTEROL: 0 MG   FAT: 3.8 G   FIBER: 0.9 G
PROTEIN: 1.9 G   SODIUM: 30 MG   CALCIUM: 14 MG

Citrus-Ginger Crisps

YIELD: 42 COOKIES

¼ cup plus 2 tablespoons margarine or butter, softened to room temperature
¾ cup sugar
¼ cup plus 2 tablespoons pure maple syrup
¼ cup orange juice
1 teaspoon vanilla extract
1½ cups whole wheat pastry flour
¾ cup plus 2 tablespoons unbleached flour
1 teaspoon baking soda
1½ to 2 teaspoons ground ginger
1 teaspoon ground cinnamon
¼ teaspoon dried grated lemon rind

COATING
3 tablespoons sugar

1. Place the margarine or butter, the ¾ cup sugar, and the maple syrup in a large bowl and beat with an electric mixer until smooth. Add the orange juice and the vanilla extract, and beat to mix well.

2. Combine the flours, baking soda, ginger, cinnamon, and lemon rind in a small bowl, and stir to mix well. Add the flour mixture to the margarine or butter mixture, and beat to mix well. Place the dough in the freezer for about 5 minutes, or just until firm enough to shape.

3. Coat a baking sheet with nonstick cooking spray. Using your hands, shape the dough into 1-inch balls. Roll the balls in the sugar coating; then arrange on the baking sheet, spacing them 1½ inches apart

4. Bake at 325°F for about 13 to 15 minutes, or until the tops are crackled and the centers are almost set. Cool the cookies on the pan for 3 minutes. Then transfer to wire racks, and cool completely. Serve immediately, or transfer to an airtight container. If the cookies become too chewy during storage, tear off several 1-inch chunks of bread, add to the container with the cookies, and let sit for several hours or overnight. The moisture from the bread will seep into the cookies and soften them.

Nutritional Facts (per cookie)
CALORIES: 62 CARBOHYDRATES: 11 G CHOLESTEROL: 0 MG FAT: 1.7 G FIBER: 0.6 G
PROTEIN: 0.9 G SODIUM: 47 MG CALCIUM: 3 MG

Variation:

To make **Cinnamon-Cocoa Crisps,** omit the ginger and lemon rind, reduce the unbleached flour to ¾ cup, and add ¼ cup plus 2 tablespoons Dutch processed cocoa powder to the dry ingredients.

Nutritional Facts (per cookie)
CALORIES: 60 CARBOHYDRATES: 11 G CHOLESTEROL: 0 MG FAT: 1.9 G FIBER: 0.9 G
PROTEIN: 0.9 G SODIUM: 47 MG CALCIUM: 4 MG

Cranberry Crunch Biscotti

YIELD: 36 BISCOTTI

1 cup plus 2 tablespoons whole wheat pastry flour
1 cup plus 2 tablespoons unbleached flour

1 cup sugar

2 teaspoons baking powder

¼ teaspoon dried grated lemon or orange rind

½ cup plus 2 tablespoons fat-free egg substitute or 3 large eggs, lightly beaten

2 tablespoons melted margarine or butter

1½ teaspoons vanilla extract

1 cup dried sweetened cranberries or pitted dried sweet cherries

1 cup chopped toasted almonds, pecans, or hazelnuts (page 30)

1. Place the flours, sugar, baking powder, and lemon or orange rind in a large bowl, and stir to mix well.

2. Place the egg substitute or eggs, margarine or butter, and vanilla extract in a small bowl, and stir to mix well.

3. Add the egg mixture along with the cranberries or cherries and nuts to the flour mixture, and stir just until the dry ingredients are moistened and the dough holds together and leaves the sides of the bowl.

4. Turn the dough onto a floured surface and divide the dough into two pieces. Shape each piece into a 12-by-2-inch log. Coat a large baking sheet with nonstick cooking spray, and place the logs on the sheet, spacing them at least 4 inches apart to allow for spreading. Bake at 350°F for about 25 minutes, or until lightly browned and firm to the touch.

5. Remove the pan from the oven, and let the logs cool on the pan for at least 30 minutes. Transfer the logs to a cutting board, and use a serrated knife to slice them diagonally into ½-inch-thick slices.

6. Arrange the biscotti slices, standing upright, on the cookie sheet, and bake at 300°F for 15 to 20 minutes, or until dry and lightly browned. Transfer the biscotti to wire racks, and cool completely. Serve immediately, or transfer to an airtight container.

Nutritional Facts (per cookie)
CALORIES: 86   CARBOHYDRATES: 14 G   CHOLESTEROL: 0 MG   FAT: 2.5 G   FIBER: 1.2 G
PROTEIN: 2 G   SODIUM: 42 MG   CALCIUM: 26 MG

Variation:

To make **Cocoa Crunch Biscotti,** reduce the whole wheat and unbleached flours to ¾ cup each and add ¾ cup Dutch processed cocoa powder to the dry ingredients. Substitute ground cinnamon for the lemon or orange rind. Substitute semisweet chocolate chips for the dried cranberries.

Nutritional Facts (per cookie)
CALORIES: 93 CARBOHYDRATES: 14 G CHOLESTEROL: 0 MG FAT: 3.9 G FIBER: 1.6 G
PROTEIN: 2.3 G SODIUM: 45 MG CALCIUM: 30 MG

Meringue Kisses

✸ *For best results, make these crispy treats on a nonhumid day and be sure there is no yolk mixed in with the egg whites.*

YIELD: 48 COOKIES

4 large egg whites, warmed to room temperature
¼ teaspoon cream of tartar
⅛ teaspoon salt
¾ cup sugar
1½ teaspoons vanilla extract

1. Place the egg whites in the bowl of an electric mixer and beat on high speed for about 1 minute, or until foamy. Add the cream of tartar and salt, and continue beating until soft peaks form when the beaters are raised. Still beating, slowly add the sugar, 1 tablespoon at a time. Beat the mixture just until stiff peaks form when the beaters are raised. Beat in the vanilla extract.

2. Line 2 large baking sheets with aluminum foil. (Do not grease the sheet or coat it with cooking spray.) Drop slightly rounded tablespoons of the mixture onto the baking sheet, spacing them 1 inch apart.

3. Bake at 250°F for 25 minutes, switch the positions of the pans in the oven, and bake for an additional 25 minutes, or until firm to the touch. Turn the oven off, and allow the meringues to cool in the oven for 30 minutes with the door closed. Remove the pans from the oven, cool to room temperature, and peel the meringues from the foil. Serve immediately, or transfer to an airtight container.

Nutritional Facts (per cookie)
CALORIES: 13   CARBOHYDRATES: 3 G   CHOLESTEROL: 0 MG   FAT: 0 G   FIBER: 0 G
PROTEIN: 0.3 G   SODIUM: 10 MG   CALCIUM: 0 MG

Variations:

To make **Brown Sugar Meringues,** substitute light brown sugar for the white sugar. If desired, add nuts or chocolate chips as directed in any of the following variations.

Nutritional Facts (per cookie)
CALORIES: 13   CARBOHYDRATES: 3 G   CHOLESTEROL: 0 MG   FAT: 0 G   FIBER: 0 G
PROTEIN: 0.3 G   SODIUM: 16 MG   CALCIUM: 0 MG

To make **Cocoa Meringues,** sift 1½ to 2 tablespoons cocoa powder over the finished meringue batter and then beat for a few seconds to mix in the cocoa. If desired, add nuts or chocolate chips as directed in any of the following variations.

Nutritional Facts (per cookie)
CALORIES: 14   CARBOHYDRATES: 3.5 G   CHOLESTEROL: 0 MG   FAT: 0 G   FIBER: 0 G
PROTEIN: 0.3 G   SODIUM: 10 MG   CALCIUM: 0 MG

To make **Nutty Meringues** fold 1 cup chopped toasted pecans, almonds, or hazelnuts (page 30) into the finished meringue batter.

Nutritional Facts (per cookie)
CALORIES: 30   CARBOHYDRATES: 3.5 G   CHOLESTEROL: 0 MG   FAT: 1.8 G   FIBER: 0.2 G
PROTEIN: 0.5 G   SODIUM: 10 MG   CALCIUM: 2 MG

To make **Cinnamon-Walnut Meringues,** fold 1 cup chopped walnuts and ¼ to ½ teaspoon ground cinnamon into the finished meringue batter.

Nutritional Facts (per cookie)
CALORIES: 30   CARBOHYDRATES: 3.5 G   CHOLESTEROL: 0 MG   FAT: 1.6 G   FIBER: 0.2 G
PROTEIN: 0.6 G   SODIUM: 10 MG   CALCIUM: 3 MG

To make **Chocolate Chip Meringues,** fold 1 cup semisweet or mint chocolate chips into the finished meringue batter.

Nutritional Facts (per cookie)
CALORIES: 30   CARBOHYDRATES: 5 G   CHOLESTEROL: 0 MG   FAT: 1 G   FIBER: 0.2 G
PROTEIN: 0.4 G   SODIUM: 11 MG   CALCIUM: 1 MG

To make **Chocolate-Pecan Meringues,** fold ½ cup coarsely chopped semisweet or bittersweet chocolate or semisweet chocolate chips and ½ cup chopped toasted pecans (page 30) into the finished meringue batter.

Nutritional Facts (per cookie)
CALORIES: 30 CARBOHYDRATES: 4 G CHOLESTEROL: 0 MG FAT: 1.4 G FIBER: 0.2 G
PROTEIN: 0.5 G SODIUM: 11 MG CALCIUM: 1.7 MG

To make **Coconut Meringues,** fold 1¼ cups shredded sweetened coconut into the finished meringue batter.

Nutritional Facts (per cookie)
CALORIES: 25 CARBOHYDRATES: 4 G CHOLESTEROL: 0 MG FAT: 0.9 G FIBER: 0.1 G
PROTEIN: 0.3 G SODIUM: 11 MG CALCIUM: 1 MG

Cherry-Vanilla Trifle

✺ *For variety, substitute cheesecake pudding mix for the vanilla.*

YIELD: 9 SERVINGS

2 cups skim or low-fat milk
1 package (4-serving size) cook-and-serve or instant vanilla pudding mix
8 slices (½ inch each) fat-free vanilla loaf cake or low-fat pound cake
3 tablespoons amaretto liqueur
1 can (20 ounces) light (reduced-sugar) cherry pie filling

TOPPING
2 cups nonfat or light whipped topping
¾ cup nonfat or low-fat vanilla yogurt
3 tablespoons sliced toasted almonds (page 30)

1. Use the milk to prepare the pudding according to package directions. Cover the mixture and refrigerate until well chilled and thickened.

2. Arrange 4 of the cake slices in a single layer over the bottom of a 2-quart glass bowl, and drizzle half of the liqueur over the cake. Spread half of the pudding over the cake, and follow with a layer of half of the pie filling. Repeat the cake, liqueur, pudding, and pie filling layers.

3. To make the topping, place the whipped topping in a medium-sized bowl, and gently fold in the yogurt. Spread the mixture over the top of the pie filling.

4. Cover the dish, and chill for at least 3 to 8 hours before serving. Sprinkle the almonds over the top just before serving.

Nutritional Facts (per serving)
CALORIES: 227 CARBOHYDRATES: 45 G CHOLESTEROL: 0 MG FAT: 1.9 G FIBER: 1.2 G
PROTEIN: 4.2 G SODIUM: 292 MG CALCIUM: 114 MG

Tiramisu Treats

YIELD: 6 SERVINGS

15 ladyfingers (about 4 ounces)
8 to 10 tablespoons coffee liqueur
¾ cup nonfat or light whipped topping
2 to 3 teaspoons Dutch processed cocoa powder
¼ cup Glazed Almonds (page 322) (optional)

PUDDING MIXTURE
4 ounces block-style reduced-fat (Neufchâtel) cream cheese, softened to room temperature
2 cups skim or low-fat milk
1 package (4-serving size) instant cheesecake or vanilla pudding mix

1. To make the pudding mixture, place the cream cheese in a medium-sized bowl and beat until smooth. Add ¼ cup of the milk and beat to mix well. Slowly beat in the remaining milk, and then add the pudding mix, and beat for 2 additional minutes or until well mixed and thickened.

2. To assemble the desserts, coarsely crumble 1¼ ladyfingers into the bottom of each of six 8-ounce balloon wineglasses. Top the ladyfingers with 2 to 2½ teaspoons of the liqueur and

about 3 tablespoons of the pudding. Repeat the layers, and top each serving with some of the whipped topping. Sift some of the cocoa powder over the top of each dessert. Cover the desserts and refrigerate for 4 to 24 hours before serving. If desired, top each serving with a sprinkling of the Glazed Almonds just before serving.

Nutritional Facts (per serving)

CALORIES: 249 CARBOHYDRATES: 34 G CHOLESTEROL: 46 MG FAT: 5.5 G FIBER: 0.4 G PROTEIN: 6.9 G SODIUM: 483 MG CALCIUM: 153 MG

Variation:

For variety and extra color, top each layer of ladyfingers with a rounded tablespoon of fresh raspberries or diced fresh apricots.

Glazed Almonds

✸ *Crisp and sweet, Glazed Almonds add a simple but elegant touch to a variety of holiday dishes. Use as a garnish for ice cream, puddings, parfaits, cakes, tortes, and many other confections. Or sprinkle over fresh fruit or a fresh green salad to add great texture and flavor.*

YIELD: 2½ CUPS

½ cup sugar
Pinch salt
2 tablespoons water
2 cups sliced almonds

1. Place the sugar, salt, and water in a medium-sized bowl, and stir to mix well. Add the almonds, and stir to mix. Coat a large nonstick baking sheet with nonstick cooking spray, and spread the almond mixture evenly over the sheet.
2. Bake at 325°F for 12 to 15 minutes, stirring every 3 minutes, or until the coating is dry and the almonds are very lightly browned. (Watch the almonds closely during the last few min-

utes, as once they begin to turn color they can burn quickly.) Remove the pan from the oven, and let the almonds cool to room temperature. To maintain freshness, transfer to an airtight container, and refrigerate for up to 3 weeks or freeze for up to 3 months.

Nutritional Facts (per tablespoon)
CALORIES: 37 CARBOHYDRATES: 3.3 G CHOLESTEROL: 0 MG FAT: 2.5 G FIBER: 0.6 G
PROTEIN: 1.1 G SODIUM: 8 MG CALCIUM: 10 MG

Praline Pumpkin Custards

✳ *As these custards bake, two delicious layers will form—a creamy custard layer and a light and luscious pumpkin layer.*

YIELD: 6 SERVINGS

½ cup cooked mashed or canned pumpkin
½ cup light brown sugar
¾ cup fat-free egg substitute
12-ounce can evaporated skim or low-fat milk
½ cup skim or low-fat milk
¾ teaspoon ground cinnamon
2½ teaspoons vanilla extract

TOPPING
3 tablespoons light brown sugar
2 tablespoons finely ground toasted pecans (page 30)

1. To make the topping, place the brown sugar and pecans in a small bowl, and stir to mix well. Set aside. Coat six 6-ounce custard cups with nonstick cooking spray. Set aside.
2. Place the pumpkin, brown sugar, egg substitute, evaporated milk, skim or low-fat milk, cinnamon, and vanilla extract in a blender, and blend for about 1 minute, or until well mixed. Pour the pumpkin mixture into the prepared custard cups.

3. Place the custards in a 9-by-13-inch pan, and add hot tap water to the pan until it reaches halfway up the sides of the custard cups. Bake at 350°F for 25 minutes. Sprinkle about 1 tablespoon of the topping over each custard, and bake for 20 minutes more, or until a sharp knife inserted midway between the center of the custard and the rim of the dish comes out clean.

4. Remove the custards from the pan, and allow to cool for at least 45 minutes. Serve immediately, or cover the custards with plastic wrap, and chill for at least 2 hours before serving.

Nutritional Facts (per serving)
CALORIES: 181 CARBOHYDRATES: 34 G CHOLESTEROL: 2 MG FAT: 1.6 G FIBER: 0.8 G
PROTEIN: 8 G SODIUM: 149 MG CALCIUM: 228 MG

Spiced Pumpkin Mousse

YIELD: 5 SERVINGS

1 package (4-serving size) instant butterscotch pudding mix
1 cup cooked mashed or canned pumpkin
1 cup skim or low-fat milk
1 to 1½ teaspoons pumpkin pie spice
2 cups nonfat or light whipped topping
5 gingersnap cookies

1. Place the pudding mix, pumpkin, milk, and pie spice in a large bowl. Stir with a wire whisk or beat with an electric mixer for 2 minutes, or until well mixed. Place the mixture in the refrigerator for 5 to 10 minutes to thicken.

2. Gently fold the whipped topping into the pumpkin mixture. Divide the mixture among five 8-ounce wineglasses, and chill for at least 2 hours before serving. Crumble a gingersnap cookie over the top of each dessert just before serving.

Nutritional Facts (per ¾-cup serving)
CALORIES: 180 CARBOHYDRATES: 38 G CHOLESTEROL: 1 MG FAT: 1.9 G FIBER: 1.6 G
PROTEIN: 2.6 G SODIUM: 350 MG CALCIUM: 93 MG

Very Cranberry Mousse

YIELD: 5 SERVINGS

½ cup boiling water

1 package (4-serving size) cranberry gelatin mix (sugar-free or regular)

½ cup whole-berry cranberry sauce

1¾ cups nonfat or low-fat vanilla yogurt (sugar-free or regular)

2 cups nonfat or light whipped topping

3 tablespoons Glazed Almonds (page 322) (optional)

1. Pour the boiling water into a large bowl. Sprinkle the gelatin mix over the top, and stir with a wire whisk for 3 minutes, or until the gelatin mix is completely dissolved. Set the mixture aside for about 20 minutes, or until it reaches room temperature.

2. When the gelatin mixture has cooled to room temperature, whisk in first the cranberry sauce and then the yogurt. Chill for 15 minutes. Stir the mixture; it should be the consistency of pudding. If it is too thin, return it to the refrigerator for a few minutes.

3. When the gelatin mixture has reached the proper consistency, stir it with a wire whisk until smooth. Gently fold in the whipped topping.

4. Divide the mixture among five 8-ounce wineglasses, cover, and chill for at least 3 hours, or until set before serving. If desired, top each serving with a sprinkling of the Glazed Almonds just before serving.

Nutritional Facts (per ¾-cup serving)
CALORIES: 148   CARBOHYDRATES: 29 G   CHOLESTEROL: 2 MG   FAT: 1 G   FIBER: 0.3 G
PROTEIN: 5.2 G   SODIUM: 131 MG   CALCIUM: 141 MG

Cherry Chiffon Pudding

YIELD: 6 SERVINGS

1⅓ cups light (reduced-sugar) cherry pie filling

1 can (8 ounces) crushed pineapple in juice, well drained

1 cup vanilla yogurt cheese (page 15)

⅔ cup mini marshmallows

⅓ cup chopped toasted almonds or pecans (page 30)

2 cups nonfat or light whipped topping

1. Place the cherry pie filling, drained pineapple, and the yogurt cheese in a large bowl, and stir gently to mix well. Stir in the marshmallows and almonds or pecans. Gently fold in the whipped topping.
2. Divide the pudding among six 8-ounce wineglasses or dessert dishes. Cover the desserts, and refrigerate for at least 2 hours before serving.

Nutritional Facts (per ¾-cup serving)
CALORIES: 179 CARBOHYDRATES: 33 G CHOLESTEROL: 1 MG FAT: 4 G FIBER: 12 G
PROTEIN: 4.5 G SODIUM: 50 MG CALCIUM: 98 MG

Festive Bread Pudding

YIELD: 8 SERVINGS

5¼ cups crustless ½-inch stale oatmeal, sourdough,
  or challah bread cubes (about 6½ slices)

½ cup sugar

⅛ teaspoon ground cinnamon

½ cup fat-free egg substitute or 2 large eggs plus 1 egg white, lightly beaten

12-ounce can skim or low-fat evaporated milk

1 cup plus 2 tablespoons skim or low-fat milk

1½ teaspoons vanilla extract
¼ cup dried sweetened cranberries or dried pitted sweet cherries

SAUCE
¼ cup orange marmalade or apricot jam
2 tablespoons brandy
2 tablespoons butter

1. Put the bread cubes in a large bowl. Set aside. Combine 1 tablespoon of the sugar and all of the cinnamon in a small bowl, and stir to mix well. Set aside.
2. Combine the remaining sugar and the egg substitute or eggs in a large bowl and stir with a wire whisk until the sugar is completely dissolved. Whisk in the evaporated milk, the nonfat or low-fat milk, and the vanilla extract. Pour the milk mixture over the bread cubes and set aside for 10 minutes to allow the bread to soften and soak up some of the milk. Stir in the cranberries or cherries.
3. Coat a 2-quart casserole dish with nonstick cooking spray and pour the mixture into the dish. Sprinkle the cinnamon-sugar mixture over the pudding.
4. Place the dish in a large pan filled with 1 inch of hot tap water. Bake uncovered at 350°F for about 1 hour, or until a sharp knife inserted halfway between the center of the dish and the rim comes out clean. Allow the pudding to cool at room temperature for 45 minutes before serving.
5. To make the sauce, place all of the sauce ingredients in a small pot. Cook and stir over medium heat for a minute or two or until hot and runny. Serve the pudding warm or at room temperature, topping each serving with a tablespoon of the sauce. Refrigerate any leftovers. (Note: This dish can be prepared to the point of baking and refrigerated for up to 24 hours. When ready to bake, remove the pudding from the refrigerator and let sit at room temperature for 30 to 60 minutes.)

Nutritional Facts (per ¾-cup serving)
CALORIES: 219 CARBOHYDRATES: 38 G CHOLESTEROL: 9 MG FAT: 3.8 G FIBER: 0.9 G
PROTEIN: 7 G SODIUM: 236 MG CALCIUM: 187 MG

Pumpkin Spice Bread

YIELD: 18 SLICES

1¾ cups unbleached flour

¼ cup plus 2 tablespoons toasted wheat germ or flaxmeal

¾ cup sugar

2 teaspoons baking powder

½ teaspoon baking soda

2 teaspoons pumpkin pie spice

⅛ teaspoon salt

1 cup cooked mashed or canned pumpkin

½ cup orange or apple juice

¼ cup canola oil

¼ cup fat-free egg substitute or 2 egg whites, lightly beaten

1 teaspoon vanilla extract

½ cup chopped toasted pecans (page 30) (optional)

1. Place the flour, wheat germ or flaxmeal, sugar, baking powder, baking soda, pumpkin pie spice, and salt in a large bowl, and stir to mix well. Put the pumpkin, orange or apple juice, oil, egg substitute or egg whites, and vanilla extract in a medium-sized bowl, and stir to mix well. Add the pumpkin mixture to the flour mixture and stir just until the dry ingredients are moistened. Fold in the pecans if desired.

2. Coat a 9-by-5-inch pan with nonstick cooking spray. Spread the batter evenly in the pan and bake at 350°F for about 45 minutes, or just until a wooden toothpick inserted in the center of the loaf comes out clean.

3. Remove the bread from the oven and let sit for 15 minutes. Invert the loaf onto a wire rack, turn right side up, and cool to room temperature before slicing and serving.

Nutritional Facts (per slice)
CALORIES: 116   CARBOHYDRATES: 19 G   CHOLESTEROL: 0 MG   FAT: 3.3 G   FIBER: 1 G
PROTEIN: 2.4 G   SODIUM: 97 MG   CALCIUM: 36 MG

Cranberry-Applesauce Bread

1¾ cups whole wheat pastry flour

⅓ cup toasted wheat germ or flaxmeal

⅔ cup sugar

2 teaspoons baking powder

¼ teaspoon baking soda

⅛ teaspoon salt

1 cup plus 2 tablespoons unsweetened applesauce

¼ cup canola oil

¼ cup fat-free egg substitute or 2 egg whites, lightly beaten

1 teaspoon vanilla extract

½ cup dried sweetened cranberries

½ cup chopped walnuts (optional)

1. Place the flour, wheat germ or flaxmeal, sugar, baking powder, baking soda, and salt in a large bowl, and stir to mix well. Put the applesauce, oil, egg substitute or egg white, and vanilla extract in a medium-sized bowl, and stir to mix well. Add the applesauce mixture to the flour mixture and stir just until the dry ingredients are moistened. Fold in the cranberries and, if desired, the walnuts.

2. Coat a 9-by-5-inch pan with nonstick cooking spray. Spread the batter evenly in the pan and bake at 350°F for about 45 minutes, or just until a wooden toothpick inserted in the center of the loaf comes out clean.

3. Remove the bread from the oven and let sit for 15 minutes. Invert the loaf onto a wire rack, turn right side up, and cool to room temperature before slicing and serving.

Nutritional Facts (per slice)

CALORIES: 131 CARBOHYDRATES: 24 G CHOLESTEROL: 0 MG FAT: 3.3 G FIBER: 1.2 G
PROTEIN: 2.2 G SODIUM: 79 MG CALCIUM: 34 MG

Golden Apricot Bread

YIELD: 18 SLICES

1-pound can apricots in juice or light syrup

1¾ cups unbleached flour

⅓ cup toasted wheat germ

⅔ cup sugar

2 teaspoons baking powder

¼ teaspoon baking soda

⅛ teaspoon salt

¼ cup canola oil

¼ cup fat-free egg substitute or 2 egg whites, lightly beaten

1 teaspoon vanilla extract

⅓ cup finely chopped dried apricots

½ cup chopped toasted pecans or hazelnuts (page 30) (optional)

1. Drain the apricots, reserving the juice, and place in a blender. Process the apricots until smooth and pour into a 2-cup measure. Add enough of the reserved juice to bring the volume up to 1 cup plus 2 tablespoons. Set aside.
2. Place the flour, wheat germ, sugar, baking powder, baking soda, and salt in a large bowl, and stir to mix well. Put the blended apricot mixture, oil, egg substitute or egg whites, and vanilla extract in a medium-sized bowl, and stir to mix well. Add the apricot mixture to the flour mixture and stir just until the dry ingredients are moistened. Fold in the dried apricots and, if desired, the nuts.
3. Coat a 9-by-5-inch pan with nonstick cooking spray. Spread the batter evenly in the pan and bake at 350°F for about 45 minutes, or just until a wooden toothpick inserted in the center of the loaf comes out clean.
4. Remove the bread from the oven and let sit for 15 minutes. Invert the loaf onto a wire rack, turn right side up, and cool to room temperature before slicing and serving.

Nutritional Facts (per slice)
CALORIES: 119 CARBOHYDRATES: 20 G CHOLESTEROL: 0 MG FAT: 3.3 G FIBER: 1 G
PROTEIN: 2.3 G SODIUM: 79 MG CALCIUM: 35 MG

Index

processed meats, 25
protein, 10, 13
provolone, 14
prunes
    spiced beef brisket with carrots and, 180–81
    Sweet Potato and Carrot Tzimmes, 169–70
puddings
    bread, 326–27
    cherry chiffon, 326
    cranberry-apple rice, 140–41
pumpkin
    cake roll, 299–300
    deep-dish pie, 111–12
    gingerbread, 284–85
    mousse, spiced, 324
    and praline custards, 323–24
    spice bread, 328
punches, 81–82

Q

quesadillas, 49–51

R

raisin, cinnamon, and walnut spread, 79
raspberries
    and cranberry ring, 136–37
    and cranberry trifle, 125
    and chocolate cake, 207–8, 290
    and chocolate sundaes, 231
    mixed baby salad greens with, 227
    parfaits, 255
    Pavlova with, 175–76
    vinaigrette, spring greens with, 199–200
    and walnut bars, 314–15
relishes, cranberry, 106–10
rice, brown, 27, 215–16
    and broccoli pilaf, 230

rice, wild, and cranberry pilaf, 119–20
rice pudding, cranberry-apple, 140–41
ricotta, 15
Rosemary Roasted Tenderloins, 200–201
rutabaga, savory, 133

S

sage, and herb stuffing, 98–99
Saint Patrick's Day, food for, 233–43
salad dressing, 18–20
salad, 32, 34
    asparagus, 247–48
    broccoli and cauliflower, 217–18
    cabbage, 157–58, 271
    Caesar, slim, 145–46
    carrot, 203–4
    coleslaw, 171–72, 262, 281–82
    cucumber, dilled, 146–47
    gelatin
        Ambrosia Gelatin Salad, 220–21
        Cran-Raspberry Ring, 136–37
        golden glow, 282–83
        Mandarin-Cranberry Ring, 135–36
    green, 116–17
        with apples, cranberries, and pecans, 172
        with balsamic vinaigrette, 246–47
        with fresh raspberries, 227
        with raspberry vinaigrette, 199–200
    layered, 270
    orange-avocado, 282
    orange-onion, 158
    potato, 252–53, 259–60
    primavera pasta, 260–61

shamrock fruit, 240–41
spinach, 218
spinach and mushroom, 234–35
squash, 183
three-bean, 263
tomato-basil, 261–62
Waldorf, 103–4
winter fruit, 219–20
salmon, lemon-herb steaks, 144–45
salsa dips, 69, 70
sandwiches, 62–63. *See also* spreads
sauces, 35
sausage, 25
    savory stuffing, 100
Sesame Sugar Snap Peas, 206
shortcakes, berry, 264–65
shrimp
    Cantonese grilled, 269–70
    penne with sun-dried tomatoes and, 228
    skewers, 42–44
    with spicy cocktail sauce, 62
side dishes, 32, 35
sodium, 12
soups, 34
    chicken, with matzo balls, 166–67
    chunky split pea, 238
    golden matzo ball, 179–80
sour cream, 17
    and chive mashed potatoes, 101
    salsa dip, 70
soy products, 11, 19
spinach
    and artichoke spread, hot, 57
    and bacon quesadillas, 50
    dip, 73–74
    and mushroom salad, 234–35
    and noodle kugel, 148–49
    pinwheels, 65–66
    salad, 218
    sweet and savory, 184–85
    tomatoes stuffed with, 185–86
split pea soup, 238